THE WHIRLWIND IN CULTURE

THE WHIRLWIND IN CULTURE

Frontiers in Theology

— IN HONOR OF LANGDON GILKEY —

Edited by
Donald W. Musser and Joseph L. Price

MEYER
STONE
BOOKS

Published in the United States by Meyer-Stone Books,
a division of Meyer, Stone, and Company, Inc.,
2014 South Yost Avenue, Bloomington, IN 47403

Cover design: Terry Dugan Design

Typesetting output: T$_{\!E}$XSource, Houston

Manufactured in the United States of America
92 91 90 89 88   5 4 3 2 1

Library of Congress Cataloging in Publication Data

The Whirlwind in culture.

   Biblipgraphy: p.
   1. Theology.   2. Gilkey, Langdon Brown, 1919-
I. Gilkey, Langdon Brown, 1919-   II. Musser,
Donald W., 1942-   III. Price, Joseph L., 1949-
BR50.W525   1988   261   88-42731
ISBN 0-940989-43-3
ISBN 0-940989-39-5 (pbk.)

Contents

v

Theology and the Social Sciences

II. THEOLOGY ENGAGES THE WHIRLWIND

III. THEOLOGY INTERSECTS RELIGIOUS PLURALISM

Preface

THE RICH CAREER OF LANGDON GILKEY has spanned more than three decades, touched five continents, and influenced the study and practice of religion in academic and parish contexts. He has served on three American university faculties, taught in Japanese and Dutch universities, and lectured throughout the world to academic and ecclesiastical groups. He has published a score of books and dozens of essays and reviews, and he served as the president of the American Academy of Religion during 1979. Yet those of us who know and love Gilkey do not think first of the accolades that have been bestowed upon him, nor do we think primarily of his works — despite the popularity now of the image of the "Whirlwind" that he has introduced to modern theological audiences. Foremost among our memories are those of Gilkey the person, Gilkey the storyteller, Gilkey the sailor, Gilkey the baseball fan. Inevitably and quickly, however, thoughts of Gilkey do turn to the significance of culture for religion and religion for culture, for his stories and experiences articulate the theological significance of experience — both his own and that of persons in general — and the religious dimensions of culture. In this regard, he is a pioneer. At heart he is always lured by a frontier: He does not regard the disciplines of the universities as establishing ownership of turf in specialized areas of understanding and insight. He dares to hazard adventure into the regions of the social sciences, the natural sciences, and the humanities in order to sort out the dimensions of experience that beg for explanation and understanding.

This volume of essays reflects the diverse interests and desire for understanding that have characterized the scholarly career of Langdon Gilkey. Yet unlike other *Festschriften,* this volume includes a major essay by the person being honored: Gilkey has written an intellectual autobiography specifically for inclusion in this volume. With customary grace and perceptivity, he offers a theological interpretation of his own trek through life, providing insights and anecdotes about the contingencies and forces of history that have affected his life and thought. By including his contribution in a volume of essays that celebrates his life and work, we also press into a new frontier, for we allow his own life and work — his storytelling — to set the context for the essays that advance the interests and concerns that have occupied his attention for the past four decades. Of all contemporary theologians who correlate religion and culture, none have been more rigorous in living the interplay of the theological and cultural worlds than has Gilkey: He has addressed artists and physicians, scientists and social theorists, politicians and historians. And in each address he has dared also to listen, to enter into conversation with his audience and to be informed by them. By including his essay in a *Festschrift* for him, we recognize the serious nature of the forum on theology and culture and the significance of his voice in that particular discussion.

The other contributors to the volume include Gilkey's peers in theological studies, his colleagues in the academy, and his recent doctoral advisees. In most of the essays they do not address directly or reflect upon his own writings, yet all of them do honor him by dealing with recurrent themes that emerge from his work — as theology *encounters* culture, as theology *engages* the whirlwind, and as theology *intersects* religious pluralism. All of the verbs in this series of themes imply movement, going "into"; they also suggest that in the venture some conflict, some wrestle, some grappling takes place. "Encounter" signifies the unexpected dimensions of a meeting and the possible conflicts that emerge. "Engagement" suggests that something or someone has occupied one's attention and has been secured or contracted for use. "Intersection" calls to mind the common territory or overlapping principles, rituals, or values that are held by two or more distinct groups. With such risk of movement outward, Gilkey has taken theology to greater understanding of itself and its own mission, as in *Naming the Whirlwind,* and he has illuminated the identity of the newly encountered, engaged, or intersected territory of culture, as in *Creationism on Trial.*

The first theme, theology's encounter with culture, singles out his creative appropriation of concepts and ideas from the humanities, natural sciences, and social sciences in order to make his theological ponderings intelligible and relevant to contemporary culture. This theme also recognizes his contributions to the specialized discourses of artists, doctors, scientists, and social theorists. The second theme, theology's engagement with the whirlwind, is admittedly tautological; nevertheless, it bears the sense of his concern for the contemporary meaning of the entire range of theological symbols of the Christian tradition. In this section, each of the essays analyzes some aspect of the symbol "God," which is the theological symbol of central concern to Gilkey. Here, in non-traditional ways the essays deal with the traditional characterization of God as providence, God as creator, and God as savior. The third cluster of essays, under the rubric of theology's intersection with religious pluralism, focuses on one of Gilkey's most recent scholarly pursuits — understanding the relationships among different religious traditions and the implications that these relationships bear for Christian theology.

By no means, however, is the placement of the essays constrictive, for several of them could be classified adequately and appropriately in areas other than those of their appearance. This multidisciplinarity of concerns and resources in the essays affirms the boundary-breaking inspiration of Langdon Gilkey, as does the venturesomeness of several of the contributors who embrace methods, perspectives, and insights from disciplines other than those of their previous expertise.

With this volume, then, we celebrate the life and career of Langdon Gilkey, whose professional and personal contributions have enabled us to hear, somewhat like Job, the prophetic response of God in and through the whirlwind — to prepare for action, to perceive the significance of culture for things beyond culture, and to seek justice for and within the culture blown by the whirlwind.

J.L.P. and D.W.M.

Introduction

A Retrospective Glance at My Work

LANGDON GILKEY

W HEN I LOOK BACK ON MY LIFE WORK — on the major interests that have inspired it and the thoughts and writings that have resulted there-from — I am impressed with its unplanned character. Seen by itself, it seems to meander from this to that with no apparent order or direction. There appears to me now, however, one thread that provides whatever consistency or intelligibility it may possess, and that is the changing shape of the historical context in which these thoughts, as essentially reactions, occurred. All this was quite unconscious: at no point did I deliberately decide to pattern my thought in relation to historical events, nor was I even particularly aware that this was happening. Consciousness does reflect being, and in this case the being reflected was constituted by the historical events lying in the middle sixty years of the twentieth century. Quite unintentionally, therefore, my thought has reflected a "correlational" approach: as when a sailboat hugs a massive but variegated shoreline, its course has been determined by the twists and turns of twentieth-century events. As the little volume summing up my theology indicates, this life work reflects a dialectic of message and existence. In the end, to be sure, the explicit and therefore deliberate theological method which I use and defend has also been correlational. But that formal method is a symptom and not a cause of a more basic pattern of thinking, namely to ponder the character of our existence, both personal and historical, before God in the light of the historical and social situation, the massive contours of events, in which we find ourselves.

1

This life work is that of a theologian. Thus its elements represent a *theology:* an attempt to discern the truth about God and God's ways with us. But this is, as noted, a correlational or dialectical theology: these ways are experienced, uncovered, and articulated in relation — and only in relation — first to the changing character of personal existence in our age, including of course my own, and secondly in relation to the shifting forms of social existence and the panorama of events that those personal existences inhabit. Thus consciousness of both the career of individual personal existences and the contours of their historical environments in the mid-twentieth century is essential for any understanding of the grounds of the theology represented here. I became a theologian because of the historical context of my early adult life, and the subsequent characteristic of the theology that arose there and the issues over the decades with which it has been concerned have likewise reflected that changing historical context.

As will be evident from this unfolding story, the sequence of events from 1933 to 1986 through which as a person aware of his environment I lived represents what I have frequently termed (following Toynbee) a "Time of Troubles," the apparent beginning of a process of social disintegration and historical decline, a *fin de siècle.* Consciousness of this has slowly developed in me, and most of my theological thoughts from their inception in the late 1930s to the present reflect this character. Obviously the question is posed by this correlation of history and reflective thought: do I think this way *theologically* because of the actually perturbed history of the mid-twentieth century, or do I see that history in this particular way because I am a theologian? All I can say is, I became a theologian because it *was* such a period, and subsequently each time I have looked at it I have been more convinced of the validity of that assessment. In any case, in such a Time of Troubles, it is intelligible that questions of personal existence, of the transcendence and the mystery of God, of the fall and sin of humans, of the direction of history, of the dominance and yet the ambiguity of a secular and scientific culture, and finally of the plurality of religions should arise and increasingly pose the kinds of theological problems I have found fascinating and the issues I have found most pressing. In such a turbulent period it is not only intelligible that one should become a believer and a theologian, but also that the resulting theology should be both *existential and historical-cultural* in its emphasis.

Now I shall turn to the story itself, which will, I trust, add flesh and life to the bare bones of these generalizations. This is neither a personal autobiography nor an existential religious history of my life. Most of what has happened to me or how I felt about it will be omitted. The point of what follows is to give the existential, social, and historical background to my life's work — where the latter has "come from" insofar as it reflects the history in which it was thought out. I shall, therefore, mention only those situations and events in my life which provide the context for my theological work.

•

I appeared on earth in 1919, and I spent my boyhood in a liberal Protestant home in one of the most lively and progressive academic centers of American life, the University of Chicago. My father (Charles W. Gilkey) was the well-known and widely acclaimed minister of what was then in effect the "University Church," the Hyde Park Baptist Church; later (1928) he became the first dean of the University Chapel. My mother was equally prominent and successful: an early feminist, a superb hostess for the university community, especially its students, and a leading YWCA officer (for one term in the late 1920s she was the national president). Together they created a potent, open, morally and socially concerned home (for years my father was head of the Chicago ACLU), filled every week with visiting preachers and church persons, students, professors, and prominent religious and secular reformers.

Above all, this environment was "liberal," theologically and politically. My father's personal religious lifestyle remained relatively disciplined and Spartan (except for his sailboat); we had daily family prayers when my sister and I were children, and there was never any alcohol in our home. Nevertheless, as a family we hardly represented a strict "evangelical" home, as had been the case with my father's family; guests smoked there, we were not sabbatarian, we played cards and enjoyed theater and movies — and we talked continually about current political events, moral causes, and social changes. In this home to be "religious" — and so to be genuinely Christian — meant, as it did for so much of liberal Protestantism, the critical spirit and the social gospel: to be relatively relaxed with regard to both doctrines and rules, to be free of the obvious moral faults and the vices of tobacco and alcohol, to be vastly concerned about social and racial justice and peace — above all peace — and to be tolerant of the ideas, the habits, and mores of other groups. It was taken for granted in this atmosphere that any kind of racial or religious prejudice; any religious, racial, or patriotic fanaticism; any overt acts of materialistic or class self-interest, national aggression, or persecution were anathema to a genuine Christianity. It was also taken for granted that my parents' many Jewish and Negro (as they were then called) friends were normal visitors in this home. We were proud when father, along with many other liberals, appeared on the American Legion's "black list" of un-Americans, and when chapters of the Daughters of the American Revolution denounced both mother and father for their racial and social liberalism. Lifestyles — perhaps especially for theologians — have changed vastly since this culminating period of Protestant liberalism in the 1920s; yet this inheritance — this "taking all this for granted" — made its permanent imprint on my conscience and has never ceased to provide the foundation for whatever has been good in my makeup. I grew up hating the anti-Semitism and the segregationist customs (not to mention the laws) still characteristic then of American society, scorning the "economic royalists" of the 1930s, and utterly devoted to the permanent establishment of peace. Thus in the early '30s we all supported Roosevelt, were dismayed at the mounting aggression of the Japanese and of Mussolini, and came not only to be fearfully conscious of the dark cloud of Hitler but to shudder at its evil portent for the world. My first original research paper during my freshman year in college in 1936 was a study of the early history and the rise to dominance (1924–34) of the Nazi movement in the German Reich. That paper documented what was then public knowledge in Germany and elsewhere, namely, the mounting persecution of Jews and the determination to eradicate them from Germany's public life.

College (Harvard) represented the continuation of all of this except now on a more autonomous basis, for in college the same person lives on only now on his or her own. This meant certain real continuities: the same liberal, political, and social convictions (though the menace of social snobbishness in college life could hide behind and mock the most liberal convictions!), and the same intellectual, literary, and historical concerns. I majored in philosophy and in that study vastly preferred metaphysical, epistemological, and moral questions to logical subjects. In fact I found in myself a marked prejudice for idealism over materialism, which I rightly ascribed to my father's influence. Still, to be autonomous also meant important changes: like so many in the 1930s I smoked a pipe, drank an occasional beer or wine, and went on as many Wellesley dates and Smith weekends as I could. I found myself becoming more and more "Ivy League," in tweeds, flannels and button downs, a far cry from the less self-conscious Midwestern corduroys of my youth.

Religion, or interest in it, played absolutely no pat in my personal or my intellectual life. I knew nothing of and thought less about Christian doctrine and was not even aware of that lack in my philosophical repertoire. I went to chapel only occasionally to hear a friend of father preach and attended religious discussion groups for reasons that were vague and certainly obscure to me. It would not have occurred to me that there might be more to discuss in such religious groups than ethical and social issues. I wrote my senior honors thesis (Fall, 1939) on George Santayana, praising his elegant, sensitive naturalism and agreeing thoroughly with his charming rejection of religious belief. I found myself tolerant of religious beliefs but confident that civilization had progressed by the twentieth century beyond their mythical picture of reality. Why, I asked myself, do we need any more than ethical principles, a social conscience, and democracy to continue to progress? I was, I suppose, an ethical humanist if I was anything — besides being a fairly serious student, an even more serious competitor in tennis, and a genial if circumspect *bon vivant.*

Twentieth-century history, however, was steadily encroaching on, surrounding, and threatening to engulf this easy, genteel, academic life. In 1938 at Munich the worst nightmare of our collective youth, namely, the reappearance of war, of world war, which we had been brought up to hate, for a moment threatened to become reality — and then receded again. But in September of 1939, when the Harvard-Yale tennis team was touring in France, that dreaded war began in reality — and we barely got home, sickened, scared, and confused. We detested Hitler — but we (and here almost an entire generation spoke) detested war more. Thus on my return in senior year, along with Avery Dulles, the lanky Presbyterian son of a liberal lawyer, I helped form the Keep America Out of the War Committee. I remained active in it until Boston Irish tirades against the British empire ("the two empires, Hitler's and the British, are identical") drove Avery and me out. The war remained a ghastly specter during most of that winter: a dominant fact in the news, it yet seemed unreal, a possible portent of untold and meaningless horrors, but as yet only a threat and so now and again quite forgettable. Then suddenly in the spring of a senior year replete with romantic weekends, tennis victories, scholastic honors, and all sorts of personal culminations, that spectral potency became an abysmally dark actuality: Hitler's armies quickly overran the smaller lands of western Europe, France fell, and apparently even England was about to be engulfed.

I recall moving with genial unreality through the events of that senior spring, as confused inside as the world was outside. Since we were concerned and devoted liberals, we found ourselves in that year driven irresistibly along two quite contradictory courses: on the one hand, out of commitment to peace, we were determined to avoid war at all costs; on the other hand, out of commitment to justice, equality and freedom, we could not but loathe Nazism and be equally determined to resist it. I was stretched between two moral absolutes, peace and justice, and quite unable to qualify or to relinquish either one. Further, I found that for my humanism to survive these must remain *absolute* requirements, else all descend into cynicism. In fact, I recall the cynical alternative becoming my increasingly frequent recourse. On one boat race weekend, relaxed, sunny, and beery, I remember arguing, that after all, these moral ideals were irrelevant to history's course, that Europe did need at some point to be forcibly unified, and that such a process was (as liberal historians say about the past but almost never about their own present) always a cruel matter but one nevertheless justified by the necessities of history. Why shouldn't Hitler do it as well as anyone? — and so (I concluded) let us leave it to the march of history to work out Europe's unhappy destiny. Having intellectually won the argument, I hated myself for so thoroughly betraying myself and my world. Gone were the social ideals and the confidence in progress towards justice that heretofore — though I had not fully realized it — buoyed up and guided my spiritual existence. I was left a clever cynic, directed only by the requirements of self-interest in a world going nowhere. The cold blast of historical reality had made my intellectual and moral humanism come apart at the seams; I realized I detested myself and the world I lived in.

Into this state of slowly developing inner confusion and disillusion-ment — it was not quite yet clear — something unexpected entered, providing the new possibility of a realistic and not deluded spiritual existence and yet one replete with understanding and self-understanding, with moral direction and spiritual centeredness. On a Sunday in early April — when Hitler's armies were beginning to move and my spiritual world was therefore beginning to crumble — I went to the Harvard chapel to listen to an old friend of father. The latter had repeatedly said, "You ought to go hear Reinnie preach sometime." And, knowing nothing else but that, I wandered in. Suddenly, as the torrent of insight poured from the pulpit, my world in disarray spun completely around, steadied, and then settled into a new and quite firm and intelligible structure.

As I listened to Niebuhr's utterly sober and realistic analysis of the power struggles among the nations, I thought to myself: "Now I am in touch with *reality* and not with the illusions of humanistic idealism"; and then as I listened to the strong moral judgments on that rebellious world that ushered forth from the same analysis, and the impassioned call — despite our failures — to be humble, to seek justice, and to show mercy, I realized that in *this* framework (he called it, to my astonishment, "biblical") one could be realistic and yet morally concerned, one could look the facts in the face and yet have confidence and hope. The dichotomy that had wrecked my humanism — *either* believe in moral ideals and the moral capacities of human groups at the price of ignoring the sordid realities of social life *or* be realistic about those realities and therefore cynical — had dissipated into a new understanding. We are separated or estranged from the ideal, and thus is humanism impossible; but that does not mean the ideal has vanished from reality and only our alienated collective existence remains. For there is God, transcendent to the fallen, warring world and yet seeking to bring it back to its true self and all of us to our own true selves. The new "duality" of dubious, stricken world and transcendent God, of an estranged self and true self — and yet the continual relation between the two — made it possible for me to be again, to understand again, and to hope again. That personal and theological principle (theological and yet also ethical) of a divine transcendence and yet a continual relevance and relatedness Niebuhr gave to me at that chosen moment — and it has remained absolutely central to my life and my work ever since.

My conversion — and that is the right word — was quick and complete. I heard him, as did hundreds more, twice again that day, afternoon and evening; and I bought, read and reread all his books then in print (up to *Beyond Tragedy*, 1936). At the end of two more weeks, I was a "Niebuhrian." In fact, during the next week I quite rearranged the course I was to teach the next year in Peking for the Yenching English Department on "Modern Western Thought." The new edition did not culminate, as I had first planned it, with the humanism of H. G. Wells, Bernard Shaw, Santayana, and Dewey, but with Niebuhr as the critique of that "now irrelevant" and evolutionary humanism and the appearance, or the reappearance, of a new religious understanding. As I slowly grew into this new viewpoint over the next two or three months, I was astounded with myself and with this "new world of the Bible," as Barth had put it — though I had then never even heard of Barth. The notion that Christian faith could be "realistic" about human evil rather than overlook it in favor of the "goodness of people" fascinated me. The concept that something could transcend and yet be related to nature, culture, and people was utterly new and intriguing; and perhaps most significant, the idea that Christianity had something to declare about the nature of reality — a philosophy or a theology — and that it implied a new personal relation to reality as well as a set of ethical rules, took me completely by surprise. Because it had been my "world," my understanding of human existence and of history, that had crumbled, not so much my ethical social norms, it was the *theological* message of Niebuhr that gripped me, and the theological teachings of the Christian tradition that captured my interest. Thus my former undergraduate interest in metaphysical philosophy was transferred lock, stock, and barrel to a concern for theology, and by and large it has since remained there. Whereas prior to that Sunday morning, naturalistic humanism appeared to me to represent hard-headed "reality" and religious doctrines a worthy but sentimental set of "illusions," now naturalistic humanism — despite its claim to scientific realism — seemed to me hopelessly mired in optimistic and naive illusions about progress and about human rational and moral goodness. On the other hand, Christian faith, initially irrational by the standards of the secular culture, now appeared in the end alone to make sense of our personal and social existence and so to be in touch with the only reality we can directly encounter. I learned then to trust the requirements of *existence* and of normal *praxis* rather than those of "objective inquiry" whenever ultimate questions about reality are at stake — although I had not at that point ever heard of Kierkegaard. Meanwhile I graduated in June. I was unsettled and confused, torn still between two worlds, on the boundary between my college humanism and the new intimations of divine reality that had so recently been opened up for me.

•

The summer of 1940, therefore, brought exciting new possibilities for my personal life at the same time that it represented terrifying and tragic possibilities for the world. While Hitler's legions were poised on the Channel prepared to gobble up England, the one remaining center of resistance, I embarked in mid-August for Peking to teach the English language at Yenching University, an American-British university for Chinese students. As this brief history makes clear, I did not go as a missionary: uninterested at that point in further academic study and restless with all the seemingly boring alternatives open to a college graduate in the United States (business, prep school teaching, etc.). I had in mid-winter signed up — thanks to a friend from China — with Yenching University for a two-year contract ($10 per month plus travel!) to teach introductory English classes (in English!). Since in early 1940 we were more than a year and a half away from the later actual war with Japan, this sojourn in Peking seemed to be sensible enough, and in August I sailed via Yokahama and Kobe to Peking. This experience in the Orient — I did not return home for five years — represented without question the most significant and formative period of my life. Whenever subsequently I have asked myself: "What is real and true in human experience? Where can I go to touch *reality*?" I find myself returning to that sequence of experiences.

When I arrived in 1940, China — and the entire Orient with it — reflected on every side the old colonial world. The British, Dutch, and French empires were still intact, and so European power dominated most of east Asia, as did British power in India, and British, French, and Belgian power in the Near East and Africa. Although China was technically a sovereign nation, it too had been completely dominated by the Western nations, especially Great Britain. The treaty ports (Tien Tsin, Tsing Tao, and Shanghai) were British, and there British law ruled. Elsewhere Westerners had all manner of extraterritorial rights, and without question any of them, rich or poor, powerful or powerless, prominent or insignificant, existed as members of a superior and so dominant race of beings amid, to them, the faceless sea of Chinese. One felt all this at once on arrival, this unaccustomed status of unquestioned superiority. I recall with some chagrin inwardly basking in its warmth, though I was also horrified at the gauche arrogance of many (though not all) of the British, French, and Americans I encountered in Peking. This aura of superiority was, moreover, total, covering every level of cultural life. It ranged from the levels of technology, industry, science, and medicine, to those of law and politics (democracy and individual rights), on up to attitudes of equality (e.g., of the sexes) and of humanitarian concern for others, to issues of the purity and absoluteness of religion. All up and down the line, therefore, the West and Westerners assumed that their own civilization, and with it their religions (and themselves!), were innately and indubitably superior. What is worse, most outside the orbit of the West who were thus looked down upon, subconsciously if not consciously, and certainly unwillingly, assented to that arrogant assessment of superiority. I remember being very conscious of this (while still enjoying its perquisites!) and saying to myself: "Seeing this dominance

and superiority of the West, I can now understand why the Japanese are
so irrationally angry, absurdly arrogant, and fanatically Shinto (as they
were indeed), despite their advanced scientific, technical, and industrial
culture." Then I recall adding, "Wait until the even prouder Chinese
(now our allies) are able to become conscious of and so to articulate
fully these same hostile and explosive feelings." As *A Passage to India*
documented this same social and spiritual situation of absolute Western dominance and superiority in the British Raj of the 1920s, so my
brief experience in Peking in 1940-41 was saturated with the identical
delectable but infinitely destructive aura of our superiority, except that
the twilight of that imperial supremacy had now deepened in 1940; I
was there only moments before it was to be eclipsed forever.

The other dominant political impression of that "free" year and
a quarter (September 1940 — December 1941) in Peking was of the
ruthless brutality and the oppressive weight of the Japanese occupation
of China, established in eastern China, and so in effect all around us
roughly from 1936 on. Since that time a number of similarly brutal
military occupations of civilian populations have horrified the world,
with the result that few but the Chinese remember the outrageous character of this one. Still, contact with it convinced me that historical evil
could at times become so vast that resistance to that evil becomes inescapable. I knew that in a situation where my help was possible and
relevant, I would take up arms against such oppression. I had for at
least that period of my life ceased to be a pacifist in principle and so to
abjure all resort under any circumstances to military violence. Meanwhile, the fascination of China grew apace; I was enthralled daily by
what I saw all around me. Old China hands always told the newcomer:
"Once here, you cannot but return." I had laughed then — now I can
hardly wait to get back again and again.

When the war began in December of 1941, we "enemy nationals"
were rounded up at once and put under a sort of house arrest. During
that time of forced inaction, I busied myself reading theology and teaching classes to missionaries on volume one of Niebuhr's *The Nature and
Destiny of Man*, which volume my father had sent to me in October of
1941 just before the war began. (I had to wait until the end of the war
to read volume two and so to hear from Niebuhr any hint of grace!).
A year and a quarter later, in March 1943, we enemy nationals (mostly
British and Americans) were sent to an internment camp in Shantung
province, and there I remained until the war ended in August of 1945.
Since the full story of that experience is contained in *Shantung Com-*

pound (1966), I shall mention only briefly here its major impact on my convictions and my thinking.

The internment camp, populated by some 1,500 to 2,000 civilians including men, women, and children, represented a kind of laboratory experiment in social living. We had to organize ourselves politically, administer our common labor, do all our own cooking, baking, and stoking, repair our buildings and equipment, and discipline and entertain ourselves, in other words, construct and maintain a miniature civilization. Our task was limited radically by an absolute lack of machinery of any sort, a minimum of equipment, supplies, and conveniences, by an overcrowded and cramped space, and by continual and deep anxiety about the future. It was a life suffused with frustration, hunger, and insecurity, despite its many very real achievements and frequent joys, not least the personal relations — and the loving relations — that could characterize even such a comfortless and precarious life. For a young healthy person the inconveniences and frustrations of that life were of minimal importance, being far less than soldiers suffered. And for me the fascination of our common enterprise of civilization-building was endless.

More and more I was impressed by the moral necessities of such communal living: without self-discipline and order our civilization quickly disintegrated into anarchy, yet without equal justice it threatened to erupt into an equally destructive violence and discord. Moral decay — which made both order and justice impossible — was thus as dangerous to our life as was a stoppage of supplies or a bad epidemic. Yet obviously nothing was more difficult under these circumstances than to be self-disciplined enough to share space and supplies with others or to be self-disciplined enough not to steal common goods. However well we organized our labor corps and our production of goods, still such was our universal self-concern that we "fell" continually in the face of these difficult spiritual requirements — we refused to cooperate or share, we hoarded goods to ourselves, we stole. As a consequence our common life suffered recurrent and increasing crises. Communal life — civilization — requires moral strength: self-control, justice, equality, and autonomy, as much as it does knowledge, rationality, and technical expertise. And yet it was evident that nothing is more elusive in human existence than that same moral strength: we are apparently made for it, yet continually we reject and deny it. Again, therefore, these two and a half years of vivid experience had (for me) validated the Christian understanding of our situation as one lived in the presence of a moral and yet loving God, a life living out a predominant and very destructive self-concern and yet one continually replete with new possibilities of repentance, trust, renewal, and self-giving. I was more convinced than ever of the relevance of the symbols of sin and estrangement, and the necessity of moral awareness and responsibility, of spiritual self-understanding and repentance, and most important, of a deep trust in God if creative personal and communal life is to be possible. As I had not been able to understand the war world of 1939 and 1940 without that theological framework, so now it was only on the same terms that I could deal with the long, arduous but utterly fascinating experience of an internment camp.

I was returned on a troop ship to the United States in November of 1945, underweight, confused about myself and my future, and inwardly estranged from the new victorious, materialistic, militaristic, and above all self-righteous spirit now so pervasive in America. Noting the vast difference of all this from the less strident, certainly more pacifistic and humble America of the 1930s, I said to myself, "Nothing is so corrupting of a people as victory in a righteous war." Consequently, the parallels between our moral failures in the camp and the nationalism and self-concern of prosperous America soon struck me, and I began to speak to social clubs, schools, and churches about those parallels — the seed of the later volume of theological reflections on the camp experience. Meanwhile after being bored to distraction in a course on international law in preparation for a possible career in diplomacy, I decided to begin formal study of theology, philosophy of religion, and ethics in preparation for teaching those subjects. There was no question of where I would go to study: only Union Theological Seminary in New York interested me because it was there that my "spiritual father," Reinhold Niebuhr, taught. And so a year later I entered the Union-Columbia program and officially began my theological career. At twenty-seven I felt infinitely old and thoroughly experienced (both quite in error!); but all I was familiar with in theology was Niebuhr's work (which I knew line by line) and some of the early Brunner (whose books a missionary friend had loaned to me in Peking). As yet, I knew absolutely nothing else in theology, biblical studies, historical theology, or the rest of religious studies. So there was a lot to do.

•

I shall now turn to the next decade and a half (1947 to 1962). It was full of learning, personal relationships and vivid, if often painful, experiences; and I shall mention only those matters or events that now seem to me to have shaped the continuing development of my thought. I came to Union and to my first teaching jobs (at Vassar, 1951–54, and Vanderbilt, 1954–63) as a committed, articulate and enthusiastic — I am tempted now to say "aggressive" — neo-orthodox, at any rate, a Niebuhrian (I had still not read a bit of Barth). This theological viewpoint seemed to me eminently true because it had been validated to me by twentieth-century events and by my own experiences; and it was to me, after a few years of devoted study, clearly also what the "tradition," biblical and historical, had said all along — except, I told myself, where that tradition had been misunderstood (for example, by the early church, by the Catholics, by the Protestant orthodox, and by the Protestant liberals!). This is still my general orientation, to be sure; but I see it now *very* differently. I am aware now of the essentially "liberal" elements within it as I was not then when in the 1940s and 1950s the main struggle was against an expiring liberal establishment. After many more years of historical reading, moreover, I see how varied the entire tradition actually was and how fortunate that variety has been for its richness and its truth. Above all, I now see (or think I do) the very significant weaknesses in that burst of theological genius and vigor associated with the dialectical or crisis theology that appeared after World War I in Europe and in America in the '30s and '40s.

In any case, for me the main elements, the sinews, of that theology — one could call it a "doctrinal system" in spirit if not in actuality — had been directly correlated with and validated by my personal (and historical) experience: the pervasiveness of sin and meaninglessness continually threatening, even in the modern age, human history and personal existence; the ambiguous and ultimately self-destructive tendencies of a civilization built on secular grounds alone, even a scientific and technical civilization; the absolute necessity of revelation and grace for any help or renewal to appear in such a situation; and as a consequence the centrality and uniqueness of the appearance and presence of God in Jesus Christ and of the community that witnesses to that revelation. The fact that this set of theological "symbols" was interpreted by all of us in a *liberal* and not an orthodox (literalistic) manner tended to escape our attention; and the fact that we all assumed without question the critical spirit and the concern for social justice that the liberals had established also went unnoticed. One might make the caustic comment that as an erstwhile liberal I was tolerant of every view except liberalism, and that I was orthodox about what was in fact a very unorthodox way of doing theology! My first three books: *Maker of Heaven and Earth* (1959), *How the Church Can Minister to the World Without Losing Itself* (1964), and *Shantung Compound* (1966) illustrate well this firm "neo-orthodox" (though quite non-Barthian) emphasis on transcendence, sin, revelation, and grace — and on correct theology. Fortunately, they also equally represent the strong correlation of theology with experience and of the divine with personal existence and the social world that I have already noted.

Two otherwise quite insignificant events illustrate this strange mixture of themes and attitudes within a fairly tightly woven theological viewpoint. Toward the end of my theological studies (1948) I was invited to be a Kent Fellow and so attended the famous Council on Religion and Higher Education's "Week of Work" held that year at a college campus in Maryland. One morning at breakfast I found myself sitting across from perhaps the best — and deservedly so — liberal philosopher of religion in the older generation, Edgar Brightman. He was one of the men who for that reason was viewed by all of us as the leader of the "other side." He and I had a spritely, not too hostile, conversation about theology in which we quickly — in fact before the shredded wheat was eaten — located our sharp points of disagreement. I had to admit I found him, somewhat to my surprise, a very charming and intelligent man. I recall we were both particularly delighted with the way we agreed about our disagreements: he said, "I believe in God *because* I believe that history represents a steady moral progress," to which I replied, "I believe in God because to me history precisely *does not* represent such a progress."

The same week the Council on Religion and Higher Education experienced a soul-revealing controversy; it was over a "liberal" social issue (racial justice), but it surely illustrated what the neo-orthodox were saying about human existence, even that of Kent Fellows! It was a terribly hot week, and we were meeting in segregated Maryland. The unexpected and shocking result was that the black members of our community were barred from the large public pool available to the rest of us. It seemed to me perfectly obvious that under these conditions *none* of our community should use the pool, and I said so at one of the early nightly meetings. Even more unexpectedly, a bitter, very existential debate followed, about half of our group finding (with the help of a newly appointed young professor of Christian ethics at Princeton!) exceedingly intellectual and intricate reasons why those families who could use the pool should do so, meanwhile feeling very sorry for and "spiritually identified with" those unfortunate families who could not! Our guest speaker, Professor Paul Weiss, said that he was "disgusted" with this so-called Christian group and would never return. I agreed and never have.

The second event illustrative of our complex if not confused theological situation happened about the same time (the late '40s). There was a lively, interesting group of young "theologians" who were American (northern) Baptists: Bob Handy, Bill Hamilton, Bob Spike, Howard Moody, myself, and a young student of the history of religions, Chuck Long. We all came together for the first time at a conference of American Baptist clergy to discuss theology at Green Lake, Wisconsin. Since the denomination had long since been split asunder by a bitter conflict between conservative evangelicals and liberals, it was expected that this debate would continue. To everyone's surprise, however, the "young Turks," who seemed so much like the liberals, sided on the whole with the evangelicals, calling for a theology of revelation, sin, and grace and rejecting the older liberal progressivism. It was the first time either conservatives or older liberals had run into this new breed, and they were astounded. I remember in one session giving a short speech about history in which I said that the traditional eschatological symbols, especially those of "divine judgment and the Second Coming," were essential for interpreting history in our age; Bob Handy rose to second my remarks. Afterwards a kind, older evangelical came up to us and said very enthusiastically: "I can't tell you how wonderful it is to hear the younger men talking this way about the Second Coming! It's going to come soon, isn't it? And where do you think it will be? Just outside Jerusalem?" Bob and I looked at each other in astonishment. We hadn't meant *that!* As I admitted to Bob later, I was a bit ashamed that all I could think of was the incredibly crowded situation on Jerusalem's highways and in its motels when that event culminating world history took place! With this amusing encounter I realized for the first time how "liberal," not to say "secular," at least how "unsupernaturalistic," we were about the objective course of history, and thus how very symbolic was our use of traditional theological concepts, such as judgment, last judgment, and Second Coming. The problem of what we *did* mean by these theological symbols, however intelligible they seemed to be in relation to all the evidence and in the encounter with Brightman, was beginning to appear on my horizon. To round out the confusion, that night, when all of us went off to find some beer to go with our theological discussions, I heard one of the liberals — another very kind middle-aged gentleman — remark, "Well, on these issues those neo-orthodox boys are too liberal for me!"

Two further events might be mentioned that had a much deeper effect on my developing existence and therefore ultimately on my professional career. Because during graduate school I found myself unable to carry through an engagement that I was sure I really wanted, I began to see a young analyst who worked near Union Seminary in New York. From the beginning I realized he was an even more gifted therapist than he was the outstanding theoretician for which he later became famous; his name was Rollo May. These biweekly sessions for three years did an incredible amount for me, though it is not easy to say just how. They showed me how vital feelings are, and being in touch with one's own feelings; they revealed how empty "attributes," even impressive ones, can be; how unreal and destructive is the intellect alone, its theories and arguments, if the self is unrelated to itself and therefore empty. In sum, they uncovered for me the heretofore buried *existential* level of self-feeling, of self-affirmation, of appropriating and being oneself, through which alone relations with others and creative action in the world become possible. From within I discovered what Kierkegaard meant by "choosing" oneself despite all that one was, and what Tillich was saying when he spoke of the "courage to be." If what I wrote after these sessions was outwardly little changed in its general theoretical shape, nevertheless its meaning for me became entirely different. Through Rollo May I discovered the *person* behind the words, the *self* behind the theories, *being* as the substratum of intellect and of consciousness — and I was given the chance to enjoy a healthy if always stormy personal and family life.

The other event came a decade or so later, when I was teaching at the Divinity School at Vanderbilt University in Nashville. By 1959 all seemed to be going exceedingly well for the young theologian: happily (so it seemed to me) married to a lovely and charming Virginia lady, a successful first book just out, and above all a wonderful adopted baby son. But other things were also brewing. Although there had been since I came there in 1954 a few black students at the Vanderbilt University Divinity School, still the university as a whole, the city of Nashville, and the entire region of the middle south remained in 1959 and 1960 thoroughly segregated — hard as it is now to believe! During that year black college students in North Carolina, in Knoxville and at home in Nashville (from Fisk and Tennessee A & I) began the "sit-ins" in protest against the most blatant injustices of that culture, especially the law that black people could not eat in so-called white restaurants downtown — in the same areas in which they were also expected to shop! These students sat down at the lunch counters and refused to move, even though they were subjected not only to verbal and physical abuse but also to arrest. At the Divinity School we had admired and supported their protests against what we all regarded without question as a set of unjust and oppressive laws that would have to change sooner or later (and that view was shared by 90 percent of the *southern* students of the Divinity School). To us it was obvious that nonviolent protest against such unjust laws was thoroughly justified morally and religiously, in fact incumbent on a responsible Christian. How else could creative change occur? How else could one be dedicated to the Kingdom? This was, however, by no means obvious to Nashville. Proud of its astounding level of church attendance, Nashville felt humiliated at this nationally publicized moral protest against its customs. Even more, it was scared, and rightly, that this situation could well result in a sea of blood flowing in the streets of downtown. That it was the white toughs who would initiate and largely commit the violence did not matter; it was the "uppity" blacks who were causing it all by breaking the law and by shattering the peace of "this lovely Christian city." It was like a chapter from Niebuhr's *Moral Man and Immoral Society* of 1933!

Suddenly, with the arrest of a number of Fisk students, it was discovered that one of *our* Vanderbilt students at the Divinity School, a very able and courageous man named James Lawson, had been "coaching" the protesters in nonviolence. We were proud of him, but the town was not. Instead of giving him its highest honors for saving the city from violence, as they should, they were shocked that a Vanderbilt student was, first, black and, second, involved in what was to them virtual insurrection. How could a Christian break the law in a Christian country and especially in a Christian city? He must be communist! The heretofore forward-looking and progressive chancellor of the university, wary of his conservative board and determined to follow his own schedule into liberalism, was furious and expelled Lawson forthwith. Knowing the convictions on such issues of the world Christian community (especially since Hitler's day), not to say of the liberal academic world, we on the faculty of the Divinity School were dumbfounded. We knew that our school would disappear without a trace if it supported such an authoritarian defense of segregation as this; and likewise we knew that our own integrity as Christian teachers would be fatally compromised. How could we, Christian professors and students, support this act of expulsion, *our* version of the British Raj and the Amritsar massacre, *our* form of Hitler's persecution of the Jews? So the entire faculty (except one) itself revolted, announced to the Chancellor their refusal to approve his action of expulsion, and went on national radio and television as frequently as we could to make this position of faculty and students alike clear to the country. As the senior member of the theological department (age forty-two), and almost of that whole young faculty, I quite naturally became the spokesman for this public protest.

The chancellor never spoke to me again, and subsequently others, especially Lou Silberman, Bard Thompson, and Jim Sellers, had to carry on the long negotiations. For three months (March–June) we negotiated with the stubborn university, insisting (on I don't know how many grounds) that they allow Lawson to re-enter the Divinity School. Finally in June *we* readmitted him and warned the university that a refusal to recognize that readmission would result in our mass resignations. They refused, so we resigned. Meanwhile key members of the medical school (four full professors and the dean) had from the beginning been urging us not to procrastinate further but to resign at once. So now that we had resigned, we told them to measure up themselves to their own words. This the five of them immediately did. The administration of the university was now itself dumbfounded: to lose a Divinity School is (in the South) possibly an irritation, but to lose a great medical school represents a major academic disaster! So now the chancellor got on the phone, accepted our terms, and readmitted Lawson. To his amazement and ours, the genteel southern board did not concur and adamantly refused to allow him to come back. With this the rest of the faculty of the university, having been mainly against us from the beginning, swung violently in our favor: they could not bear being run by the board! So the chancellor overruled the board, readmitted Lawson, and we won our fight. Lawson, meanwhile, had been admitted to Boston University and decided to stay there. Though we hoped he would come back, we could not really blame him for not doing so. It was a wild, chaotic sequence, and unbelievably lucky in its nonviolent outcome. Ironically the town integrated its restaurants in May, a full month before the "liberal" university capitulated in June (1960)! Looking at the racially mixed character of present-day southern (and northern) life, at least on the surface, in universities, colleges, football teams, hotels, restaurants, and so on ad infinitum, this whole drama seems incredible, and to have occurred in some other epoch rather than a mere twenty-six years ago!

Although objectively this struggle resulted in a significant victory, it was devastating — for the moment at least — to my personal existence. Slowly over the years we as a couple, and especially my Virginia wife, had become part of the younger Nashville social scene. The Lawson event, however, horrified most of the community, and quite clearly our status among them was badly shaken. My doctor's wife remarked that I was the first communist she had ever met! Close personal friends remained utterly loyal and open, but things had really changed. This fact did not make any imprint on me — my wife had left in April to visit her family in Virginia — until summer when it became clear to me that my family had by now thoroughly disintegrated, though certainly the Lawson case was by no means the sole cause. We spent an uneasy and alienated fall and winter on sabbatical leave in Munich, but that spring (1961) my wife left Munich to live alone with our son in New York. The following summer on my return from Germany she refused to accompany me back to Nashville, and so I agreed to seek a divorce. Ironically, I had gone to Germany to write a volume on the theological faith in providence; I returned with little faith in anything, certainly none in myself as a person or a theologian. It was not that I condemned divorce; nevertheless, it was one of those things that I had thought inconceivable for myself, and it was shattering to have to face it. I had also discovered how fallible I was: how much I had been myself at fault in this broken family, and how unable I was to handle with any grace such a personal crisis. All this seemed to represent the end: I had lost (I felt) my son, and with that all hope of creative family life; I had been a failure in the most important of life's endeavors; thus I was void of any real sense of worth or even of cleanness. Because of all this, I felt I could hardly function any longer as a theologian, as a witness to the power either of faith or of grace. Thus — so I told myself — when I recovered a bit, I would have to see what else at forty-two I might take up.

The divine power does, however, work in our life, and grace is very real and effective. There *are* new beginnings, and so things are never necessarily really at an end. This is not because of our own strength and virtue — important as they are — because these do arrive at an end, as mine clearly had done. The new beginnings come from a power not our own. A new loving relationship did appear, a much more creative one with a superbly attractive and talented Dutch woman. A year and a quarter later (1963) with remarriage we started a new home, and I accepted a new position teaching theology at Chicago. And in the years since a new and wonderful family, the clear center of my own existence, has grown and prospered.

There was, however, a vast difference in my self-feeling about this new marriage, the family, and this new career: truly they were of grace and not merit. I was now newly conscious of how precarious every aspect of good fortune is, how deeply confused and misguided we remain, and how uncertain is every step we take. In 1960 for our twentieth class reunion, I had written smugly of my then obvious beginnings of success: a full professorship, a new book, a happy marriage, a new child. For the twenty-fifth in 1965 I wrote a very different summation of my existence to date: how easily, I said, even the most well planned and well established securities fall apart, how fragile our valued relations and accomplishments are, and how uncertain is every fortune — and how we must proceed by faith if we are to proceed at all.

Because of this new and creative beginning followed by the appearance of a marvelous new family in the form of two children, I was able to begin to ponder again, now from a quite existential standpoint, the symbol of providence. The traditional and orthodox themes of sin and grace, of human fall and providence, of crisis, disillusionment, and new beginnings, established as presuppositions in the last days of college and forged in the war experiences of the camp, continued as dominant in my experience as these decades unfolded. However, whereas at the beginning all of this existed as a set of concepts, one may say an almost *frozen theology,* now, through the painful ups and downs of social and personal life, they became less frozen as concepts and more ingredient in existence. And consequently, as is appropriate, the theology itself, like the self thinking it, became progressively more tentative, more (ironically) "liberal," more open to the new.

•

Many changes occurred in this new world: a new and creative marriage, a new job in a new (but to me old) university and community, and a new family — and after all this was also the 1960s when all sorts of new attitudes, new costumes, and new mores appeared. During the next years we enjoyed two long sessions in Europe, one for six months in Rome in 1965 and then one for fifteen months in Holland in 1970–71. At home we gradually become acclimatized to the very different lifestyles of Hyde Park. By the end of the decade not only was I surrounded by a charming, bilingual family, but also I was outwardly almost completely transformed: a knotted scarf instead of a tie, longish hair, a mustache or a beard, and an earring in my left ear. I had in 1970–71 noticed an earring in the left ear of each massive sailor in North Holland and in Crete. As one Greek sailor explained, "Poseidon wears one, why shouldn't we?" As a consequence, since I sailed a small boat on the Maine coast, I decided to wear one, which I continued to do (except at the trial in Arkansas in 1981) until a year or so ago in 1985.

Most influential of all in this set of rather dramatic changes, outwardly visible in the shift from short to long hair but effective on much deeper levels as well, was certainly my wife. A very gifted sculptress and now an equally gifted therapist, she was even more a free spirit; she could exist creatively in all communities but did not fit snugly into any one: suburban-business, academic-scholarly, church-theological. Everything she touched bore its own stamp, represented an original creation, something developed from within rather than reflected from without. As a consequence our home became under her hand in its own modest way quite unique: in decor, in its atmosphere and feel, and in the lifestyles that were present there. If I too became more myself or more original in appearance, dress, attitudes, and inner being, it was owed largely to her, who had been that way (as I had not) since she appeared on earth.

The first new personal, and as a consequence also professional, interest that appeared in this new Chicago existence came as a kind of accident. In 1964 we discovered that after two years of teaching, my wife and I could in 1965 enjoy (if we could organize it) a quarter off somewhere abroad. Both of us wanted to live in and explore Italy — but heretofore Rome had hardly been a fruitful pasture in which Protestant theologians might graze! Then, all of a sudden I awoke to the implications of Vatican II, whose astounding course I had been following since it had started in 1961. I recall saying to myself: "There *must* be some creative theology lying back of these massive changes — if there is *not,* then what we theologians do is vastly irrelevant!"

Thus as an act of faith, if I may put it that way, I applied for a grant "to study the new theological movements so evidently at work in the exciting new developments of reform in the Roman Catholic church." Since I was (apparently) about the first Protestant theologian to propose such a trek to Rome to study these new theological movements (many were already there, of course, as observers of the Council), I received a fellowship, and we embarked via Amsterdam for Rome in the summer of 1965. That fall and early winter I read much of Karl Rahner and Bernard Lonergan, and all else I could on the "new theology" in Roman circles. Together we went to seminars for the observers at the Council (and heard there the young Hans Küng and Edward Schillebeeckx, among others) and to several Vatican II sessions — and we ate as only two enthusiasts can in Rome! All of this introduced me — though, to be sure, only in part — to the fascination and power of the Roman ecclesia: the reality and depth of its community, the seemingly (to a WASP) infinite class, ethnic, and cultural varieties of its manifestations, its real (and also its unreal) rationalism, its seemingly limitless intellectual and moral potentialities, and therefore the immensely creative moral and religious role it might play in the post-Christian *and* in the post-modern world.

I had barely returned to Chicago in early 1966 when Catholic students in increasing numbers began to apply to our graduate theological program. I felt (humorously) grateful that our yearnings for the aesthetic treasures of Italy had, as a kind of "assist," resulted in a provisional acquaintance with the intellectual power of present Catholic theology. Two years later, our first, and stunning, Catholic appointments were made in the theological area, and the new age of ecumenical learning and teaching theology, even more of deep ecumenical friendship, dawned. To my surprise and delight soon I found myself lecturing and speaking as frequently at Catholic seminaries, colleges, and universities as at Protestant or secular ones.

As a result of all this I became aware of the frequent feelings of ineptness and of self-doubt that plagued Catholics conscious of the inadequacies of their recent "orthodox" tradition, and their consequent lack of self-confidence that this tradition, even if "revised," could cope adequately with the modern situation. Increasingly, therefore, my addresses spoke of the difficulties — as a Protestant well knew — of any religious community in the secular modern age and, further, of what to me were the unique "gifts" that the Catholic tradition, as Catholic — if brought into focus with the cultural life it inhabited — could bring to the modern crisis. I came to feel that Protestantism would in the decades ahead need them as much, perhaps even more, than the reverse, and thus, that it was important for the entire Christian enterprise that they be not only "brought up to date," but that they mange to do this in a genuinely *Catholic* form. Thus resulted in 1975 a book on Catholicism "from a Protestant perspective," one I entitled *Crisis and Promise* but which the publishers labeled *Catholicism Confronts Modernity.*

Much else also was new in the theological world in the 1960s and early '70s. This was the era when (as in the older liberal era a half century earlier) the world was enthusiastically accepted, and so in new ways entered, served, and admired by the churches and so by the theological community: in dress and styles of life, in social causes and social action (especially, of course, vis-à-vis race and Vietnam), in many of its moral norms and attitudes, and now also in aspects of its "secularity," its fundamental attitudes about reality, and its standards of truth. Thus the active social protests inherited from our common liberal background continually appeared and reappeared in this new era: almost the whole faculty at the Divinity School at the University of Chicago marched at Selma in 1965, and in 1972 David Tracy, Bernard McGinn, and I went twice to Washington to join the rallies against the war in Vietnam.

One important theological result of this new set of relations to the world was the "God is Dead" theology. By accident, and also by interest, I had a hand in the founding of that potent if brief movement. In the early fall of 1963 I finally read my old friend Bill Hamilton's earlier but relatively unnoticed book, *The New Essence of Christianity.* I was intrigued and yet horrified by his "abandonment of the word God" and the very cogent reasons he gave for this new move in theology. Two weeks later I met the vivacious and brilliant Tom Altizer at the Eliade's, who at dinner also declared that God was now thoroughly dead. I told him to call Bill, whom he had never heard of, on the phone. The next week at an ecumenical conference in Swift Hall I heard a very good paper by a young Episcopal theologian from Austin. When I told him afterwards how much I liked his paper, he introduced himself as Paul Van Buren and told me a new book would soon be out that I would like even better. It is called, he said, *The Secular Meaning of the Gospel,* and "it does theology without God." I gave him the numbers of both Bill and Tom.

The movement utterly fascinated me. Declarations of the death of God from secular academics were part of the staple diet of my youth in Chicago, in college at Harvard, and certainly in the Columbia of the 1940s — but coming from *theologians* this had a different feel and a different relevance. Incidentally, none of these meant what European theologians said they meant by the death of God, namely, that the Christian God was hidden to the world's profane gaze and had revealed himself only in Christ's death.

I did not agree with this new secular theology at all; my cumulative experience of twenty-five years had assured me in countless ways of the reality, the power, and the grace of God. In addition, personal and social experience had also far too thoroughly convinced me of the relevance and validity of the classical symbols of theology for this. Nevertheless, I could feel in myself the powerful tug of their arguments. Secular at-

titudes and standards had also been part of my spiritual reality from
the beginning, and certainly they had grown again in my consciousness
since coming to Chicago. I knew I needed to find some deeper theological grounding for my continuing allegiance to the Christian symbols
than their (to me) obvious relevance in interpreting experience. How
did I know, how could I know, in the secular world we all inhabited
that the divine we spoke of and witnessed to was *real,* as a part of our
most fundamental experience? I could feel how powerful their arguments were — and see their effects on many of my friends (many of
whom have later become "closet" God-is-dead theologians!). Could I
also feel and then articulate an *answer* to these arguments, a defense of
the religious discourse they found now so meaningless?

Clearly, to appeal to *revelation* as most European neo-orthodox theologians did was useless; this was one of the elements of God language
that was now being radically doubted in the name of secularity. Likewise
any argument *metaphysically* to the reality of God (as process theology
suggested) was futile since most current philosophy was doubting the
possibility and legitimacy of metaphysical argument fully as radically as
this theology was questioning the authority of divine revelation. So I
turned to what we all had in common, to our fundamental experience,
the experience of being and becoming ourselves in the world, in society, and in history, our "ontic" experience as *existing,* as searching for
meaning, and so seeking to be and to achieve *value.* I was convinced
that at this existential level — whatever our intellectual or theoretical interpretation of reality may be — the modern age felt, acted, and trusted
religiously, that is to say, in relation to what I called a dimension of ultimacy. Our fundamental anxieties reflected such a dimension, even in a
secular world; and our "secular" answers to these anxieties, our ideologies, also reflected such a dimension. In a secular culture our existence
is in opposition to our understanding of it and certainly to our theories about that existence. For in our actual existence we *are* religious
whether we wish to be so or not. Thus religious language — for example, the ideological language of politics — has "meaning," even secular
meaning, because it was this sort of language alone that could articulate
(thematize) this dimension of experience.

The results of this effort to answer the God is Dead theology were two
books published in 1969 and 1970. The first, *Naming the Whirlwind,*
was certainly the better of the two. After a discussion of the sources of
secular theology and a critique of its coherence, it represented an examination (phenomenological I called it) of ordinary, common, and so

secular experience of a mostly personal sort to uncover the religious dimension latent there — its dimension of ultimacy — and so to show the
meaning and thus in that sense the use of religious discourse as language
articulating that dimension of experience. The second book, *Religion
and the Scientific Future,* was an inquiry into modern science, the heart
of modern secular culture, to show the religious dimension latent there
as well, first in the dimension of ultimacy present in all scientific knowing, and secondly in the inescapable use of "myth" whenever science
sought to understand not only the natural order outside itself but even
more in its efforts to understand itself and its place in human life. Neither one of these volumes represented a systematic theology; for positive
theology depends on a *particular* manifestation of the divine reality pervasive in our life, that is to say, on what Christians call revelation. This
was an attempt to uncover, so to speak, the "shadow" of that divine
presence in daily, secular experience as the possibility of and the basis for the meaning of the symbols that articulate our special relation
to it in revelation and faith, namely theological symbols. I called this,
therefore, *a prolegomenon* to theology proper, necessary to establish the
grounds for the meaning of any set of theological symbols but not sufficient for establishing either the validity or the particular meaning of
a special religious faith. As is evident, I was seeking here to preserve
what I regarded as the essential core of my earlier neo-orthodoxy while
giving to that core a now much needed ground or base in common experience. There is little question that in this analysis, Tillich had now
joined Niebuhr as the central models for my theological efforts.

My next large theological effort, *Reaping the Whirlwind* (1976), represented in my mind an application to one major symbol in systematic
theology (providence) of the method worked out in *Naming.* It also
represented the culmination of many years of puzzlement and reflection
on what I came to regard as the central existential and religious (if not
philosophical) issue of the twentieth century, the question of the meaning of history. Thus the book begins with an examination of ordinary
experience to see how the questions of the meaning of time and of history inevitably arise there, and how with those questions a dimension of
ultimacy, a religious dimension, illustrated by the ideological character
of all politics, inescapably also arises. The volume concludes with an
effort to rethink the traditional theological answers to this question.

Certainly along with the issues of human nature and personal existence, that of history has been central for most of my theological thought
since the 1930s, when the rise of Hitler and the fall of France had raised

so sharply for my generation the question of where history was going. In this work, therefore, I was reflecting consciously on the issue that subconsciously has dominated my theological thinking from the beginning, namely, the question of the structure and career of history and its events. Central to this question in its contemporary form were three cultural/historical facts that I had come to take for granted. The first was that history was continually full of novelty; the second that "learning," especially scientific knowledge and technological expertise, did cumulatively rise in history; nevertheless, third, that despite this progress in knowledge, our mid-century had come to celebrate, not at all the death of God, but rather precisely the death of the belief in progress. Although the level of knowledge, theoretical and technical, may steadily rise, our ability to use it creatively does not, nor do self-concern and irrationality recede. Thus civilization remains as ambiguous and precarious a venture as ever, as suffused with suffering and with tendencies toward self-destruction. I knew well, of course, that this belief in the progress of civilization was not yet dead in the scientific and academic worlds; still, it seemed obvious to me that the historical grounds for it certainly were. This merely shows that with regard to ultimate issues of belief, falsification is as irrelevant with regard to "secular" as to "orthodox" faiths. Since belief in the progress of history represented, I felt, the "religious substance" or spiritual basis of modern culture, whether liberal capitalist or Marxist, this "death" heralded a major spiritual crisis, a crisis centering on the question: if history is *not* progressing, how are we to understand ourselves and our existence in time, and what *now* do we have to believe in, to put our hope on? In answer, I sought to spell out a new understanding of God and of God's providence as providing a firmer and less precarious ground for a renewed confidence in history. Instead of the progress in which the modern West has believed, a "biblical" understanding of history would, I argued, understand history and the work of providence as characterized by covenant or creative beginning; betrayal, judgment, and crisis or breakdown; and creative new beginnings again.

This effort to articulate a theological interpretation, a "revised Christian theology," on the basis of the method of phenomenological prolegomenon and existential correlation — ordinary experience providing the ultimacy, the crisis of anxiety, and so the "question," and the reinterpreted theological symbol providing the answer — was continued (and concluded) in a short ("baby") systematic theology called *Message and Existence* (1979).

Two convictions basic to this theological viewpoint had grown in me during the decade of the 1970s while this theological analysis of history and of personal existence had been under construction and, of course, while the historical career of our scientific and technological culture had been developing. The first was that Western culture appeared to be more and more in a situation of crisis, a "Time of Troubles" as Toynbee had put it, when its own scientific, technical, and industrial achievements, not to mention its development of nationalism, were now increasing its dilemmas rather than resolving them. As a consequence, as in many other epochs of decline, fanaticism and irrationality could only be expected to grow rather than to diminish. The second conviction followed from the first: this was that however secular it may still consider itself to be, modern culture continued to be "religious" in its essential existence, and that this religious character was growing in this period of recurrent crises, manifesting itself not only in the spread of new religious cults and in the expansion of older orthodoxies, but also in the increasingly religious character of its political myths, those of American capitalism on the one hand and those of Marxism on the other. Like many another earlier epoch, our "secular" one was suffering from what were essentially *religious* conflicts, only now set within the terms of the awesome power of modern scientific and industrial culture. These thoughts, developed in addresses and papers in the later 1970s, were published in the series of essays entitled *Society and the Sacred: Towards a Theology of Culture in Decline* (1981).

•

The next interest came as a complete surprise, and yet it continued — in fact added the stamp of specific empirical validation to — many of the reflections about religion and modern culture already set down in *Society and the Sacred.* In late summer of 1981 I was invited, after a rigorous testing process, to be a witness for the ACLU at the upcoming "Creationist Trial" at Little Rock in Arkansas. A state law mandating the teaching of "Creation Science" alongside "evolution science" had been passed, and most of the churches and synagogues of Little Rock, aided by the ACLU, were challenging that law. I, of course, accepted. I proceeded to study Creation Science as thoroughly as I could, and then I worked out slowly and carefully with Tony Siano, one of the lawyers on the case, my testimony as an "expert" theologian and philosopher of religion.

I found this participation in a significant legal process (provided one is innocent!) utterly fascinating, especially since it illuminated for me much of the obscurity of our complex scientific and technological culture and showed the unexpected ways religion and science join forces there. To the media and to most of the scientific observers of this controversy, the latter represented merely the latest skirmish in the "eternal warfare" of objective and mature science against fanatical and immature religion. In fact, as I discovered, it was anything but this.

In the first place, the creationist law was being challenged largely by religious forces: clergy, church groups, and Jewish congregations. Almost all the mainline Protestant, Catholic, and Jewish communities, and only one scientific group, were represented among the plaintiffs. Secondly, the major leaders — writers, debaters, theoreticians, etc. — among the creationists were persons trained in science, possessing Ph.D.'s from reputable universities in one or another of the natural sciences. Thus, despite the fact that it was contrary both to the methods of science and to the content of modern science in all its branches, "Creation Science" could only be the strange, even deviant product of scientists and of a wider scientific culture. That it was in fact contrary to science was obvious. Since it insisted that the universe was only ten to twenty thousand years old and that *none* of its essential forms (nebulae, stars, earth, mountains and valleys, forms of vegetable and animal life) had changed since the beginning, it was as destructive of the methods and conclusions of astrophysics, astronomy, and geology as it was those of biology. Nevertheless, it represents not so much a religious attack on science as such as a new, and deviant, *amalgam* of modern fundamentalist religion and modern science, a "deviant union" of the two. In Creation Science fundamentalists were not at all denying or rejecting Science as such, as they had done in the 1920s; rather, now fully participants in modern culture (e.g., Sunday morning TV), they were absorbing science and in so doing reshaping it into their own quite different forms. As I now saw it, such an amalgamation appears in an advanced scientific culture when political, social, and historical anxieties mount and so where absolutistic certainty becomes necessary and fanaticism grows. In such situations absolute types of religion unite with science — as they also do with technology — to create this sort of strange species.

When I saw this, I realized that Creation Science was no isolated instance of this process of amalgamation in our century; on the contrary, it had repeatedly been preceded by far more dangerous examples. Japan was perhaps the first. In the 1920s and '30s the rapidly developing science, technology, and industry of Japan shifted dramatically away from its liberal culture base (established at the end of the nineteenth century) to one founded upon a strident nationalism and a Shinto mythology. The same development appeared again in the 1930s in Germany, the most advanced scientific nation in the early twentieth century. There at the advent of Nazi "religious" ideology most of the scientific establishment — academic, medical, and industrial — capitulated lock, stock, and barrel and proceeded during the next decade to form "Nazi science." In slightly different form Stalinist Russia created a rather rigid "Marxist science," and now, reworked and liberalized a bit, there is certainly still a Marxist science at Russian university centers. Had he lasted longer, Mao would have created in China a Maoist science — and probably in the end some form of Shi'ite science will appear in Iran. Both religion and science are here to stay. As these repeated cases in our century show, these two do not so much conflict (though particular forms of each will conflict with other particular forms) as they jostle with each other until they find ways of forming a viable union satisfactory to both — but frequently one as wildly deviant from liberal science as from liberal religion. And when they form such a union, each of them (science and religion) reshapes the other, twentieth-century experience showing that it is more frequently the scientific side that is reshaped than it is the religious side. In a Time of Troubles, and so an age of uncertainty and anxiety, the religious element in society's life tends to expand, to become more fanatical, and in the end to dominate, refashion, and then direct the scientific and technical sides of the culture. Religion is, to be sure, permanent and significant — but it is also extremely dangerous.

One conclusion from all this is that the health of science and of technology depends not so much on the internal developments of science, as our culture has thought; much more does that health depend on the health and strength of the legal, political, moral, and especially the religious context of the culture within which science functions. A developed scientific establishment (universities, laboratories, advanced research, etc.) lodged within an absolutistic ideology or religion remains powerful and important — but now infinitely dangerous. Thus science needs the humanities if it would preserve itself. All of this has been set down in my latest volume, the story of the Arkansas trial and reflections thereon: *Creationism on Trial: Evolution and God in Little Rock* (1985).

The most recent interest that has dominated my thoughts and my writings for the past three to four years has also represented a quite new departure. And like the controversy with the creationists, it seems to represent a sharp turn toward the "liberal" side of my intellectual history, if not a step beyond even that. I refer to the interest in dialogue with other religions, especially Buddhism, and a corresponding theoretical concern for the theological challenge that is represented by this new sense of plurality in religion.

This interest really began with a trip by the entire family to Japan to teach for four months at Kyoto University in 1975. This was my first return to the Orient and my first touch again with Japan since we had been at war thirty or more years before and I had been a prisoner. It reawakened all the slumbering fascination with the Orient that I had felt as a young man, and happily my wife and children now fully shared that fascination. Japan was, of course, transformed, infinitely more *modernized* than in 1940 when I had stopped there briefly on my way to Peking. But, as I now realized in living and working there, it was hardly more "Westernized," since all it social structures and fundamental ways of doing things, its customs and mores — home life, university, industry, corporations, and so on — remained thoroughly Japanese and so thoroughly different from our own. It had sufficiently and creatively absorbed modern culture, made it its own, and now it was proceeding to set all this into *Japanese* form. I realized with a start that the West was not spreading *its* culture around the globe, as it had told itself it was in speaking over and over of "Westernization"; it had merely "passed on" to the Orient the modern culture Europe and America had developed in their own forms. Thus, that culture *in these Western forms* was not becoming any more universal than it had been in the age of colonial empires; "modern culture" was now appearing and reappearing in countless novel and non-Western forms in a *newly* plural world. These last thoughts, moreover, received vivid confirmation later that summer when the whole family returned to Europe and Holland westward via the Trans-Siberian railway. In those nine days crossing the seemingly limitless expanse of Russia, we witnessed still another very different, vastly poorer, and (to me) more depressive form of modern culture.

The colleague at Kyoto University who had issued the invitation to me and with whom I taught a seminar on technology and religion, was the distinguished Buddhist philosopher Takeuchi Yoshinori. Through my frequent talks with him about "doing theology" in the midst of a modern scientific culture, I found myself continually intrigued by our common set of problems and yet eager as well to explore our important differences. On that extraordinarily warm and fruitful personal level, therefore, my interest in dialogue began — and it has continued as the predominant concern of my thinking ever since.

Another factor, also very personal, has added to this growing interest. Anyone living through the later 1960s and especially the early '70s in an urban and academic community could not help becoming aware of the many religious movements newly appearing in American life; in our case this also meant participation in them. Over the next few years our family, especially through my wife's increasing devotion to yoga, became involved with the Sikh movement in America, and in 1974 she entered the Sikh Khalsa as one of its members. As a consequence, our family lifestyle changed rather radically; I have, moreover, found myself since then doing yoga weekly in my wife's class and participating in tantric yoga on several weekends each year and for ten days at summer solstice in New Mexico. Thus, to the interchanges with Buddhism have been added this continual and intimate set of relations to modern Sikhism, frequent contacts with its extraordinary leader, Yogi Bhajan, and a growing understanding of — and admiration for — the community of Sikhs in the Western nations. There were several things here that were quite new to me: an Indian religion powerfully practiced (and so transformed) on Western soil by Europeans and Americans, incidentally former Protestants, Catholics, and Jews; a religion based on the practice of traditional techniques (especially yoga) and on strict personal discipline that clearly, despite its obviously "works" or "self-help" character, led to a deep and self-validating experience of the divine and to a transformation or renewal of personal existence; and, finally, a religion in which neither theological beliefs nor philosophical viewpoints played any noticeable role in conversion or in loyalty, but rather followed entirely from (rather than leading to, as in my own case) an experience of a high consciousness and a renewed personal life. In all of this — as in my continual contacts with Buddhists — I realized on a new and sharper level the lacks and weaknesses, as well as the strengths, of my own tradition. For it was obvious on every hand that each member of the Khalsa had found in this very different stream of Indian tradition something significantly needed and yet quite lacking in their own experience of a Christian or a Jewish community. That these "non-biblical" religious traditions possessed their own spiritual power (truth and grace, as we would say it in Christian terms) and had so much to teach us, as well as much to learn, was now too obvious even to wonder seriously about. The new task, therefore, was to understand this *theologically;* that is, to understand my own faith all over again in the new light of

this incontestable "plurality." What I have later called the new experience in our time of "the rough parity" among religions came to me
with unanswerable certainty in these experiences and has set for me the
major theological task of the next years.

These were personal experiences with the wider religious culture beyond the West, with the Orient; as personal they carried great weight in
my thinking. They were to me, however, at the same time increasingly
and vividly viewed (and understood) in relation to the most significant
changes that had transpired in the wider historical background of our
epoch. The deep dilemmas of modern Western culture, its potentialities for infinite evil, had been apparent since my youth in the 1930s.
With the shattering experiences of the Bomb in the '50s and later of the
crisis of the environment in the '70s, this sense of the crisis of Western civilization deepened and the term "time of troubles" for the West
became an important theme of my theological writing. Now, however,
these renewed experiences with the Orient, beginning in 1973 to 1975,
added a new dimension. For it became evident to me how dramatically
the relations of the West with the Orient, in fact with the rest of the entire world, had changed during the course of my own lifetime. In 1940
when I went to China the West was still dominant and so "superior"
on almost every level. All of this was now quite gone: on every front
parity reigned. Western flaws, lacks, and sins have moved to the forefront of consciousness everywhere, much (let us recall) as the flaws in
Oriental cultures were in the forefront of every Western consciousness
in the nineteenth and early twentieth centuries. Correspondingly, a re-
vitalization of non-Western religions and a sense of the new power of
non-Western traditions has accompanied that new consciousness. After
400 years of unquestioned Western dominance, a quite new set of relations between the national powers and the cultural traditions of our
world has appeared.

My own life's experience, from the Japanese humiliation of Westerners in East Asia in 1941 to these cumulative events of the immediate
present, has witnessed and so validated this change. The era of Western
military dominance and cultural superiority (and not just of *Europe's*
empires) is over. A new parity of cultures and of powers is upon us.
American as well as European power represents now only one among a
number of power centers, and Western culture and its religions represent one among a number of equally vital cultural and religious possibilities. The rise of Islam as an economic, political, and religious reality
is merely a more vivid illustration of this same theme. The deepest

source, not so much for the parity of religions, but for our new ability to *recognize, appropriate, and possibly understand that parity* is this change in our world's historical and cultural context apparent since mid-century, a context in which the dramatic loss of the dominance of the West, along with the excessive, even "demonic" power of science and technology, represents perhaps its major characteristic. It is within this new age that we must now do theology, an age in which the plethora of national and ideological conflicts and crises — and the accompanying temptations to absolutism — may by no means be new, but in which the self-understanding of each tradition, in its relations to other traditions, is entirely new. For the first time, each tradition, like it or not, now finds itself one among many in a *plural* world, in a sort of "rough parity" with the others.

How does one do theology in this new context? Can one at the same time affirm and articulate a genuine and viable spiritual commitment, an existence centered on the relation to the divine beyond relativity, and yet also recognize, as now apparently we must, the "parity" of one's own stance with that of others and so the relativity in some sense of all our affirmations? Does not the relativity of religious viewpoints implied here swallow up all religious validity and so all existential or theoretical affirmation or witness? How can a "relative" religious faith subsist, as it must, as an ultimate concern, an ultimate center of trust and confidence? Are we not then left with only relative religious viewpoints through none of which, therefore, we can receive any illumination or arrive at any certainty? But to relativize all religious viewpoints is necessarily to make some *other* viewpoint, probably that of a secular humanism based on science and democracy, ultimate. And our age has even more emphatically shown the relativism, in fact the parochialism as well as the barrenness, of that humanistic and scientific center of modern Western intellectual and spiritual life. Such a humanistic faith had seemed to be universal in the period of Western cultural dominance. Then the dream of a universal scientific and humanistic culture as the spiritual substance of future history more or less defined the notion of progress so important to "modern" culture. As we have noted, such a dream of a universal culture — as an extension of *our* culture — still inspires most of academia. My point, however, is that in fact the possibility of the universality of *that* culture has vanished as thoroughly as has that of a universally triumphant Christianity. There is no aspiring center, be it traditionally religious, secular humanistic or Marxist, that is not equally challenged by this new relativism, and as a consequence that can avoid coming to terms with it.

On the other hand, if our history since the 1930s has shown anything, it is that one cannot live a human existence, especially in a stormy epoch, on relativism: uncommitted, undirected, empty of norms and of ultimate trust. The shock of Hitler had shown this point to us all: one must stand *somewhere* if one is to resist such evil when it appears in power — and resist one must or lose one's soul completely. For to take no stand is not to be neutral but to join with, to participate in, and so to acquiesce to an unacceptable evil. Such a stance is not to be applauded as "objective" and "neutral" but is to be condemned as cynical, loveless, and cowardly. Nothing since, whether it be the racial conflicts, the Vietnam debacle, or the new issues of liberation, has but validated this point. Humans in history, and especially in a time of troubles, must act and act creatively; to do this they inescapably relate themselves to something ultimate, and must do so in terms of commitment, self-surrender, and self-giving, if they are to live creatively. Our age has revealed both the necessity of a relation to the absolute — the *necessity*, if you will, of the religious; and at the same time, it has revealed the relativity of all such relations — the *danger* of the religious. It has manifested the demonic character both of an unquestioned absolutism and of an uncommitted relativism. Theology is still utterly essential; but in a new way and on a new level, it has now to be a relativized theology.

To interpret theologically the rough parity of the religions and so in that sense the relativity of each is, however, a puzzling and frustrating, as well as a new, task. For all theology, as with the faith or the religious existence that theology expresses, seems to begin with some center, some absolute starting point that cannot itself be relativized, be it revelation, holy tradition, special religious experience, or even reason. But in a situation of recognized parity, where each viewpoint shares truth and grace with others, the usual unconditional starting point for each tradition seems to have dissolved and constructive reflection of any sort appears to be frustrated. In an infinity of possible centers, where can one begin to build? One solution to this has been the effort to find a "post-Christian" starting point, one that lies beyond every particular religious tradition and thus seems (at first glance) to include them all. On this basis, the theology of the future can be built. So say many wise and influential voices today, each in a different ways. Frithjof Schuon, Huston Smith, Wilfred Cantwell Smith, John Hick, Paul Knitter. I have found, however, that I cannot follow this route: such a reflected essence of religion, whatever it may be, is itself too parochial and relative; it represents — try as it may to avoid it — a particular way of being religious and so a particular interpretation of religion. Thus it has to *misinterpret* every other tradition in order to incorporate them into its own scheme of understanding. In the end, therefore, it represents in a new form the same religious colonialism that Christianity used to practice so effectively: the interpretation of an alien viewpoint in terms of one's own religious center and so an incorporation of that viewpoint into our own system of understanding, our own quite particular religious orientation.

A path that's sounder and more redolent with creative possibilities, it seems to me, is the enterprise of theological reinterpretation of one's own standpoint in the light of parity. One is, therefore, still "at home" with one's own symbols, sources, and authority — and thus in continuity with the theological tradition one is now seeking in a new way to articulate. Yet one is seeking to reinterpret that tradition in a new way, as in parity with others, as a valid but particular representation of the ultimate reality (or non-reality) all are seeking to express. Can Christianity be legitimately understood in this "relative-absolute" way? That is the question with which now I am concerned, and only a bare beginning of thinking that question through has been accomplished. I am convinced that within the Christian tradition itself there are multiple symbols and themes, biblical and traditional, that support such an interpretation and will contribute to it; and it seems already apparent that many themes and symbols from other traditions — Buddhist, Sikh, Confucian, to name a few — are there that may aid in this effort. As is evident, this last volume is still only a dim shape on the distant horizon.

Far too long, this story has now come to a close. I have here only referred to and hinted at the theological content, the discussions of method, symbols and norms for praxis, dominant at each of its stages. This is because that content, and not the personal history out of which it arose, is itself the subject of the books and articles that I have written. I have here been concerned with the personal and historical context that helped give rise to those theological reflections. Looking back at this history of my history, I think that this narrative has shown unquestionably that whatever else they may represent, these reflections appeared in the shape that they did because of the changing history, both personal and global, in which my life was set — which is, to me at least, to end squarely on the most emphatically "biblical" theme of all.

PART I

THEOLOGY ENCOUNTERS CULTURE

Chapter 1

The House of Intellect in an Age of Carnival: Some Hermeneutical Reflections

NATHAN A. SCOTT, JR.

I SHOULD LIKE IN WHAT FOLLOWS to offer a few observations about the kind of larger cultural atmosphere in which those of us who are today engaged in the various fields of religious studies must carry on our work and in relation to which we must think about the hermeneutical problem. And, once my reflections began to be focalized by this general theme, I found myself brought back again, as I frequently have been on previous occasions over the past twenty years, to one of the great moments in the history of modern spirituality. And the moment to which I refer is a certain evening in late December of 1817 when John Keats was walking back from London to Hampstead and when, all of a sudden, "several things dovetailed" in his mind. He was in the company of his good friends and Hampstead neighbors Charles Armitage Brown and Charles Wentworth Dilke, the three having been in to London for the Boxing Day opening of a pantomime in the Drury Lane theater. Brown was a young Scotsman with strong literary interests who owned a house adjoining Dilke's on the edge of Hampstead Heath. And Dilke himself, though at the time holding a post in the Navy Pay Office, was already launching what was to become a long and successful career as essayist and editor. Between these three there was much warmly affectionate liking, and, on this particular night, they were having (as Keats later reported in a letter to his brothers George and Tom) "not a dispute but a disquisition." Dilke was a man who, as Keats later said, could not even "feel he [had]...a personal identity unless he [had]...made up his Mind about every thing": he was one "incapable of remaining content with half knowledge" — which prompted Keats to suspect that he might "never come at a truth as long as he lives; because he is always trying at it."[1] So, as the three young men thrashed out whatever it was they were ventilating, Dilke was very probably laying about in his customary manner, being confident of the genial tolerance of his friends. And, said Keats, as their "disquisition" proceeded, "several things dovetailed in my mind, and at once it struck me, what quality went to form a Man of Achievement especially in Literature.... I mean *Negative Capability*, that is when man is capable of being in uncertainties, Mysteries, doubts, without any irritable reaching after fact and reason."[2]

Now Keats's word about Negative Capability, this proposal that a sure sign of strength and competence and poise is a capacity for tolerance of complexity, of the ambiguous and the uncertain, of what is dark and fugitive — this is a proposal whose well-nigh scriptural status today attests to its being one of the great testimonies of modern spirituality. And it is surely a testimony that carries an immense relevance to the present time, for ours is a period when all is in uncertainty and doubt: indeed, the title that the French novelist Nathalie Surraute bestowed on a collection of her essays in the 1960s gives us the very name of the age — "the age of suspicion."[3]

In the opening decade of this century William James was vigorously opposing his doctrine of "radical pluralism" to all absolutist and "monistic" conceptions of truth, to the whole notion, as he phrased it, of "Truth with a big T, and in the singular."[4] But, were he a part of the current scene, James would surely not find it necessary any longer to conduct this particular polemic, since on every side the present age is prepared to regard the search for "truth with a big T, and in the singular," as constituting the very essence of "false consciousness." Indeed, nothing is regarded with greater mistrust than "totalistic" visions of unity and simplicity, for we accord a privileged status to multiplicity and fragmentation and diversity. Wrenching things apart and breaking them up is more attractive for contemporary sensibility than hierarchically subsuming things under principles of order: which is to say — again, in the terminology of William James — that we prefer to dwell in a "multiverse" rather than in a "universe."[5] And this preference is itself most deeply rooted in an extreme intolerance of any kind of universalistic philosophy or metaphysic. What is taken for granted is that "the world

[has] become...a place not only vacant of gods, but also empty of a generously regular and peacefully abiding nature."[6] So it is further assumed (as the title of a famous play of Pirandello's puts it) that "tonight we improvise...."

Moreover, contemporary skepticism tells us that, again, it is a sign of "false consciousness" for us to try in any way to legitimate our improvisings, whether in religious thought or in poetic art or in philosophy or in politics and social theory — since the attempt at legitimating a given mode of cultural enterprise will almost always entail an appeal to some kind of metadiscourse and will thus inevitably reinstate the old superstition that the world has indeed a regular and abiding nature that can be known. It is just this consideration, for example, that accounts for the fury with which the French philosopher Jean-François Lyotard rejects the program of the Frankfurter Jürgen Habermas. For the project that Habermas has pursued over the past twenty years, beginning with his early book *Knowledge and Human Interests* and culminating in his recent book *The Theory of Communicative Action,* has involved most essentially an effort at finding a way of rationally justifying the normative standards that may undergird a critical theory of society; and he has supposed that, if this effort is futile, then the furtherance of human emancipation must itself lack any firm rationale. But Lyotard dismisses the whole project that Habermas has undertaken as a radical misconception, since he conceives it to be a fundamental error for any science to seek "to legitimate the rules of its own game," for what it then produces is simply "a discourse of legitimation." As he lays it down in his book *The Postmodern Condition,* "any science that legitimates itself with reference to a metadiscourse of this kind [is merely by way of] making an explicit appeal to some grand narrative, such as the dialectics of Spirit...[or] the hermeneutics of meaning."[7] And he takes the speciousness of such a procedure to be confirmed by the absolute "incredulity toward metanarratives"[8] that is a hallmark of postmodern consciousness.

So if, in our search for barometers of the period, we turn to those who have lately come to be accounted as our representative Wise Men, if we turn to such figures as Jean-François Lyotard and Jacques Derrida and the late Roland Barthes and perhaps the late Michel Foucault, it would seem indeed that ours is not only an age of suspicion but also an age of carnival, in Mikhail Bakhtin's sense of the term. The concept of carnival is, of course, an essential element of Bakhtin's theory of literature, for he considers the novel — which is for him the genre above all others —

to be saturated with the carnival spirit.[9] I do not want, however, on this present occasion to attempt any review of his highly complex argument about the role that is played in fiction by the carnivalesque, but, rather, I want only to recall his conception of carnival as such, in its purest ideality. And, in this connection, the first thing to be said is that, for Bakhtin, a time of carnival is one in which "life [is] drawn out of its *usual* rut" or is in some radical way " 'turned inside out.' "[10] That is to say, all the customary hierarchical structures and all the conventional norms and protocols are suspended, as the common life is invaded by a great wave of riotous antinomianism that makes everywhere for bizarre *mésalliances.* Things that are normally separate and distinct are brought together, so that "the sacred [combines] with the profane, the lofty with the low, the great with the insignificant, the wise with the stupid."[11] And the presiding spirit of blasphemy finds its quintessential expression in the ritual of the mock crowning and subsequent decrowning of the carnival king — who is the very antithesis of a real king, since he is in fact often a slave or a jester. In short, everything is topsy-turvy, and the disarray thus engenders an uproarious kind of laughter. But the laughter belonging to carnival is no more the laughter of absolute negation than it is the laughter of absolute affirmation, for what Bakhtin takes to be the most fundamental fact about carnival is that, under its strange kind of dispensation, ambivalence of viewpoint is the prevailing sentiment: *nothing* is accorded a privileged status, and *everything* is relativized.

So I say that, in Bakhtin's sense of the term, ours seems now to be an age of carnival. For, amidst the radical pluralism that distinguishes the contemporary intellectual scene, the time when truth "with a big T" ("and in the singular") prevailed seems very remote indeed, and any attempt at reviving that former age is greeted with a suspiciousness that does not trouble to conceal its resolute hostility. We are all, it seems, engaged in what the philosopher Nelson Goodman calls "worldmaking"[12]: theologians make theirs, and literary theorists make theirs, and philosophers theirs. Moreover, the practitioners of a single *Wissenschaft* are making not one world but multiple worlds. Within the field of literary studies, for example, there is an immense diversity of worlds: there are the worlds of deconstruction, of feminist criticism, of *Rezeptionsaesthetik,* of Marxist criticism, of psychoanalytic criticism, of readerresponse criticism, of structuralism, and of semiotics, to mention but a few. Nor will one find it at all difficult to remark a similar diversity of "worlds" in theology and philosophy and historiography and philology and jurisprudence and all the other departments of humanistic studies.

And, of course, if we are to be denied any resort to what Jean-François Lyotard speaks of as "metadiscourse," then the time must surely come when it will be said of us — as Melville says of that motley crew over whom Ahab presides aboard the *Pequod* — that "they were nearly all Islanders..., each... living on a separate continent of his own."

Indeed, it is precisely the myriad disjunctions that fractionize and disunite cultural discourse in our period, making all our forums a scene of babel — it is just these disjunctions that make it inevitable that the humanistic enterprise today should be in some measure an enterprise of hermeneutics, whether in the field of *Religionswissenschaft,* or literary theory, or philosophy or any other area of the human sciences. What is clear beyond question is the extreme unlikelihood that the people of the West shall ever again be presented with any great, overarching *speculum mentis* that subdues all the entanglements of modern intellectual life and integrates the various fields of culture, assigning to each its proper place within the terms of some magnificently comprehensive map of the human universe. Nothing, indeed, could be more phantasmal, for the name of the game that we are fated to play (the game that organizes *our* culture and *our* consciousness) is pluralism. Which means that, instead of irritably reaching after what Keats calls "fact and reason," we must seek to win that special virtue which will enable us equably to dwell amid uncertainty and ambiguity and contrariety — and this, of course, is the virtue that Keats speaks of as Negative Capability.

We are, in short, given the pervasive cultural fragmentation of this late time, irrevocably committed to an ethos of encounter, to the stance of attentiveness and listening: ours, in other words, is an irreversibly hermeneutical situation in which the most serious undertaking is that of learning, without recourse to any sort of reductionism, how to understand and interpret the multitudinous messages and voices that press in upon us, each clamoring for attention and for pride of place. And in such a situation the real essence of "false consciousness" will be disclosed in any effort at bullying the world into granting its suffrage to some unilateral position that is claimed to be foundational in respect to the rest of culture and therefore capable of adjudicating the claims of all other points of view.

Choking off in this way what Michael Oakeshott calls "the conversation of mankind"[13] will, to be sure, doubtless be a recurrent temptation. Amid all the exactions entailed in a cultural situation that is radically pluralistic we are likely over and again to be assailed by the impulse impatiently to obliterate "dialogue" (as Bakhtin would say) by some form of "monologue." But, then, a still further complication may present itself in the form of a hermeneutics whose opposition to monologism gives it a certain attractiveness — which turns out, however, to be deceptive, once we discover that the subversion of monologism is not at all intended to support any sort of really genuine affirmation of plurality;[14] and it is precisely this that I believe to be the case with deconstruction. Some of the most interesting figures in religious thought on the American scene just now are, to be sure, being deeply drawn to Jacques Derrida's general program. I have in mind, for example, such people as Carl Raschke and Thomas Altizer and Charles Winquist, and most especially do I think of Mark Taylor and his brilliant book of 1984 (*Erring: A Postmodern A/theology*). And I have no doubt but that the subtlety and acuteness of their work will have the effect of persuasively commending their general outlook to various others. But, as for myself, I cannot allay certain misgivings, principal among which is my conviction that, for all its animosity toward "logocentrism," deconstruction is itself simply another absolutism that is therefore uncalculated to facilitate any vital dialogue between religious thought and other modes of cultural discourse.

The great lesson, of course, that Derrida wants to lay down is that language is without any foundation outside itself in which the play of language may be grounded, since anything that is accessible to the mind is itself "always already" organized by some system of signs and is thus merely another language. There is, in other words, absolutely nothing outside language itself, nothing that is immediately present to us as something which is elemental and self-confirming, as something in which language may find its "center" and with reference to which the determinate meaning of a given utterance may be established. Language in short, as the deconstructionists say, is not "motivated" ontologically by anything beyond itself: so, as the familiar figure of the late Paul de Man puts it, there is a certain "blindness" that is ineradicably a part of all discourse, since, however carefully supervised it may be, it can, in the final analysis, do nothing other than dramatize its own self-reflexiveness.

Now what kind of *Gesprächspartner* might we expect a good deconstructionist to be? Jürgen Habermas suggests, and I think rightly, that there can be no true dialogue apart from an ethos of generous democracy that rules out any element of "force" or "domination": the participants must, in other words, in some real sense accord one another the status of equality.[15] But, of course, the very nature of the deconstructionist project militates against its according equality to any other cultural project; it is simply a matter of fundamental method: the deconstructionist is not, in Wordsworth's phrase, "a man speaking to men" but, rather, one who sets out to construe only for the sake of deconstruing. From Schleiermacher to Emilio Betti and from Dilthey to Gadamer and Ricoeur the tradition of hermeneutical reflection is to be found reminding us over and again that the process of understanding does perforce involve dialogue with whomever or whatever we are seeking to comprehend. True dialogue will, to be sure, doubtless involve interrogation and dispute, but the essential integrity of whoever or whatever is in front of us will not be initially contested, for such a procedure would cut the vital nerve of the dialogical possibility itself at the very outset. Yet this is precisely the procedure of deconstruction: it wants from the very beginning to dismantle, to root up, to eliminate, to erase: it intends to demonstrate that whatever it confronts is at cross purposes with itself. Which means that, within the intellectual forum, it considers dialogue to be an antique sort of undertaking. "The point here is," as one commentator has said, "that you can't enter into a discussion with someone or something that has got you under analysis, and this is where deconstruction has always got you," for it puts you into the "position of not having a say, or not being able to answer back."[16] And thus, as it seems to me, Jacques Derrida and his various epigones are not to be counted on for any good guidance, as we seek today to reckon with the challenge and the opportunity that are presented by the radically polyglot culture in which we find ourselves.

To speak, however, of the pluralistic character of our culture as polyglot may not be altogether appropriate, since in this context the notion of the polyglot may seem to reinforce what is, I think, a mistaken view: namely, the presumption — fostered no doubt in part by Wittgenstein's posthumous influence — that the multiplicity of theory and doctrine and belief that we face in our time represents a great swarm of "language games" each of which, in being closed off from all the others, is a kind of "windowless monad." But, as Habermas reminds us,

We are never locked within a single grammar. Rather, the first grammar that we learn to master already puts us in a position to step out of it and to interpret what is foreign, to make comprehensible what is incomprehensible, to assimilate in our own words what at first escapes them.[17]

And thus the relativism entailed in a pluralistically ordered culture may not be so absolute as we are at first inclined to suppose.

Which is what we will also be reminded of by one of the crucial ideas of the great Russian literary theorist Mikhail Bakhtin. In his book on Dostoevsky and in the four long essays making up his book *The Dialogic Imagination* Bakhtin develops a kind of speech-act theory that, despite its essential uniqueness, may be felt by English-speaking readers to bear certain resemblances to the thought of the Oxford philosopher, the late J. L. Austin. His guiding assumption is that the human order, in its most fundamental character, is dialogical and (as he says) "polyphonic." And this is why he regards the novel as the genre above all others, because he takes it to render a more adequate kind of justice to the polyphonic nature of human life than any other literary form. He consistently holds to a social conception of selfhood not unlike that of the American thinker George Herbert Mead, and thus he considers the essential reality of the individual to be resident not in the detached, solitary ego but in the whole matrix of relations by which every person is formed. I am, for example, the result of a *paideia* administered by family, by church, by certain educational institutions, by class, by nation, and countless other agencies. And the language I employ in spoken and written utterance is one that contrapuntally adjusts to one another all the voices emergent from these various places of my origin. My language, in other words, is not really mine, for one does "not, after all [get one's language] out of a dictionary": "it exists in other people's mouths, in other people's contexts, serving other people's intentions: it is from there that one must take the word, and make it one's own."[18] Indeed, says Bakhtin, "The word in language is half someone else's."[19] So no speech act, whether in spoken or written utterance, can be claimed to be wholly original, for the world that we hold in common is comprised of many voices and many languages; the term that Bakhtin coined for this plurality is "heteroglossia," which is the condition in which "concrete discourse finds the object at which...it [is] directed already...charged with value," since it is "shot through with...[other] thoughts...[and] points of view." Human life in short is a great polyphony of languages and voices that are constantly impinging upon and permeating one another in "a dialogically agitated...environment."[20] And the stance of the monologist, in its servitude to merely one language, is for Bakhtin the very type and example of *in*authenticity.

But, then, given the "heteroglossia" that is our fate and given the multiplicity of hermeneutical programs that are presently jostling with one another for priority of place, in which direction should religious thought be turning for a hermeneutic that will foster the kind of Negative Capability that is requisite for dwelling with poise and level-headedness in a radically pluralistic culture? Michael Holquist, the Yale scholar who is perhaps Bakhtin's ablest interpreter on the American scene, suggests that his entire project of building a dialogical theory of literature and rhetoric may be regarded as an extended "phenomenological medita-tion" on that great word of Christ's in the Sermon on the Mount which says: "All things...whatsoever ye would that men should do unto you, even so do ye also unto them" (Matthew 7:12).[21] Here, as Professor Holquist feels, is the ethic that Bakhtin takes to be the controlling prin-ciple of cultural exchange, when it is truly responsive to the essential logic of dialogue. But where does one turn for a hermeneutic that will keep us on such a high road — in an age of carnival?

Certainly, I should think, as I have already suggested, that one will not turn to the deconstructionists, to the New Inquisitors who receive their instructions from Paris. But Bakhtin himself, I would propose, will make a good point of departure. And then in which other directions ought we also to be turning?

The remarkable sensitiveness with which Paul Ricoeur has addressed himself to the issues of religious apologetics and to their involvement in the whole tangle of hermeneutical problems in the human sciences will surely at once put us in mind of him. And his special relevance to an age of carnival, to a time of radical pluralism, stems, I believe, precisely from the clarity with which he perceives that ours is a pe-riod ineluctably marked by "conflict of interpretations."[22] Nor is the elaborate hermeneutical theory that Ricoeur has developed in any way calculated to obliterate this "conflict" by "totalizing" the multiplicity of interpretations toward the end of some kind of "absolute synthesis." Indeed, from his standpoint nothing could be more delusive than the dream of such a synthesis, since he considers the pluralistic character of our situation to be not merely a result of the cultural exigencies belong-ing to late modernity but, more fundamentally, a result of the essential "finitude of [human] reflection"[23] or of what he speaks of as "the per-spectival limitation of perception" which "causes every view...to be a *point of view.*" And this partiality of perspective that contaminates the entire enterprise of thought is irremediable, because it is rooted in our finitude that may not itself simply be transcended. So any kind of "absolute knowledge is impossible."[24] All "totalistic" schemes, in other words, deserve to be distrusted, and thus, far from wanting to dissolve or annul the "heteroglossia" in which we find ourselves, Ricoeur's great purpose has been that of making manifest "the modalities... of interanimation between [the various] modes of discourse"[25] that give our culture its distinctive buzz and hum. As he says, "When Odysseus completes the circles and returns to his island of Ithaca there is slaughter and destruction. For me the philosophical task is not to close the circle, [or] to centralize or totalize knowledge, but to keep open the irreducible plurality of discourse," and he reminds us that, in order "to show how the different discourses may interrelate or intersect... one must resist the temptation to make them identical"[26] or to fashion some sort of monistic system whereby they may be hierarchically ordered and dominated. Which is to say that the only way of reckoning with a situation of radical pluralism in cultural life is to accept it and live *through* it, since it is only by way of such a "detour" that fundamental meanings and values in any field of inquiry are to be "retrieved."

Now it is just his intention to lay down a similar lesson that qualifies, I believe, Jürgen Habermas to be regarded as still another good guide through the thickets of late modernity (*pace* J. F. Lyotard). True, like Bakhtin, he is not a specialist in the interpretation of religion but is, rather, one who, if he can be said to have a particular specialty at all, might be identified with what we speak of as the sociology of knowledge. Yet, like his predecessors in the Frankfurt School, like Walter Benjamin and Max Horkheimer and Theodor Adorno, he represents an immense breadth of cultural interest; and his deep engagement with classical German philosophy, with American pragmatism, with British analytic philosophy, and with the modern European tradition of Nietzsche, Marx, Weber, Lukács, Heidegger, and Derrida exemplifies a kind of intellectual mastery that one encounters only very rarely among the personnel of American sociology. The body of ideas that he has brought into play in such books as *Knowledge and Human Interests* (trans. Jeremy Shapiro; Boston: Beacon Press, 1970), *Theory and Practice* (trans. John Viertel; Boston: Beacon Press, 1973), *Legitimation Crisis* (trans. Thomas McCarthy; Boston: Beacon Press, 1975), and *The Theory of Communicative Action* (trans. Thomas McCarthy; Boston: Beacon Press, 1984) is far too various and intricate to allow of any swift and comprehensive summary. Suffice it to say that over the past decade or so his basic project has come to entail a study of the particular kind of social action that he calls "communicative action" — which is not so much a special kind of action as it is the decisively constitutive action performed within a given society, since the end toward which communicative action is oriented is what Habermas speaks of as "the intersubjective mutuality of reciprocal understanding."[27] And, of course, in a radically pluralistic society the *consensus omnium* is the very definition of social peace. The consensus prevailing in a polity made up of numerous groups representing diverse interests and values is always, in the nature of the case, something fragile and in a state of contestation, for one group is forever calling into question the rightness and honesty of the position taken by another. And the cause of justice and rationality is by no means guaranteed, as Enlightenment *philosophes* supposed, by simply inculcating in the general populace a reverence for reason, since mere reason can easily be converted into *Zweckrationalität,* into the kind of rationality that is only concerned to find ways of efficiently adjusting means to ends — and this is an orientation, as Max Weber was long ago reminding us, that prepares the way for our being tyrannized over by all the cabals of bureaucratic procurators who are eager for the power to define what's good for us. The guardians of reason, in other words, as Habermas would argue, must aim at something larger and more humane that *Zweckrationalität,* if a genuinely democratic consensus is to be achieved. And such a consensus, he maintains, which rests not on any kind of force or coercion but on unmanipulated, free agreement — such a consensus is to be realized only by way of an unshackled public discourse in which, as the arguments between the various participating parties spurt back and forth, unanimity and concord are restored by nothing other than the force of the better argument.

This is, to be sure, a view of social and political process which Habermas's antagonists have sometimes dismissed as an affair of little more than "utopian rationalism," contending that he has things the wrong way round, that, instead of communicative action generating legitimate institutions, it is "legitimate institutions (legitimate power)...[that] set free communicative action as a mechanism of social coordination."[28] But, whether it be the one or the other, his point is that legitimacy itself is the final outcome of a complex process whereby conflicting rhetorics are adjudicated. Which is to say that, at bottom, his thought finds its center of gravity in the contention that, amid all the "heteroglossia" of a pluralistic society, we shall be preserved at once from anarchy and from tyranny by nothing so much as by the steady promotion of disciplined and candid dialogue — or, as it might be put, Habermas considers it to be hermeneutics alone that can unite *theoria* and *praxis*. And thus it is in his strenuous undertakings with respect to the idea of communicative action that religious thought in our period may, I believe, find another exemplary model, as it seeks to reckon with the difficult hermeneutical issues that are presented by so heterogeneous a culture as our own.

But, then, it is surely Hans-Georg Gadamer who, perhaps beyond all others, deserves to be thought of as the master strategist in the modern period of dialogical approaches to the hermeneutical problem; and his great book *Truth and Method* is today an unignorable text. Long before his work began to win any attention in literary circles on the American scene, it had, of course, already won a limited currency in the theological community, as a result of its having exerted some influence on that German insurgency of Gerhard Ebeling and Ernest Fuchs and Heinrich Ott, which James Robinson introduced in the 1960s as "the New Hermeneutic."[29] And in this country over the past twenty years he has become a great looming presence for all those who are engaged with fundamental questions in theory of interpretation.

His work is, of course, by no means without its problematic elements. Unlike Habermas, he is more than a little touched by that cultural insularity so characteristic of German scholarship that has allowed him to neglect large ranges of Anglo-American thought from which, given the nature of his project, he might have been expected to take profit. And on other grounds his theoretical studies have been vigorously questioned by Habermas, Emilio Betti, Wolfhart Pannenberg, E. D. Hirsch, and various others. But the heart of his program retains a powerful appeal. And perhaps his most fundamental proposal is simply that the event of understanding is one in which, forswearing any intention of seeking to control or manipulate that which is to be comprehended, we undertake instead to be utterly open to what it wants to say to us. Though his *magnum opus,* to be sure, is entitled *Truth and Method,* Gadamer's thought (as David Linge reminds us) is distinguished not so much by any new hermeneutical method he advances as by his description of "what actually takes place in every event of understanding."[30] And this he likens unto what happens in really genuine conversation, for he takes understanding itself to be a form of dialogue.

When two persons are engaged in true conversation, the relation between them does, of course, represent a complete inversion of the master-slave relationship, for neither is seeking to dominate the other: on the contrary, each is seeking to be fully open to and to listen to the other. To be sure, both conversation-partners live and move and have their being within their own horizons: each has his or her own established ways of construing experience, and these will not be merely suspended for the sake of the exchange. But, in the degree to which the conversation has real depth and seriousness, the cross-questioning that goes back and forth will entail each partner's conception of how the world is ordered being submitted to stringent interrogation which, as it progressively deepens down, brings the interlocutors ever nearer that moment in which a real "fusion of horizons" may occur. This, for Gadamer, is the moment of understanding, the moment in which the whole hermeneutical effort wins through at last to fulfillment. And it is on the basis of this fundamental premise that his entire theory of interpretation stands.

Now Mikhail Bakhtin, Paul Ricoeur, Jürgen Habermas, and Hans-Georg Gadamer do most assuredly form a very diverse group indeed. Yet, for all the divergences of interest and doctrine that they reflect when considered together, they do present a significant unanimity in their principled hospitality to difference and variety in the cultural forums of the modern world. Indeed, they make us feel — and this is perhaps what is most quickening — that they conceive the health of the kind of *polis* in which we dwell in this late time to be guaranteed above all else by difference and variety freely submitting themselves to a morality of mutual respect. And it is toward the end of promoting such a morality that they urge that cultural discourse be obedient to the dialogical principle.

Yet, important as candid and courteous dialogue may be in such an age as ours, if we are to be delivered from the frustrating impasse of simply interminable conversation, then surely it is clear that the hermeneutical imagination must finally seek to reach for some principle beyond that of mere dialogue itself. But what should this be? When, for example, a Christian and a Buddhist or a Jew and a Hindu do truly encounter one another in a spirit of mutual respect, and when each has fully laid out before the other what it is in his or her tradition that offers a cogent and healing vision of the possibilities for human fulfillment, surely none of us is then able to invoke any hierarchical principle of valuation that, with reference to some universal and transhistorical "truth," can establish the veracity of the one tradition and the error of the other. And this consideration holds not only with respect to inter-religious or interconfessional dialogue: it also holds with respect to the dialogue that goes on amongst the various parties within a given religious tradition, as it furthermore holds with respect to the conversations that proceed between interpreters of religious tradition and spokesmen for the various influential secular outlooks of our period. The fact of the matter is that the truth is scattered, but, as one of the supremely intelligent men of the nineteenth century, John Stuart Mill, is reminding us in his famous essay *On Liberty:*

> Not violent conflict between parts of the truth, but the quiet sup-
> pression of half of it, is the formidable evil; there is always hope
> when people are forced to listen to both sides; it is when they at-
> tend only to one that errors harden into prejudices, and truth itself
> ceases to have the effect of truth, by being exaggerated into false-
> hood. And since there are few mental attributes more rare than
> that judicial faculty which can sit in intelligent judgment between
> two sides of a question, of which only one is represented by an
> advocate before it, truth has no chance but in proportion as every
> side of it, every opinion which embodies any fraction of the truth,
> not only finds advocates, but is so advocated as to be listened to.[31]

So, fatuous as some may consider the recommendation of dialogue to be amid all the "heteroglossia" that at times appears to be engulfing us, it is, nevertheless, indispensable to that "open society" which alone serves the cause of truth.

But, then, the hermeneutical transaction must at last eventuate in an act whereby we *assess* the validity of the given text or system of thought with which we are dealing. It is my present conviction, how-ever, that this assessment is not properly made with reference to any kind of "totalistic" or absolute doctrine of truth "with a big T." On the contrary, it seems to me that we do well to follow the guidance of a certain kind of revisionist pragmatism in recent philosophy whose way of adjudicating discourse descends from something like the notion of "forms of life" that Wittgenstein advanced in the *Philosophical Investi-gations;* and, in accordance with this mode of judgment, we will say that a particular scheme of argument or poetic representation either does or does not exhibit "rightness of fit"[32] with respect to that *Lebenswelt* to whose authority it would seem to be appealing. And if this *Lebenswelt* does not itself appear to be something demonic or impossibly bizarre or irrelevant or unaccommodable to an open society, then one will say acquiescently, "Yes, I understand..."

It is, I believe, only by way of some such protocol as this that we may dwell happily together not only within the religious community but also within the larger frameworks of cultural and political life, where we must always be prepared to reckon with the fact that, as Hannah Arendt puts it, "Plurality is the law of the earth."[33]

NOTES

1. *The Letters of John Keats,* vol. 2, ed. Hyder Edward Rollins (Cambridge: Harvard University Press, 1958), p. 213.

2. *The Letters of John Keats,* vol. 1, ed. Hyder Edward Rollins (Cambridge: Harvard University Press, 1958), p. 193.

3. See Nathalie Surraute, *The Age of Suspicion: Essays on the Novel,* trans. Maria Jolas (New York: George Braziller, 1963).

4. William James, *Pragmatism* (New York: Longmans Green, and Co., 1907), p. 232.

5. William James, *A Pluralistic Universe* (Cambridge: Harvard University Press, 1977), p. 146.

6. William H. Gass, *Fiction and the Figures of Life* (New York: Vintage Books, 1972), pp. 23-24.

7. Jean-François Lyotard, *The Postmodern Condition: A Report on Knowledge,* trans. Geoff Bennington and Brian Massumi (Minneapolis: University of Minnesota Press, 1984), p. xxiii.

8. Ibid., p. xxiv.

9. See Mikhail Bakhtin, *Problems of Dostoevsky's Poetics,* ed. and trans. Caryl Emerson (Minneapolis: University of Minnesota Press, 1984), pp. 101-180; see also his *Rabelais and His World,* trans. Helene Iswolsky (Cambridge: MIT Press, 1968), *passim.*

10. Ibid., *Problems of Dostoevsky's Poetics,* p. 122.

11. Ibid., p. 123.

12. See Nelson Goodman, *Ways of Worldmaking* (Indianapolis: Hackett Publishing Co., 1978).

13. See Michael Oakeshott, *The Voice of Poetry in the Conversation of Mankind* (London: Bowes and Bowes, 1959).

14. See in this connection Matei Calinescu's interesting observations on what he calls "negative monologism" in three of his essays — "L'intellectuel et le dialogue," in *Cadmos,* vol. 2, no. 7 (1979), pp. 59-83; "Persuasion, dialogue, autorité," in *Cadmos,* vol. 3, no. 11 (1980), pp. 16-36; and "From the One to the Many: Pluralism in Today's Thought," in *Innovation/Renovation: New Perspectives on the Humanities,* ed. Ihab Hassan and Sally Hassan (Madison: University of Wisconsin Press, 1983), pp. 272-273.

15. Jürgen Habermas, "The Hermeneutic Claim to Universality" ("Der Universalitätsanspruch der Hermeneutik," in his *Kultur und Kritik* [Frankfurt: Suhrkamp, 1973]), trans. Josef Bleicher, included in his *Contemporary Hermeneutics: Hermeneutics as Method, Philosophy and Critique* (London: Routledge and Kegan Paul, 1980), pp. 204-206.

16. Gerald L. Bruns, "Structualism, Deconstruction, and Hermeneutics," in *Diacritics,* vol. 14, no. 1 (Spring 1984), p. 14.

17. Jürgen Habermas, "A Review of Gadamer's *Truth and Method,*" in *Understanding and Social Inquiry,* ed. Fred Dallmayr and Thomas McCarthy (Notre Dame: University of Notre Dame Press, 1977), pp. 335-336.

18. Mikhail Bakhtin, *The Dialogic Imagination,* ed. Michael Holquist and trans. Caryl Emerson and M. Holquist (Austin: University of Texas Press, 1981), p. 294.

19. Ibid., p. 293.

20. Ibid., p. 276.

21. Michael Holquist, "The Politics of Representation," in *Allegory and Representation,* ed. Stephen L. Greenblatt (Baltimore: Johns Hopkins University Press, 1981), pp. 171-172.

22. See Paul Ricoeur, *The Conflict of Interpretations: Essays in Hermeneutics,* ed. Don Ihde and trans. by several hands (Evanston: Northwestern University Press, 1974).

23. Paul Ricoeur, *Freud and Philosophy: An Essay on Interpretation,* trans. Denis Savage (New Haven: Yale University Press, 1970), p. 379.

24. Ibid., p. 527.

25. Paul Ricoeur, *The Rule of Metaphor*, trans. Robert Czerny *et al.* (Toronto: University of Toronto Press, 1977), p. 258.

26. "Dialogues with Paul Ricoeur," in Richard Kearney, *Dialogues with Contemporary Continental Thinkers* (Manchester: Manchester University Press, 1984), p. 27.

27. Jürgen Habermas, *Communication and the Evolution of Society,* trans. Thomas McCarthy (Boston: Beacon Press, 1979), p. 3.

28. Albrecht Wellmer, "Reason, Utopia, and the *Dialectic of Enlightenment,*" in *Habermas and Modernity,* ed. Richard J. Bernstein (Cambridge: MIT Press, 1985), p. 59.

29. See James M. Robinson and John B. Cobb, Jr., eds., *New Frontiers in Theology,* vol. 1: *The Later Heidegger and Theology* (New York: Harper and Row, 1963), and vol. 2: *The New Hermeneutic* (New York: Harper and Row, 1964).

30. "Editor's Introduction," in Hans-Georg Gadamer, *Philosophical Hermeneutics,* trans. and ed. David E. Linge (Berkeley: University of California Press, 1977), p. xxvi.

31. John Stuart Mill, *On Liberty,* ed. David Spitz (New York: W. W. Norton, 1975), p. 50.

32. Nelson Goodman, *Ways of Worldmaking,* p. 132.

33. Hannah Arendt, *The Life of the Mind,* vol. 1 (New York: Harcourt Brace Jovanovich, 1978), p. 19.

Chapter 2

The Surface of the Deep:
Deconstruction in the Study of Religion

CHARLES E. WINQUIST

Is there in experience any transcendent dimension for which religious or theological language is necessary and in relation to which
it makes sense?" The theological debate has moved from the question of the character of God to the more radical question of God's
reality, and from the question of the nature and form of religious
language to the more radical question of its possibility as a mode
of meaningful discourse.[1]

In some it is their deprivations that philosophize; in others, their
riches and strengths. The former *need* their philosophy, whether
it be as prop, sedative, medicine, redemption, elevation, or self-
alienation. For the latter it is merely a beautiful luxury — in
the best cases, the voluptuousness of a triumphant gratitude that
eventually has to inscribe itself in cosmic letters on the heaven of
concepts.[2]

Oh, those Greeks! They knew how to live. What is required for
that is to stop courageously at the surface, the fold, the skin, to
adore appearance, to believe in forms, tones, words, in the whole
Olympus of appearance. Those Greeks were superficial — *out of
profundity.*[3]

Anyone whose goal is "something Higher" must expect someday to suffer vertigo. What is vertigo?... It is the voice of the emptiness below us that tempts and lures us; it is the desire to fall, against which, terrified, we defend ourselves.[4]

The desire for depth, certainty, foundations, and beginnings has discovered in its own fulfillment a surface of uncertainty, ambivalence, and ambiguity. As a result, postmodernist theories of discourse have abandoned traditions of self-certainty and have accepted responsibility for their erring ways.

The journey into selfhood is now understood to be a wayward pilgrimage. If the study of religion is to be part of the journey into selfhood, it must range over the surface of deep traditions and make clearings for otherness in experience. This is a deconstructive task.

The deconstruction of discourse importantly resembles the transcendental critique of Immanuel Kant when he posed the question as to what are the conditions that make objective knowledge possible. It is not, however, objective knowledge but discourse itself that is interrogated and turned on its own possibilities. Contemporary religious thought in general, theology in particular, and speculative philosophy have shared in a collective semantic anxiety about the meaningfulness and significance of their discourses. A suspicion has surfaced within the academic community of theologians that the theological use of language is a play of signifiers without any determined or determinable reference outside of its own play.

This is not immediately a problem for the allied disciplines in the field of the study of religion when their discourse is properly understood to be historical, sociological, anthropological, or phenomenological. They appear to have an object for their study even when that object is the history of theological discourse. If theology could be contained, talk of deconstruction in the study of religion could be resisted and silenced. But theology is not only an object to be studied. There is also a theological exigency in thinking because of the desire for depth, certainty, and foundations in all discursive disciplines. Theology and the study of religions become vertiginous disciplines unless an artificial restriction prohibits the entertainment of radical ideas. Theological concepts such as Nirvana, that than which nothing greater can be conceived, the Atman-Brahman synthesis, Allah as Lord of the Worlds, or creation out of nothing too much populate the religious world to isolate the foundational problems of theology.

"The voluptuousness of a triumphant gratitude that eventually has to inscribe itself in cosmic letters on the heaven of concepts" marks the desire for a vertical intrusion and transformation of dreary ordinariness revealing a height or a depth of experience that is heavy with being. In the secular and academic world, temples have become museums, pilgrimages have become vacations, and rituals have become mannerisms. They are to be studied and justify research grants but they do not orient us to the cosmos. The worlds of theological necessity are sharply contrasted with our own world that Milan Kundera has characterized with the title *The Unbearable Lightness of Being.* The objective phenomena that present themselves before the eye of the student of religion are sites of lack, loss, and desire.

The proclamation of the death of God by the nineteenth-century philosophers Hegel and Nietzsche and by the twentieth-century theologians Altizer, Hamilton, and Rubenstein, as well as the development of a deconstructionist a/theology express a lack of reference and a loss of significance. This lack and loss are the conditions for a felt desire. Theological eros ranges over the otherness of culture seeking a home for this homeless desire. Desire posits an otherness. What is desired is what the experience of the self is not.

The secular self that we have come to know in the confidence of rational inquiry is most importantly a being toward death. The vale of our soul-making is a valley of death.[5] The autonomy that we have come to value is also an aloneness in a world that is *real* only in as much as it presents itself as contingent, relative, and transient.[6] We live in the negative implications of Nietzsche's doctrine of eternal recurrence which means, as Milan Kundera states, "that a life which disappears once and for all, which does not return, is like a shadow, without weight, dead in advance, and whether it was horrible, beautiful, or sublime, its honor, sublimity, and beauty mean nothing."[7] Who thinks about the horror of the genocide of the Armenians? Dachau is a memorial. The ditch of blood is now a row of flowers. The grandeur, the beauty, the horror, the abjection of history float unbearably lightly in the theater of memory. The substitutive reality of the memory image is a presence that reveals the absence of substantive reality in mind. Presence of mind is an epiphenomenon of imaginal lightness that follows the trace of reality. Mind is present always in passing. We can't bolt down the conceptual furniture of secular understanding.

A unified field theory has eluded our grasp. Principles of incompleteness, indeterminateness, and uncertainty complement the darken-

ing turn of enlightenment rationality when David Hume could not find
a simple sense experience of necessary connection and declared that the
whole world of a posteriori synthetic judgments could be only probable.
Seams in the modernism of enlightenment rationalism were beginning
to show. A suspicion that language cannot be a mirror of nature was
introduced that was to be deepened by Marx, Nietzsche, and Freud —
the evangelists of suspicion. The conscious center of rationalism could
not hold in descriptions of experience that focused on ideology, the unconscious, and the will to power. There simply is no identifiable ground
on which to stand and build totalizing or holistic systems from minimal empirical affirmations. There is also no purity of consciousness free
from the possibilities of displacement, disguise, and ideologically stereo-
typed symbolizations that can be reflected on itself as a foundation for
phenomenological description.

We can have faith in the intelligibility of experience and we can experiment in order to discover the truth, but our deepest problem is that
we can't get outside of ourselves. We are situated in the contingency of
the given. The blind forces of our material world reveal no purpose in
themselves. The order of things is the production of a text. We are the
makers of meaning and therein resides the deepest problem. We know
the world in alienation. This alienation has been described philosophically by Jacques Derrida as the inscription of identity in difference.
We defer reality and thereby make it differ from itself to be part of a
semiotic system governed by rules of syntax and the lexicon. The word
"dog" does not materially resemble a dog but we know a dog by thinking
it in a language. As Jacques Lacan has pointed out, it is in the mirror
stage that we can take a reflection of ourselves, what we are not, assign
our name to the image, and know ourselves semiotically. Identity is in
difference. This substitution at the origin of self-understanding is an
alienation of ourselves. The experience of self is an experience of lack
and loss. The irony of the search for the self is that its achievements are
metaphorical substitutions and further complexifications of our alienation. Desire is not satisfied but intensified. Desire is for the otherness
of what we know.

When Alphonso Lingis writes about his descent into the ocean and
the rapture of the deep, he is writing about the desire for the other and
for our alterity.

When one descends into the deep, regresses to the depths, the eye
detached from the grasping hand, the mobilizing posture, is de-

tached from its look, moved now by its own voluptuous desire. The voluptuous eye does not seek to comprehend the unity in the surface dispersion of shapes, to penetrate to the substance beneath the chromatic appearances, to comprehensively apprise itself of the functions and relationships; it caresses, is caressed by the surface effects of an alien domain. It is seeking the invisible. The invisible that the eroticized eye seeks is no longer the substances, the principles, the causes of the alien; it is the alien look.[8]

Lingis, like Nietzsche and in the tradition of Nietzsche, seeks the surface of the deep — out of profundity. He also knows that this seeking is a work about which he travelled across several continents with an anthropological and philosophical eye. He looked outwardly in order to release the alien look that could look inwardly.

The pilgrimage of his thinking was a journey into exotic worlds that few of us will directly experience; but the erotic root driving his cultural and geographical wanderings is the desire and accompanying vertigo in the face of the other that is all of our experience. It is desire that experientially constitutes the significance of otherness and also leaves us unfulfilled and insecure. We seek the gaze of the other and seek to overcome the gaze of the other, and this oxymoronic state of affairs is our dilemma and dissatisfaction. We, ironically, seek the gaze of the "Tiger! Tiger! burning bright" not "In the forests of the night" but in a zoo. Our culture is a zoo story, and although we see the tiger, we don't see the tiger. Only if we go into the forests of the night is the tiger truly other. Only there is the tiger experienced as fate and destiny and not as an interesting distraction from an ordinary afternoon.

It is my suspicion that we are tired of ordinary afternoons and we are at the same time afraid of tigers. We want our lives to be deep, but we don't want to know the deep or live on the surface of the deep. The fascination with the mysterious depths of eastern cultures, psychoanalysis, or quantum mechanics and particle physics pulls us toward foundational concepts that, when fully valenced for ordinary understanding of life and culture, would change and challenge our understanding of mastery and wholeness. Indeterminacy, incompleteness, uncertainty, nothingness, and the order of the nonrealized are characteristics of the face of otherness that shows itself at the extremities of foundational thinking. For example, civilization and its discontents are implications of psychoanalytic understanding of dream work. It is the implicated world and implicated self-understanding that usually leads us to compartmentalize master concepts and develop pragmatic competencies that obscure the importance of these root ideas for the revolution of radical thinking. We blunt the imagination with a belief in a hidden order of things that is neither experienced nor capable of being experienced if what we do experience at the extremities of thinking is any measure of the credibility of consciousness. This notion of an order of things at once both hidden and good has no experiential credibility except as an ideological prefiguration begging the question of its own belief. This hidden order of things is the production of a text that can serve as a prop, sedative, medicine, or center of redemption as long as it does not convolute at its extremities and reveal itself as a discursive mask. Thinking the concept of the hidden order of things is a false consciousness of the deep because it is consciousness only of a belief in the deep. It never has to go beyond itself and meet the gaze of the other. Its thinking always stops short of that which transcends it and of that which comprises its transcendental conditions.

Unless an unrestricted interrogative concept is instantiated in the development of a discursive discipline, the notion of humanness can be defined so that its inclusive range falls far short of the range of human experience. The deep then is a metaphorical evocation of the ideological prefiguration of the human. Thought references itself, and the otherness of thought becomes both anomalous and abject. It falls outside the order of things and is glimpsed only as a shadow or disappearing trace. There may be an awareness of a forgetfulness but not an awareness of what is forgotten.

One of the more poignant examples of a critique of a deep forgetting is James Hillman's critique of humanism's psychology:

> Humanism's psychology starts off by forgiving and forgetting. Its very use of the word "human" forgets what it means. By making it mean "humane" the shadow in the word is forgiven. But the human touch is also the hand that holds the flamethrower and tosses the grenade. Correctly speaking, to humanize means not just loving and forgetting: it means as well torturing and vengeance and every cravenness history will not let us forgive.[9]

If we ideologically prefigure forgiveness, we can forget the whole history of political abjection, death camps, racism, sexism, and the systematic violence of economic colonialism, and we can fashion a holistic image of the human that is the terminus of our growth. Here even the growth metaphor is seriously attenuated so that our growth is the growth of a toddler learning to walk and not the growth into the decrepitude of advanced old age where we can no longer walk. Growth is arrested somewhere in the realm of yuppie self-realization. The inevitability of disease, decrepitude, and death as the terminal point in the trajectory of growth would appear to be an anomalous recognition for the industry of growth seminars and in the consciousness raising of humanism's psychology. We seem to forget that although death may be the otherness of life it is an essential part of our humanness. It is our finitude and our fate. It is the emptiness that is also our vertigo tempting us to go deep.

It is the desire to fall into the deep, Freud's death instinct, that makes us uneasy with humanism's metaphors of attenuated growth. We know we have not yet drawn close enough to the human enigma. We are given life, but without necessity and without infinity. The infinity of semiotic replication floats without anchorage in the human enigma that is flush with its finite animality. Desire is not the desire for a closed system, but it is the desire for the other and the otherness of self. Thus, the language of desire is a mixed discourse that is always incomplete, always indeterminate, always less than a total presence. Desire in language is a duplicity. It is inside and outside the order of thinking. It is object and abject. Desire is the enigma of our humanness that challenges concepts of totality, totalizing thinking, and totalitarian praxis. It is the animal revolt against the repression of nature.

Desire in language is the vertical intrusion and transformation of dreary ordinariness from below. This return of the repressed is the whirlwind of vitality that is named in religious traditions and then unnamed as our secular consciousness has invalidated the warrant for traditional theological thinking. No simple name is credible; but the problematics of desire are no less impertinent in our settlement with the givenness of reality now than when we could reference goddesses or gods. Can there be a naming of the whirlwind that is not a substitutive dissipation of its vitality? It is clear that any forms of literalism are a disguise of the duplex complexity of the manifestation of desire in language. It is not new thoughts or new names that are needed. What is needed is a new way of thinking that can entertain desire in its purview without reducing it to itself.

The new way of thinking is not an objectivism. Straight historical studies are blind to the ideological exclusion of desire and the general tropics of discourse. The problem is no less intense than when Gilkey stated in 1969 that "[We] shall challenge the secular understanding of

secular existence... on its failure to provide symbolic forms capable of
thematizing the actual character of its own life."[10] The difference is that
now the problem appears to be less a need for a formal symbol system
than for the articulation of textual strategies that accept responsibility
in its own reflexivity for the repression of otherness. These are textual
strategies that do not compensate for loss by a fascination with exotica
but work through themselves toward the significance of otherness. Desire references what discourse is not, but it is only known discursively.
The problematic of desire in language is to acknowledge extralinguistic
reference within an internal play of linguistic signification.

It is here that we can discern a new warrant for theological thinking
and place its importance within the study of religion. Theological thinking is relevant because it is other than ordinary discourse and is itself
a discourse that can display the otherness of its semantic achievement.
What this means is that historically the fundament in theology has been
unrestricted — God, ultimate reality, Brahman, and other unrestricted
formulations — and even though an objective and descriptive literalism
is no longer credible, the definition of theology as a discursive discipline
includes responsibility for unrestricted inquiry. Notions of "that than
which nothing greater can be conceived" violate intelligible closure to
achievements of understanding within any language game. We could
characterize theology as a deconstructive agent and theological thinking as a deconstructive act within the prison house of language. If it is
important, it is here that we can define the focus of its importance.

A postmodern theology is not defined by the object of its inquiry.
What was in the center of theological thinking and why theology was
itself in the center of intellectual inquiry is now marked by a lack and
a loss. Mark Taylor's a/theology outlines the deconstruction of theology
as a progressive series of losses beginning with the death of God and
proceeding through declarations of the disappearance of the self, the
end of history, and the closure of the book. All of these moves rooted in
the fulfillment of the Hegelian project are for theology a radical ascesis,
a self-denial of its traditional subject matter. Through internal necessity
theology moved into the margins of intellectual life, which was of course
coincident with its valuation by the secular public.

Theology harbors no secret knowledge and has no access to a hidden
order of things. It has become like a nomad wandering over the surface
of the deep. But what it did not surrender in its self-denial was its
unrestricted interrogative form. Its conceptual formulations instantiate
a radical negativity simply by being thought. Questions about what we

take seriously without any reservation may not have answers, but they transgress the boundaries of any claims to totality or closure.

Theology is textual production in which the author is written into the work as a theologian by implicating the text in the exigencies of the unrestricted scope of theological inquiry. The surface of the ordinary world looks differently in the context of unrestricted questioning. We still will be reading a text but the text will be marked and sometimes re-marked by fissures wrought by limiting questions, poetic indirections, and figures of brokenness. From its marginal position theological in-verbalization and inscription will be a supplement to ordinary thinking. We might even think of theology as a supplementary evaluation of the otherness that is present only by its absence in the textual articulation of experience. It is in its postmodern articulation a method of hesita-tion on the surface, the fold, the skin, and the appearance of reality so that there can be an acute recognition of our being there in the world. There is in this recognition a consent to an otherness of reality — a pri-mal sense of nature — that is always in danger of being repressed and exploited by systems of thinking.

Theological defamiliarization can be understood as an ethical exper-iment in letting things be in their otherness. It works against the con-formation of the natural to the idealization of intellectual systems. It is in particular a lever of intervention from within language that prevents systems of totalization from pretending closure. Totalitarian praxis is denied its ideal justification.

The surface of the deep is the surface of life. To be superficial out of profundity is to work against repression and oppression. It all has to do with dogs rather than the word "dog," trees rather than the word "tree," love rather than the word "love."

When the student asks the Zen master, "What is the meaning of Bodhidharma's coming from the west?," the reply is, "The cypress tree standing in the garden."[11] Huston Smith calls this "divine ordinari-ness."[12] This releasement before things subverts the spirit of an age that still trades in enlightenment coinage.

Again consider this comment on Nietzsche from Milan Kundera:

Another image also comes to mind: Nietzsche leaving his hotel in Turin. Seeing a horse and a coachman beating it with a whip, Nie-tzsche went up to the horse and, before the coachman's very eyes, put his arms around the horse's neck and burst into tears. That took place in 1889, where Nietzsche, too, had removed himself

from the world of people. In other words, it was at the time his
mental illness had just erupted. But for that very reason I feel his
gesture had broad implication. Nietzsche was trying to apologize
to the horse for Descartes.... And that is the Nietzsche I love.[13]

And that is the Nietzsche from whom a deconstruction in the study of
religion is theologically warranted. The Cartesian captivity in the subject recognized by Nietzsche has been a repression of the body and animality in general. The "deep" became a subjective idealization without
reference to its own surface in the experience of otherness. Nietzsche's
suspicion that philosophy has been an unconscious disguise of physiological needs and an interpretation and misunderstanding of the body,
is a suspicion that what is at stake in all philosophizing is not "truth."
The "bold insanities of metaphysics" are a concealed misunderstanding
of physiological needs.[14] The body and the whole range of correlate animal experiences are known as text, and through the closure of the text
in totalizing concepts is the repression of otherness effected. We are able
to make adjustments in language to deny the otherness of otherness.

Language can be a tool of familiarity that is forgetful of its own
metaphorical achievement. When otherness is constituted metaphorically as a presence in language, it is no longer itself. Otherness remains
unthought. What is thought is the fiction of language. Otherness can
be controlled in language so that it is thought in the language of contingency, relativity, and autonomy while at the same time no longer being
contingent, relative, and autonomous. The rules of syntax can guarantee a conventional familiarity in the truth of a fiction. The ironic vision
of Nietzsche that sees the commitment to truth as an obligation to lie is
itself the warrant for a deconstruction of claims of truth. The confidence
in enlightenment strategies wavers in this challenge to the commitment
to truth.

The search for a transcendent dimension justifying the theological
use of language may still be thought of as a search for theological truth,
but the strategies for theological text production are radically revised.
The radical question about the reality of God called for by Gilkey in
Naming the Whirlwind leads not to a renewal of God-language but to
a deconstruction of God-language. Language can cover up its forgetfulness unless there is a commitment to subvert the closure of language
from within language. The trajectory of the theological use of language
is not the representation of God. It is instead, as Scharlemann has
suggested in "The Being of God When God Is Not Being God," the in-

stantiation of a radical negativity that marks the otherness of the subject or object of discourse.[15] When the word "God" is allowed to function in a radical defamiliarization of the subject and object of discourse, the strategy of theological thinking is reflexive. Language subverts itself in this dialectical release of language to its otherness. Theology is then both in and out of language even though "the referent of theological meaning is given in and as language."[16]

In this revision of the theological task, systematic theology can never come to completion and foundational theology is not a meta-analysis. Theology cannot stand outside of itself to envision its radical possibilities. Foundational theology is radical theology. It is reflexive. It turns on itself. Its radical possibilities are an achievement of its internal subversion. It cannot become a system because it works against the completeness of a system.

Theological thinking is an ongoing experiment. It may be an experiment with the truth, but it is more importantly an experiment of desire. Theology, with its radical conceptuality, implicates desire in the full range of textual achievements. Its relevance is far reaching when it enacts its radical possibilities. It does range over the surface of deep religious and cultural traditions. Entertaining the possibility of naming the whirlwind is ironically a deconstruction in the study of religion.

NOTES

1. Langdon Gilkey, *Naming the Whirlwind: The Renewal of God-Language* (Indianapolis: Bobbs-Merrill, 1969), p. 13.

2. Friedrich Nietzsche, *The Gay Science* (New York: Vintage Books, 1974), pp. 33–34.

3. Ibid., p. 38.

4. Milan Kundera, *The Unbearable Lightness of Being* (New York: Harper & Row, 1984), pp. 50–60.

5. Cf. James Hillman, *Re-Visioning Psychology* (New York: Harper and Row, 1975), pp. ix–x.

6. Gilkey, *Naming the Whirlwind*, pp. 38–71.

7. Kundera, *The Unbearable Lightness of Being*, p. 3.

8. Alphonso Lingis, *Excesses: Eros and Culture* (Albany: State University of New York Press, 1983), p. 13.

9. Hillman, *Re-Visioning Psychology*, p. 186.

10. Gilkey, *Naming the Whirlwind*, p. 250.

11. Huston Smith, *The Religions of Man* (New York: Harper and Row, 1958), p. 150.

12. Ibid., p. 151.

13. Kundera, *The Unbearable Lightness of Being*, p. 290.

14. Nietzsche, *The Gay Science*, pp. 34–35.

15. Robert Scharlemann, "The Being of God When God Is Not Being God," in *Deconstruction and Theology* (New York: Crossroad, 1982), p. 102.

16. Ibid., p. 104.

Chapter 3

Paradigm Change in Theology

HANS KÜNG

ANYONE WHO HAS A SPECIAL PERSONAL RELATIONSHIP with the Divinity School of the University of Chicago will always have one also with Langdon Gilkey. At this talent-rich school he is one of the most prominent theologians. Several distinct characteristics about him are appealing: He knows how to lead the life of a modern person with great inner freedom while at the same time remaining firmly rooted in the Christian faith; he concentrates upon the decisive elements of Christian theology within a distinctively ecumenical perspective; and he is a person of good humor and earnest sincerity. It meant a great deal to me that I was invited by the University of Chicago to spend there the fall term of 1981. Most especially important to me during this time were the conversations with Langdon Gilkey which, conducted in a spirit of friendship, were inspiring and thought provoking. Out of this guest semester a plan developed for a common symposium of the Institute for the Advanced Study of Religion of the University of Chicago, the Institute for Ecumenical Research of the University of Tübingen, and the international theological journal *Concilium* on the problem of "New Paradigms for Theology." I present here my fundamental reflections from this symposium concerning the paradigm shift in theology. That this symposium became a great, even international success, we may thank, not least of all, Langdon Gilkey. He perhaps more than any other theologian has strengthened me in the conviction that we find ourselves presently in a new paradigm shift from the modern to the postmodern period in theology.

Innovation in Theology and Theory of Knowledge

At all times and in all places, traditional theology has been extremely suspicious of the category of the *novum,* a category that the Marxist philosopher Ernst Bloch has given a new respectability for our times. Innovators who were seduced by Satan and their own doubt and who stubbornly persisted in their pride and rigid outlook were considered heresiarchs, heretics, enemies of the church, and often also enemies of the state. These "unbelievers" who incurred condemnation were to be persecuted by every available means, to be defamed and liquidated — if not physically, at least morally. But I have no desire here to enter into a "history of heretics," either of Catholic or, up to a point, of Protestant origin. I want to turn to the essential problems in the context of the theory of knowledge, which today amounts to a science of science, a theory of theory. It will quickly become clear that we are concerned here not only with the theory but also with the practice of theology, not only with an innocuous general analysis, but with an extremely dramatic history of the past and of the present time.

How is a new situation reached in science? What is involved when we hear of something new in theology? It is not without reason that *rabies theologorum* has become proverbial: It is a clear sign of how ideological and religious controversies, in particular, can stir up people's emotions, overwhelm them existentially, and enter (so to speak) into their bloodstream far more than political or aesthetic differences can arouse similar responses. This is especially the case by contrast with the controversies of natural science, which (as some natural scientists maintain, not without pride) pursue their course entirely rationally. But, is this true? Is the word "rational" the right one? I wonder. In mathematical and natural scientific thought and research, as distinct from that of theology, do subjective conditions and assumptions, standpoints and perspectives really play no part? Can they be completely eliminated for the sake of a pure objectivity?

A comparison between scientific and theological controversies, in particular, can clarify how much is at stake for theology and can indicate how the great controversies are far more than mere squabbles. Nor is it a question of tensions involved in the very nature of theology. As in the far-reaching controversies of natural science, what is really happening is that one theological "paradigm" or model of understanding is being replaced by another, a new one. That, at any rate, is what the situation looks like if it is considered at the level of the present state of epistemological discussion: It is a discussion which, after the dominance of logical positivism and critical rationalism, has entered on a new, third phase where it is beginning again to become directly interesting and fruitful for the humanities in general and for theology in particular. What at first seems an unusual comparison, particularly with the natural sciences and especially with their hard core (physics and chemistry), can help us to develop a keener awareness of problems, even in regard to the question of what is new in theology.

Despite all differences in method, today the natural and the human sciences must be seen again more in their interconnection: some contrasts in method formerly regarded as a matter of principle — for instance, speaking of "explaining" (*erklaren*) in the natural sciences, and "understanding" (*verstehen*) in the human sciences — must now be considered obsolete. For every natural science has an horizon of understanding, a hermeneutical dimension, as understood by those like Hans Georg Gadamer who are concerned with the hermeneutics of the human sciences. Nowhere — not even in the natural sciences — can absolute objectivity be sought by excluding the human subjects, the researchers themselves. Even the conclusions of the natural scientist and the technician are hermeneutically established. They are restricted to those points on which an answer is expected, simply because that is how the question is phrased. Modern physics itself, in connection with the theory of relativity and quantum mechanics, has drawn attention to the fact that the conclusions of natural science have no value in themselves, but only under certain clearly defined conditions and not under others. In the experiments of physics the method changes the object; what it reveals is always only one perspective and only one aspect.

All this is particularly relevant to a critical ecumenical theology, if the latter is meant to be something more than a denominational theological controversy.

It was Karl Popper who as early as 1935 analyzed in his book *Logik der Forschung* the rules for establishing new hypotheses and theories in natural science.[1] He concluded that new theories in natural science are not established by positive confirmation, by corroboration in experience, by "verification." In the 1920s and 1930s this was the thesis of logical positivism upheld by the Vienna Circle associated with Moritz Schlick and Rudolf Carnap, the latter producing (together with the young Ludwig Wittgenstein) his program of an anti-metaphysical "scientific theory of the world," which determined the first phase of the modern theory of knowledge. A positive verification of universal scientific propositions — for instance, "all copper in the universe conducts electricity" — is simply impossible.

Not by verification, says Popper, but by "falsification," by refutation, can new scientific hypotheses and theories be established. The discovery of black swans in Australia, for instance, refutes or "falsifies" the universal proposition that "all" swans are white, and it permits the deduction of the general (existential) proposition: "There are non-white swans." A hypothesis or theory, therefore, can be regarded as true (*wahr*) or, better, as corroborated (*be-wahrt*) when it has withstood all attempts at falsification up to the present. Thus, science appears to be a continually ongoing process of "trial and error," which leads, not to a secure possession of the truth, but to a progressive approach to the truth — a process of continuous change and development.

The question of course, which emerges with increasing clarity in the light of Popper's penetrating logical analysis, is: Although science certainly is not a subjective and irrational enterprise, is logic an adequate means of understanding it? Is progress in science adequately explained by this "logic of scientific discovery," which consists in continual falsification on the basis of strictly rational tests?

That this is not the case became clear in the third phase of the theory of knowledge: logico-critical penetration is not sufficient. (Those engaged in the human sciences had always known this.) Historical-hermeneutical consideration (as practiced particularly in the history of theology and history of dogma) is also needed; above all, psychological-sociological investigation (hitherto largely absent from theology) is required. This is an investigation of the knowledge that represents a combination of theory of knowledge, history of knowledge, and sociology of knowledge.

Hence, in the past fifty years the discussion has moved from an abstract, positivistic logic and linguistic analysis through innumerable interim corrections to taking history, the community of inquiry, and the human subject seriously again. These widespread attempts at an explanation have already achieved results.

Paradigm Change

Radically new hypotheses and theories even in natural science do not emerge simply by verification (as the Vienna positivists thought) or simply by falsification (as Popper, the critical rationalist, suggested). New hypotheses and theories emerge as a result of a highly complex and generally protracted replacement of a hitherto accepted model of interpretation, or "paradigm," by a new one. They arise from a "paradigm change" (not a sudden "paradigm switch"!) in a longer process that is neither completely rational nor completely irrational; and it is often more revolutionary than evolutionary.

This is the theory that the American physicist and historian of science Thomas S. Kuhn expounded in a book that has now become a classic of modern scientific research: *The Structure of Scientific Revolutions.*[2] I gladly admit that it was this theory that enabled me to understand more deeply and comprehensively the problems of growth in knowledge, of development, of progress, of the emergence of a new approach, and thus, in particular, of the present controversies about conceptual change in both science and theology.

I would also like to make Kuhn's terminology my own, but only up to a point. In particular, I do not want to insist on the terms "paradigm" or "revolution." For "paradigm," which originally was understood simply as "example," "classic example," or "pattern" for further experiments, has turned out to be ambiguous. For my own part I am equally happy to speak of interpretative models, explanatory models, models for understanding (*verstehensmodelle*). By this I mean what Kuhn meant by the term "paradigm": "an entire constellation of beliefs, values, techniques, and so on shared by the members of a given community."[3]

Stephen Toulmin, another leading representative of the third phase, remarks in his basic work, "The Collective Use and Evolution of Concepts," which is Part I of *Human Understanding,* that the term "paradigm" (which is more than a "conceptual system") was already used by Georg Christoph Lichtenberg, professor of natural philosophy at Göttingen in the mid-eighteenth century, to indicate certain fundamental patterns of explanation. After the eclipse of German Idealism, Lichtenberg had a great influence on Ernst Mach and Ludwig Wittgenstein, who picked up the term "paradigm" as a key to understanding how philosophical models or stereotypes act as molds (*Gussform*) or "clamps" (*Klammern*), shaping and directing our thought in predetermined and sometimes quite inappropriate directions. In this form the term entered the general philosophical discussion and was first explored in Britain by Wittgenstein's student W. H. Watson, by N. R. Hanson, and by Toulmin himself. Finally, in the early 1950s, the term arrived in the United States.

In his preface, Toulmin formulates his "central thesis," his "deeply held conviction," that in science and philosophy alike, an exclusive preoccupation with logical systematicity has been destructive of both historical understanding and rational criticism. Men demonstrate their rationality, not by ordering their concepts and beliefs in tidy formal structures, but by their preparedness to respond to novel situations with open minds — acknowledging the shortcomings of their former procedures and moving beyond them.[4]

And Toulmin agrees with Kuhn in re-establishing the neglected link between conceptual changes and their socio-historical contexts, without entirely identifying them, "by re-emphasizing the close connections between the socio-historical development of scientific schools, professions, and institutions, and the intellectual development of scientific theories themselves."[5] *In toto*, then, this constitutes a less formalistic but more historical approach than the "self-sufficient and anti-historical logical empiricism inherited from the Vienna Circle."

To be sure, there is a dispute between Kuhn and Toulmin about whether we have to speak of "revolutionary" or "evolutionary" changes; I will have to come back to this question. But more important, it seems to me, is the basic agreement of both authors that "paradigms" or "models" change. Whatever term we choose for our specific theological purpose, this term must be understood broadly enough in order to include not only concepts and judgments but "an entire constellation of beliefs, values, techniques, and so on, shared by the members of a given community."

Now, I must affirm frankly that I am involved with no slight risk in attempting here and now in the course of a single paper to examine the abundantly documented remarks of Kuhn (and Toulmin) hitherto scarcely noticed in the epistemological reflections of theologians, and to give at the same time an account of the highly complex internal developments in theology to which Kuhn himself (in contrast to Toulmin, who is only accidentally interested in the human sciences) has hitherto paid no attention. But the hermeneutical discussion alone, about valid modes, methods, and the principles of solution, persisting in both Catholic and Protestant theology, should be evidence of the fact that we are in the midst of a theological upheaval on which further reflection is sadly needed. Today this situation in theology points to the need for reflecting upon the new paradigm in terms of the theory-praxis discussion in Europe (e.g., Jürgen Habermas and Karl Otto Apel) as well as in America (besides Kuhn and Toulmin, also Richard Bernstein).

I distinguish macro-, meso-, and micromodels, as (for example) in physics: macromodels for scientific global solutions (like the Copernican, the Newtonian, and the Einsteinian models); mesomodels for the solutions of problems in intermediate fields (like the wave theory of light, the dynamic theory of heat, or Maxwell's electro-magnetic theory); and micromodels for detailed scientific solutions (like the discovery of X-rays). Similarly in theology the models can be specified: macromodels for global solutions (the Alexandrian, the Augustinian, and the Thomist models); mesomodels for the solution of problems in the intermediate field (the doctrines of creation and grace, the understanding of the sacraments); micromodels for detailed solutions (the doctrine of original sin, the hypostatic union in Christology). In our context, of course, we have to concentrate on the macromodels.

In physics, for instance, it is possible to distinguish between a Ptolemaic, a Copernican, a Newtonian, and an Einsteinian macromodel. Ought it not be possible also in theology to distinguish, for instance, between a Greek Alexandrian, a Latin Augustinian, a medieval Thomistic, and a modern-critical interpretative macromodel? Kuhn always speaks of "science" (as frequently in American and British usage) as synonymous with "natural science"; I use the term here in the European sense (*Wissenschaft*). But Kuhn sees, albeit with some scepticism, that the problems arise also for the human sciences; in fact, he admits that he himself frequently applied to the natural sciences insights far more familiar to the historiography of literature, music, the visual arts, and politics. On the other hand, the "harshness" in particular of the problems of natural science reveals completely new aspects to the practitioner of the human sciences and especially the theologian. For my own theological purpose, I use these broad terms "paradigm" and "model" interchangeably.

I speak of a "model" as a "paradigm" in order to stress also the provisional character of the project, which in fact holds only under certain assumptions and within certain limits, which does not in principle exclude other projects, but which always grasps reality only comparatively objectively, in a particular perspectivity and variability. For the scientist and theologian alike, facts are never "naked" and experiences never "raw," but always subjectively arranged and interpreted; every "seeing" takes place from the outset in a (scientific or prescientific) model of understanding. Even the best tested "classical" theories, like those of Newton or Aquinas, have turned out to be inadequate and in need of overhauling. There is no reason, therefore, to make a method, a project, a model, or a paradigm absolute; but there is certainly reason for continually starting on a new quest, for permanent criticism and rational control: going through pluralism to ever greater truth.

Analogies between Science and Theology

Although all of this sounds very abstract, it can now be expressed more concretely in view of our central question: Where are the parallels and where are the differences between progress in knowledge both in natural science and theology? The differences are more obvious. Consequently, I am attempting in this essay first of all to bring out clearly certain parallels, similarities, and analogies, so that afterwards I can deal with what is more properly theological. Here we shall discuss five main points.

1. With reference to natural science, Kuhn makes an observation that can serve as our starting point: In practice, students accept certain models of understanding less as a result of proofs than because of the authority of the textbook they study and of the teacher to whom they listen. In ancient times this function was fulfilled by the famous classics of science: Aristotle's *Physics,* Ptolemy's *Almagest;* in modern times, Newton's *Principia* and *Opticks,* Franklin's *Electricity,* Lavoisier's *Chemistry,* Lyell's *Geology,* etc.

Christian theology was distinguished from its beginning from both mythic-cultic "theology" (tales and testimonies of the gods) and philosophical "theology" (doctrine of God), which begins in the New Testament itself with Paul and John. For theology, in addition to the original apostolic witnesses, certain great teachers, "classical writers" so to speak, remain supremely important: Irenaeus, for instance, the most important theologian of the second century, in his resistance to Gnosticism, produced a first survey of Christianity; then in the third century Tertullian in the West and especially the Alexandrians Clement and Origen in the East produced theology in the course of a comprehensive discussion with the culture of their time. Theology thus has to be understood again and again as, in the words of David Tracy, "a dialectic of challenge and response."

Theological textbooks in the strict sense, however, emerged in medieval times when theology was established as a university discipline. From that time onward, theological paradigms or models of understanding therefore have become more easily conceivable.

At an earlier stage in the East, of course, works like the *Fountain of Wisdom* (*pege gnoseos*) by John Damascene, and especially its third part ("An Exposition of the Orthodox Faith"), offered a summary of Eastern theology. As one of the few Byzantine systematic theological surveys, this work exercised an influence in both the Greek and the Slavonic East throughout the whole of the Middle Ages and right up to the present time.

In the West, Latin theology bearing the imprint of Augustine was brought to the medieval scholastics by Peter Lombard (d. 1160), whose *Sentences* consisted for the most part of quotations from Augustine. In this way, Augustine's thought, together with a mainly Neo-Platonic system of ideas, came to dominate scholastic philosophy and theology in both method and content up to the middle of the thirteenth century.

At this time Thomas Aquinas (d. 1274) was still an extremely controversial theologian: Attacked and denounced as a modernist by traditionalist (Augustinian) theologians, he was recalled from Paris by his own Dominican order, eventually subjected to a formal condemnation as a representative of a "new theology" by the competent ecclesiastical authorities in Paris and Oxford, but finally given protection by his order. It was only just before the outbreak of the Reformation that his *Summa Theologiae* succeeded in gaining acceptance outside his order; the first commentary on the whole *Summa* was that of Cardinal Cajetan, classical interpreter of Aquinas and opponent of Luther; and it was only Francisco de Vittoria, father of Spanish scholasticism, who in 1526 introduced the Thomistic *Summa* as a textbook at the University of Salamanca. Louvain followed later with two professorships in Aquinas's theology and seven-year courses on the *Summa Theologiae*. During the next four centuries, ninety commentaries on the whole *Summa* were published, and 218 were written on its first part. Although their works were not on the same scale, the Reformers also produced classics and textbooks that made history: e.g., Melancthon's *Loci,* Calvin's *Institutio,* and the Anglican Hooker's *Laws of Ecclesiastical Polity.*

The fact cannot be overlooked that in theology as in natural science there is something like a "normal science": "research firmly based upon one or more past scientific achievements that some particular scientific community acknowledges for a time as supplying the foundation for its further practice."[6] These great theoretical constructions provide "exemplars," "patterns," "paradigms," "models of understanding" for everyday scientific practice.

Whether in physics it is the earlier Ptolemaic or later Copernican astronomy, the earlier Aristotelian or later Newtonian dynamics, the earlier corpuscular or later wave-optics, and whether in theology it is the earlier Alexandrian or later Augustinian or Thomistic teaching, anyone (even a student) who wants to have a say with regard to the particular science must have mastered by intensive study the model of understanding involved: the macro-, meso-, and micromodels pertaining to it.

And — this is the odd thing — real novelties within the scope of the established model are not really wanted either in natural science or in theology. Why? They would change, upset, perhaps destroy the existing model. Normal science is wholly concerned by every means to confirm its model of understanding, its paradigm, to make it more precise, to secure it, to extend its scope; it is interested in development by aggregation, accumulation, a slow process of growth in knowledge.

In practice, as we see, normal science is just not, in the last resort, interested in falsification, which would only jeopardize the model; but it is interested in solving the puzzles that remain. Consequently, it attempts to confirm the existing model and to incorporate new phenomena, counter-examples, and anomalies (if they are not at first simply denied or suppressed) into the established model and as far as possible to modify the latter or to formulate it in a new way. In this connection the case of Galileo is of equal interest to theology and physics. Not only in theology, but also in natural science, discoveries or anomalies that jeopardize the usual model are at first frequently morally discredited as "disturbers of the peace" or simply reduced to silence.

Analogies between natural science and theology then come to light especially with reference to normal science, and thus it is possible in regard to our problems of the emergence of the new to formulate a (provisional) first thesis, into which, as with the rest of the theses, distinctions will have to be introduced at a later stage.

As in natural science, so also in the theological community, there is a "normal science" with its classical authors, textbooks, and teachers, which is characterized by a cumulative growth of knowledge, by a solution of remaining problems ("puzzles"), and by resistance to everything that might result in a changing or replacement of the established paradigm.

2. One should not speak too hastily against this normal science. Scholars practice it to a certain extent and depend on it for their own thinking. But does scientific development really mean only that progress is made slowly but inexorably against a multitude of errors? Do the

natural scientific disciplines or even theology advance only by coming bit by bit a step closer to the truth?

There is no doubt that this far too simple idea of "organic development" is widespread even among natural scientists. Among theologians, especially Catholic ones, the theory became established already in the nineteenth century through the efforts of John Henry Newman and, under Hegel's influence, particularly of the Catholic Tübingen School. And paradoxically, it also became popular in Rome in order to explain organic development of new dogmas, like that of the Immaculate Conception (1854). I would like, however, to put forward for consideration the following counter-examples that point, not to a simple development, but to crises.

First let us consider physics. In the sixteenth century what was the initial position for Copernicus's astronomical revolution? In addition to other factors, the obvious crisis of Ptolemaic astronomy involved an inability to cope with increasingly clearly recognized discrepancies and even anomalies such as the persistent incapacity of normal science to solve the puzzles imposed on it, especially that of a long-range forecast of the positions of the planets. And in the eighteenth century, what was the precondition of Lavoisier's fundamental breakthrough in chemistry? It was the crisis of the prevailing phlogiston theory, which sought to explain the burning of bodies as due to a concentration of phlogiston. But since (in all its varied proliferations) it could not explain the increasingly frequently observed gains in weight in the process of combustion, Lavoisier began eventually to ignore the existence of such a warm energy substance and recognized that combustion was due to the absorption of oxygen. The foundation for a new formulation of chemistry as a whole had been established. And in the nineteenth and twentieth centuries, what preceded Einstein's theory of relativity? It was the crisis especially of the dominant ether theory, which, despite all the apparatus and experiments, was unable to explain why no movement, no current or carrying of ether (no sort of "ether wind") could be observed. Einstein therefore began simply to ignore the idea of such a sustaining medium for gravitational forces and light waves ("light ether") and was able to assume the velocity of light to be constant for all reference systems moving uniformly toward each other.

These are enough examples from natural science. Are there similar processes in theology? Are there crises in theology?

Already in the New Testament times various Jewish and Hellenistic models of understanding of the one Christ-event appeared alongside and

following one another, reaching a point of intersection especially with
Paul, the Apostle of Jews and Hellenes. The non-fulfillment of the apocalyptic model of the imminent expectation meant a first critical situation
for early Christianity: God's kingdom, expected at an early stage, did
not come. This Jewish apocalyptic model of the imminent end (Christ
as the end of time) was tacitly replaced, especially in the Lukan writings, the Pastoral Epistles, and the Second Epistle of Peter, by an early
Catholic model of interpretation in terms of salvation history with Jesus
Christ as the center of time and of an obviously longer continuing time
of the church. Incidentally, the church now increasingly forgot its Jewish
origin and became more and more Hellenized and institutionalized.

This deep penetration into the Hellenistic world led, however, to a
crisis of identity, manifested especially in the second century in Gnosticism, which completely disregarded the historical origin of Christianity
and moved towards an unhistorical-mythical theology. Several models
of theology were successively developed within the church in the face of
this challenge to its existence. In the second century there came first the
mainly philosophical theology of the Apologists, who tried to defend
both the identity and the universal validity of Christianity rationally
with the aid of borrowings from popular philosophy and invoking the
Hellenistic-Johannine Logos active everywhere in the world. Then, at
the turn from the second to the third century, Irenaeus's biblical theology, which was oriented to salvation history and which had recourse
to Scripture and apostolic tradition against the Gnostic mythologies,
appeared. Eventually in the middle of the third century, Tertullian's
theology came out in the West; and in the East the theology of the
Alexandrians Clement and Origen took shape. Boldly assimilating all
previous attempts, including the Gnostic ones, Origen developed (in discussion with Neo-Platonic philosophy) a first mature and in the long run
largely authoritative macromodel of a theology. The structural elements
of this Greek theology, both open to the world and wholly ecclesial,
both historically justified and based on philosophical reflection, were
the biblical canon, the rule of faith, and Neo-Platonic thought. Origen's
allegorical, symbolical reinterpretation of the words of Scripture and his
spiritual-pneumatic interpretation of Scripture as a whole came to prevail in theology even against the opposition of the mainly Aristotelian
and historically-grammatically oriented Antiochene School. That is to
say, a theology-model was designed here that helped to prepare the way
theologically for the Constantinian turning point. In the fourth century
it was corrected and developed further, particularly by Athanasius and

the Cappadocians (Basil, Gregory Nazianzen, Gregory of Nyssa) and became the model of Greek Orthodoxy (John Damascene).

In the West, despite all solidarity (particularly in scriptural interpretation) with the Greeks, there was a very different macromodel that in the long run became authoritative: the theology of Augustine. In the midst of the crisis of the Roman Empire, Augustine's theology emerged first of all as a result of his personal crisis, both his turning away from dualistic Manichaeism and academic scepticism and his turning to the faith of the church, to Neo-Platonism, to allegorizing, to Paul, to an ascetic Christianity, and finally to the episcopal office. But what really determined the specific development of Augustine's particular model of theology were two crises in church history and in the history of theology: the Donatist crisis, which made its mark on Augustine's conception of the church and the sacraments and then also on that of the West as a whole, and the Pelagian crisis, which decisively shaped the theology of sin and grace right up to the Reformation and Jansenism.

Here is a further example. What was it that led a man like Thomas Aquinas, the most modern theologian of the thirteenth century, to his new revaluation of reason in regard to faith, of the literal sense of Scripture in regard to the allegorical-spiritual method, of nature in regard to grace, of philosophy in regard to theology, and thus to his large-scale new theological synthesis, which, as we saw, was to determine both Spanish scholasticism and the neoscholasticism of the nineteenth and twentieth centuries? It was the crisis of Augustinianism, provoked by the general history of Europe and especially by the reception of Aristotle's work as a whole in Christian Europe. It led to confrontation with an immense accumulation of recent natural discoveries with the similarly Aristotelian-oriented Arabian philosophy. With theology now established at the university and in a new form as an academic discipline (a *scientia*, science, *Wissenschaft*), Aquinas with methodological strictness and dialectical skill fitted the Platonic-Augustinian ideas into his new philosophic-theological system, without ever indulging in polemics, but did not hesitate to reinterpret them completely or even firmly to leave them aside when they did not suit him. Again in the sixteenth century, what was Martin Luther's starting position for his new understanding of word and faith, justice of God and justification of man, and so for his earth-shattering biblical-christocentric new conception of theology as a whole, rejecting allegorizing and basing itself on strict linguistic-grammatical interpretation of Scripture? Within the framework of the crisis of the late medieval church and society, the crisis of systematic-speculative scholasticism became increasingly remote from its biblical sources, neglecting both the basic truths of faith and its existential character, while piling up a mass of purely rational conclusions.

And what was the starting position in the seventeenth and eighteenth centuries for that modern critical theology that made its definitive appearance at the time of the German Enlightenment? It sought to maintain the scientific character of theology against all pietistic biblicism, and the historical character of Christian faith against all deistic natural theology. In a spirit of strictly modern rationality it sought to give account of biblical faith; in dogmatic exegesis the doctrine of verbal inspiration was abandoned and replaced both by an assimilation in principle of the biblical writings to other literature and by an unreservedly philological-historical interpretation of Scripture. The starting position was undoubtedly the crisis of orthodox Protestantism that appeared at the end of the confessional period and its *Religions Kriege*. Looking again to Aristotle, Lutheran and Calvinist Orthodoxy had built up and consolidated a Protestant-scholastic model of theology. This, however, collapsed at the great turning point of tolerance to modern thought and the modern world-vision, when Aristotelianism ceased to be the standard mode of thought for all science. The resultant emancipation of the new philosophy, the individual sciences, and finally the state and society at large from the authority of theology and the church then led to continually fresh revolutionary moves in philosophy and the individual sciences, and eventually also to a new understanding of theology as a whole: a new modern critical paradigm!

In an "ideal typical" way, so to speak, I have outlined here the historical processes in the theological community that are extremely complex in the causation, initiation, and development, and that are scarcely ever accomplished by a single individual and certainly never overnight. (There is no mere "switch" of paradigms.) The irony of history is that, for the most part (as in natural science, so too in theology), normal science itself contributed involuntarily to the undermining of the established model. Insofar as it brought to light additional information that did not fit into the traditional model, it increasingly refined, specialized, and complicated the theory.

The more that the movements of the stars, for example, were studied and corrected in the light of the Ptolemaic system of the universe, the more material was produced for its refutation. The more that orthodox Protestantism, for instance, adopted a neo-Aristotelian approach to science, so much the more did it provoke on the one hand the unscientific "simple" biblicism of Pietism and on the other the unhistorical-rational natural theology of the Enlightenment. Or, we could say, the more that the neoscholasticism of the present century attempted to uphold certain speculative theses with reference to the church's constitution, papal primacy, and infallibility in the light of historical research, so much the more did it bring out contradictory elements that contributed to their undermining.

In theology as well as in natural science, the replacement of an explanatory model is generally preceded by a transitional period of uncertainty in which faith in the established model is shaken; people see through the existing patterns, ties are loosened, traditional schools are reduced in numbers, and an abundance of new initiatives compete for a place. Catholic theology, which had remained far behind modern developments and new Protestant theological trends, was faced with such a transitional situation at the time of Vatican II. Now the differences between the classical neoscholastic schools (Thomists and Scotists, Thomists and Molinists, etc.) no longer played any part, and in their place a whole series of competing new theological initiatives appeared that even now continue to make the future of Catholic theology seem very uncertain.

Despite all the complexity and the pluricausality of any kind of theological development, it has thus become clear that new models of theological interpretation emerge not simply because individual theologians like to handle hot potatoes or to construct new models in their studies but because the traditional model of interpretation breaks down: "Old thinkers," the "puzzle solvers" of normal theology, in the face of the new historical horizon and its new challenge, find no satisfactory answer to great new questions, and thus "model testers," "new thinkers" set in motion alongside normal theology an extra-normal, "extra-ordinary" theology.

Certainly crisis is not an "absolute prerequisite" for a change of model, as Kuhn first maintained in his book but later expressed more cautiously in his postscript of 1969: "crises need only be the usual prelude, supplying, that is, a self-correcting mechanism which ensures that the rigidity of normal science will not forever go unchallenged."[7]

In light of the above, with reference to the emergence of the new in theology, I would like to formulate a second provisional thesis:

As in natural science, so also in the theological community, awareness of a growing crisis is the starting position for the advent of a

drastic change in certain hitherto prevailing basic assumptions and
eventually causes the breakthrough of a new paradigm or model of
understanding. When the available rules and methods break down,
they lead to a search for new ones.

3. Up to now we have explained only the starting position for the
replacement of a paradigm: crisis. But how does the replacement itself
come about in a community of inquiry? Here, too, Kuhn's observations
based on the history of natural science are helpful. What is needed
for a replacement is not merely the critical state of the old paradigm
but also the rise of a new paradigm. Intuitively perceived, this is generally present even earlier than a definite system of common rules for
research and results of research. The new astronomy, the new physics,
the new chemistry, the new biology, and the general theory of relativity,
for example, make it clear that the decision to abandon an old model
is simultaneous with the decision to accept a new one. The model to
be replaced needs a worthy, credible model to succeed it before it can
retire. It needs a new "paradigm candidate."

If such a candidate is at hand, however, the replacement neither
takes place simply through continuous "organic" development nor only
through the usual cumulative process of normal science. Here it is not a
question simply of correcting course but of changing course, whether you
call it a "scientific revolution" or not; it is a fundamental reorganization
of the science as a whole, its concepts, methods, and criteria, often with
considerable socio-political consequences.

There is no need to explain all this further with reference to the great
upheavals in natural science. More important here is its application to
theology. From time to time in theology, there also are drastic changes,
not only in the limited micro- or mesosphere but also in the macro-
sphere. As in the change from the geocentric to the heliocentric theory,
from phlogiston to oxygen chemistry, from the corpuscular to the wave
theory, so in the change from one theology to another fixed and familiar
concepts are changed; laws and criteria controlling the admissibility of
certain problems and solutions are shifted; theories and methods are
upset.

In a word, the paradigm, or model of understanding, is changed,
together with the whole complex of different methods, problem areas,
and attempted solutions, as these had previously been recognized by the
theological community. The theologians get used to a different way of
seeing things, as in the context of a different model. Some things that

formerly were not seen are now perceived, and possibly some things that were formerly noticed are now overlooked. A new view of the human being, world, and God begins to prevail in the theological community where the whole and its details appear in a different light.

In times of epochal upheavals theology thus acquires a new shape, even in its literary expression; we need only compare within the field of comprehensive, systematic projects Clement's *Paidagogos* and Origen's *Periarchon* with Augustine's *Enchiridion* or *De doctrina christiana,* or later the medieval *Summae* with Luther's *Sendschreiben* of 1520 or his *Catechisms.*

As we have already seen, in New Testament times an initial radical change took place when that very model of apocalyptic imminent expectation, taken over from Judaism, was itself unobtrusively replaced by a hellenistically understood conception of Jesus Christ within salvation history as the center of time. The latter was the model that acquired its grandiose first completion by Clement and Origen, who saw the whole history of humankind as a great educational process continually leading upwards (*paideia*): The image of God in the human being shattered by guilt and sin is restored by the pedagogy of God and brought to fulfillment. In God's plan (*oikonomia*) God's becoming a human being is itself the precondition for humanity's becoming God. The primary event of salvation is regarded here as the incarnation rather than the cross and resurrection, as in the New Testament.

A drastic theological change of the same kind took place also in the West. Here that originally extremely worldly man, that intense thinker and acute dialectician, talented psychologist, brilliant stylist, and eventually passionate believer, Aurelius Augustinus, started to work out theologically his intellectual-spiritual experiences, his earlier sexual experiences, and finally his later experience of high office in the church. Like the Greeks, he too wanted to establish a synthesis between Christian faith and Neo-Platonic thought. But the detail and the whole had been changed because of the development of his personal career, his later anti-Donatist and anti-Pelagian confrontations, and the crisis of the Roman Empire. I may mention only a few characteristics of his theology: a mysterious-sinister dual predestination of some to bliss and others to damnation; a new sexually conditioned understanding of sin as original sin and *concupiscentia;* a new theology of history, of the city of God, and of the earthly city; a new psychological definition of the relationship of Father, Son, and Spirit, starting out from the one immutable divine nature. All in all, an epoch-making new theological macromodel emerged that lasted almost a millennium. Understandably, it was viewed by the Greeks with the greatest mistrust even up to the present time, although the comprehensive and thoroughgoing patristic unity of reason and faith, philosophy and theology, still remained secure.

A similar epoch-making theological change involving great struggles again took place with Aquinas and subsequently, to an even greater degree, with Luther. These examples likewise illustrate how much each of these paradigm changes had particular socio-political presuppositions and at the same time also considerable socio-political consequences. Admittedly, the consequences bore some ambivalence; for example, this is true of the Hellenistic-Christian conception of *paideia* for the Byzantine churches or Augustine's two cities or two kingdoms theory for the Middle Ages, or of Aquinas's papalist ecclesiology or Luther's new understanding of justification, church, and sacraments for the modern age. And, as already indicated, it would be possible to continue after Luther or the Lutheran and Reformed orthodoxy to give further examples of drastic theological changes. But for our purposes these examples taken from the history of theology should be sufficient to enable us to formulate a third provisional thesis:

As in natural science, so also in the theological community, an older paradigm or model of understanding is replaced when a new one is available.

4. At the same time another aspect has indirectly become clear, an aspect that might have been perceived at the very beginning of this essay: Without opposition, without struggle and personal sacrifice, as is evident from the history of all those great theologians, nothing new ever came to prevail even in the theological community and in the church. But the subjective circumstances relevant to this change of model must not be defined more exactly with reference to comprehensive scholarly research. It is taken for granted that a whole mass of diverse factors is involved when theologians — whether as initiators or recipients in what is generally a long and complex process — decide in favor of a new explanatory model. This can also be abundantly proved by reference both to Augustine's *Confessions* and letters and to Luther's life-story and self-testimonies, but this is well-known also with regard to Origen (from Eusebius's *Church History*) and Aquinas (especially with reference to the significance of the Dominican order). But for natural scientists the fact that numerous other factors are involved is proved not only in

Popper's *Logic of Scientific Discovery* but also by Kuhn's remarks that are also very consoling for the theologian.

A first observation: In great crises not only theologians, but even natural scientists, have doubts of faith when normal science and its traditional system let them down and they have to look for something new. "It was as if the ground had been pulled out from under one, with no firm foundation to be seen anywhere, upon which one could have been built." This was said, not by a theologian about theology, but by a physicist — Albert Einstein about physics.

"At the moment physics is again terribly confused. In any case, it is too difficult for me, and I wish I had been a movie actor or something of that sort and had never heard of physics." Wolfgang Pauli, later Nobel prizewinner for physics, wrote that in the months before Heisenberg's paper on matrix mechanics pointed the way to a new quantum theory.[8]

It is also well-known that in such critical situations, when no new way was found, not only have theologians lost their faith in theology, but also — and histories of science of course scarcely mention this — natural scientists have lost their faith in natural science and chosen a different calling.

A second observation: Not only in theology, but also in natural science, when there is a paradigm change, non-scientific factors, which are apart from scientific influences, also prove important. A mixture of "objective" and "subjective," individual and sociological factors play a part: The non-scientific aspects include origins, careers, and personalities of those involved; often the nationality, reputation, and teachers especially of the innovator; and, not least, the perhaps aesthetically conditioned attractiveness of the new solution — the consistency, transparency, effectiveness, and also the elegance, simplicity, and universality of the proposed paradigm.

A third observation: The influence of religious convictions on supposedly purely scientific decisions is something that Kuhn did not observe. Yet it is found not only with the great theologians but also with the great physicists — with Copernicus, Newton, and Einstein. Remarkably little was heard in his last decades of Albert Einstein, the greatest physicist of the present century, because he thought he could not participate, could not permit himself to participate in the new, epoch-making turn that physics had taken with quantum mechanics. His attitude was based on religious grounds, as can be seen in his correspondence with Max Born. His famous statement that the "old one" does not play at dice is not a joke, but it is the expression of a definite religious conviction. Einstein believed to the end in the pantheistic-deterministic God of Spinoza, something that evidently remained concealed even from Born in those discussions.

A fourth observation: Not only in theology, but even in natural science, with reference to a new model of understanding there is required something like a conversion, which cannot be purely rationally extorted. I am speaking now less of the initiator, the person who (because of a sudden intuitive experience or of a long and arduous ripening) has suggested a new model, than that of the recipients, those who have to decide for or against the new model. The defenders of the old and of the new models live in "different worlds," different worlds of ideas and of language; often they can scarcely understand each other. Translation from the old to the new language is necessary, but at the same time there must be a new conviction, a conversion.

Certainly convincing objective reasons are important for a conversion of this kind; for it is not a question here simply of an irrational process. Nevertheless, even good reasons cannot extort conversion; for it is likewise not a question merely of a rational process. In the last resort it is a question of a "decision of faith" (in the non-religious sense of the term) or, better, of a "vote of confidence." Which model copes better with the new problems and at the same time preserves most of the old solutions to problems? Which model has a future? This is not so easy to foresee. And since here it is ultimately a question of trust, discussions between the two schools of thought and language-worlds often take the form less of rational argumentations than of more or less successful attempts at recruitment, persuasion, and conversion. For both parties have, in fact, their own lists of problems, priorities, norms, and definitions — their ultimately opposite standpoints. The other party is expected to adopt one's own so obvious standpoint, to accept whatever one's own premises happen to be. In the community of inquiry, the acceptance of the new model then depends on the decision of the individual scientist as to whether to agree with this standpoint, with these particular premises. And this is not easy. For it is not a purely theoretical question.

A fifth observation: Not only in theology, but even in natural science, a new model at first has only a few, usually young advocates. Copernicus was thirty-four when he worked out the heliocentric system. Newton, the founder of classical physics, formulated the law of gravity when he was twenty-three. Lavoisier, founder of modern chemistry, was twenty-six when he deposited with the secretary of the Academie Française his famous sealed testimony expressing his doubts about the dominant phlogiston theory. And Einstein presented the special theory of relativity at the age of twenty-six. Among theologians we find a similar pattern. Origen, the first scholar in Christendom to undertake methodical research, at the age of eighteen took over successfully the Christian education work among intellectuals in Alexandria which had been neglected after Clement's departure. Augustine was thirty-two at the time of his "last" conversion, and Aquinas was not yet thirty when he began in Paris his commentary on the Sentences in the spirit of Aristotle. Finally, Luther was thirty-four when he published his theses on indulgences.

These examples of the achievement of younger men are sufficient. Certainly Kuhn's finding holds for natural science and theology that increasing numbers of scientists are converted to a new paradigm only in the course of time and then pursue more intensely their investigation into this paradigm. Not only because of the stubbornness of age, but also because of their complete attachment to the old model, the most experienced older investigators of the established model often keep up their resistance for a lifetime. A new generation is then required before the great majority of the scientific community eventually accepts the new explanatory model; no less a person than Charles Darwin has stated this with almost depressing clarity in his preface to the *Origin of Species*. Whether or not a new model eventually prevails does not depend on this or that scholar, but on the scientific community as a whole. What the great physicist Max Planck said in his *Scientific Autobiography* is true perhaps more of theologians than of physicists: "A new scientific truth does not triumph by convincing its opponents and making them see the light, but rather because its opponents eventually die, and a new generation grows up that is familiar with it."[9]

Perhaps now we have cited enough material to enable us to formulate a fourth provisional thesis:

As in natural science, so too in the theological community, in the acceptance or rejection of a new paradigm, scientific and extra-scientific factors are involved, so that the transition to a new model cannot be purely rationally extorted, but may be described as a conversion.

5. There remains one last question that can be answered briefly. Is it so certain that the new theological paradigm, the new model of understanding, will always prevail? I want to suggest that in theology,

as in the great controversies of natural science, there are in principle three possible ways out of the crisis.

The first possibility: The new explanatory model is absorbed into the old. Contrary to all appearances, normal science proves to be capable of coping with the problems that produced the crisis; it can assimilate certain new discoveries and improve the existing model without having to give it up. In theology, this was the situation with Augustinianism after Aquinas and with Thomism after Luther.

The Augustinianism of the Franciscan School, increasingly incorporating also Aristotelian ideas, was able to stay alive even after Aquinas. Then it was absorbed into "modern" Scotism and eventually came to an end in that Ockhamism to which Luther probably owed the first imprint of his theology.

Thomism also was able to continue until well into the modern age, especially in comparatively secluded regions like Spain. However, as a result of ignoring modern science and philosophy, it ceased to be the theological vanguard as it had been in the thirteenth century and it became the rearguard of the seventeenth century. And promoted by Rome with every means, it continued in this latter form during the nineteenth and twentieth centuries, losing its predominance in the Catholic church to a large extent only with Vatican II.

The second possibility: The new explanatory model prevails against normal science and replaces the old. Concretely, this means that scientific books, commonly understood descriptions, and comprehensive interpretations, based on the previous model, have to be wholly or partly rewritten. What was once entirely new now becomes old. What began as heretical *innovation* rapidly becomes venerable *tradition.*

We can observe this phenomenon with macromodels in both natural science and theology. At the same time we must note that the textbooks normally describe mainly the results of the radical change while tending to conceal the change itself and the extent of the "revolutions." To that extent a textbook of physics or chemistry, and often too a textbook of dogmatics or ethics, can give a misleading impression of the progress of science. Textbooks of this kind frequently render the radical change, the upheaval, as invisible and make it look simply like evolution, an extension of traditional knowledge. They often make it appear to be the cumulative growth of normal physics, for instance, or an organic growth of normal dogmatics.

The third possibility: The problems and possibly also the circumstances of the time resist radically new initiatives. For the time being these problems are "shelved": The new model is "put into cold storage." Shelving the model in this way can be a purely scientific process. But particularly in theology and in the church, the shelving was frequently effected by compulsion, which meant that instead of generating analogies there arose more differences between natural science and theology. These differences will be the subject of the next section. We can bring to an end the series of analogies with a fifth provisional thesis:

> *In the theological community as in natural science, it can be predicated only with difficulty, in the midst of great controversies, whether a new paradigm will be absorbed into the old, replace the old, or be shelved for a long period. But if the new model is accepted, innovation is consolidated as tradition.*

"Smashing prejudices is more difficult than smashing atoms," said Albert Einstein on one occasion. And I would add that, once they are smashed, they release forces that can perhaps move mountains. I think there is now enough material for thought with reference to a structural similarity between natural science and theology in the emergence of the new. And yet the question is thrust upon us: Does not theology, even Christian truth itself, faced by nothing but paradigm changes and new conceptions, become a victim of historical relativism, which makes it impossible any longer to perceive the Christian reality and makes every paradigm equally true, equally valid? Perhaps the natural scientist is not very much concerned with this problem, but it is of the greatest consequence for the Christian theologian. It was not without reason that we described our theses as "provisional." A theological counterpoint is overdue. We must discuss the five theses worked out with reference to Kuhn and deal with the function of Christian theology, the Christian understanding of truth, and what today paradigmatically distinguishes what I would like to call a modern critical ecumenical theology. Let us therefore pose the question: Does a paradigm change involve a total break?

The Question of Continuity

First we must consider that even in natural science — in all scientific "revolutions" — there is never any question of a total break. In fact, in every paradigm change, despite all discontinuity, there is a fundamental continuity. Thomas Kuhn stresses the fact that in natural science also it is a question of "the same bundle of data as before," which however are placed "in a new system of relations with one another."[10] The transition, for example, from Newtonian to Einsteinian mechanics does not "involve the introduction of additional objects or concepts," but only "a displacement of the conceptual network through which scientists view the world."[11] And Kuhn concludes:

> Whatever he may then see, the scientist after a revolution is still looking at the same world. Furthermore, though he may previously have employed them differently, much of his language and most of his laboratory instruments are still the same as they were before.[12]

We have to affirm even more. There is a common language for theoretical discussion and a procedure for comparing results; thus the "conversion," not necessarily an irrational event, is not without arguments sanctioning the change of the standpoint; it never breaks absolutely with the past. Stephen Toulmin is right:

> We must face the fact that paradigm-switches are never as complete as the fully-fledged definition implies; that rival paradigms never really amount to entire alternative world-views; and that intellectual discontinuities on the theoretical level of science conceal underlying continuities at a deeper, methodological level.[13]

Indeed, this is my conviction: If we ever want to understand the development of theology, we have to avoid the choice not only between an absolutist and a relativist view, but also between a radical continuity and a radical discontinuity, rationality and irrationality, conceptual stability and conceptual change, evolutionary and revolutionary elements. And if one does not like to speak about "revolutionary" changes, then one may speak about *drastic* (not only gradual) and *paradigmatic* (not only conceptual) changes, which of course include gradual and conceptual changes.

In theology (and the historical sciences) much more than in the basically un-historical natural sciences, which mention their fathers and heroes only in introductions and in the margin, it is therefore not a question of a new invention of a tradition. It is a question of a new formulation of tradition, admittedly in the light of a new paradigm. "Novelty for its own sake is not a desideratum in the sciences as it is in so many other creative fields." Consequently, new models of understanding, even though they "seldom or never possess all the capabilities of their predecessors," should "usually preserve a great deal of the most concrete parts of past achievement and always permit additional concrete problem solutions besides."[14]

For theology, the problem of continuity appears at a much deeper level. For what is involved here is something that Kuhn avoids mentioning up to the very last pages, even the word: "truth." Indeed, it is a question of the "truth of life" or, as Wittgenstein says, of the "problems of life." For the natural scientist generally starts out less directly from the problems of life: "Unlike the engineer, and many doctors, and most theologians, the [natural] scientist need not choose problems because they urgently need solution...." And because theologians are more directly concerned with the problems of life, they must also be more concerned about recognition, not only by the "experts," but by the wider public. Even "the most abstract of theologians is far more concerned than the scientist with lay approbation of his creative work, though he may be even less concerned with approbation in general."[15] Even as a scientist, then, Kuhn has no answer to the very obvious vital question of the *whither* of the vast process of development of both science and the world as a whole: "Inevitably that lacuna will have disturbed many readers." But neither has he any answer to the vital question of *whence*: "Anyone who has followed the argument thus far will nevertheless feel the need to ask why the evolutionary process should work."[16]

Here in fact we come to the frontiers of natural science, which remains and seeks to remain tied in its judgments to the horizon of our experience in space and time. Possibly we also reach the frontiers of human and social science, and (if Kant is right) even the frontiers of philosophy insofar as it is a science of pure reason. Vital questions about the whence and whither of the world and the human — i.e., about ultimate and original meanings and standards, values, and norms, and thus about an ultimate and original reality as such — are questions of a believing trust, which is certainly not irrational but utterly reasonable, or a trusting belief.

The responsibility for dealing with these questions lies with theology as a science (*Wissenschaft*), as a rational exposition or account of God (cf. Augustine, *De civitate dei,* III, 1: *de divinitate ratio sive sermo*). Theology exercises this responsibility of course in accordance with its own method. For, like questions of nature, like questions of the psyche and of society, of law, politics, history, and aesthetics, questions of morality and religion too must be treated according to their own methods and style and appropriate to their object. What does this imply?

The Differences between Natural Science and Theology

Christian theology is even less than others a "science without presuppositions." Typically, its presupposition and its object comprise the Christian message, as attested originally in Scripture, as transmitted through the centuries by the church communities, and as proclaimed also today. For all its scientific character, then, Christian theology is essentially characterized by *historicity*. In Christian theology the question of a profoundly historical truth is distinguished from the very outset (1) from the unhistorical-mythological "theologies," that is, tales and testimonies of the gods composed as myths by poets and cultic priests. At the same time as these unhistorical-mythological theologies were being composed, Plato first used and criticized the term "theology" in this sense. And from the start Christian theology distinguished historical truth (2) from the *supra*-historical philosophical "theologies," that is, the natural doctrine of God produced by the philosophers.

Christian theology is quite decidedly a rational account of the truth of the Christian faith, which is faith concerned with the cause of Jesus Christ, thus with the cause of God, and at the same time with the cause of humanity. This Jesus Christ is neither an unhistorical myth nor a suprahistorical idea, doctrine, or ideology. He is, in fact, the historical man Jesus of Nazareth, who as the Christ of God is according to the New Testament writings the standard for believers of all times and of all churches. The original testimony of faith of this Christ Jesus form the basis of Christian theology. Does this exclude a critical scholarly work? Not at all. As, for example, the historian as constitutional lawyer in critical loyalty has to interpret no other history or constitution than that which is given, so the theologian — to be and to remain a Christian theologian — in critical loyalty must consider no other testimony of faith than that originally recorded in the Old and New Testaments, which were transmitted through the ages by the church community in continually varying linguistic forms and which must be continually, freshly translated for people of the present time.

In this sense Christian theology, like natural science, is not only related to the present and the future; nor, like every historical science (history of literature, of art, of philosophy of the world), is it *only* related to tradition. Over and above all of this, it is in a wholly specific sense related to the origins. For theology the primordial event in the history of Israel and of Jesus Christ and consequently the primordial testimony, the original record, of the Old and New Testaments, remains not only the historical origin of the Christian faith but also the point to which it must constantly return.

Despite all the parallels between natural science and theology, this especially is the reason why there are important differences between a paradigm change in natural science and such a change in theology, Christian theology. It is in this light that the five provisional theses with which I attempted to explain the emergence of the new in theology must be distinguished.

1. On thesis 1 on *normal science*: For theological normal science classical authors, textbooks, and teachers are important. They provide systematically in a form that is easy to assimilate the established theological macromodel with its meso- and micromodels. But, unlike their counterparts in natural science, they have at best only a secondary, derived authority. This is true also of the conciliar and of all theological authorities to which normal theology constantly appeals and which can never be more than a standardized norm (*norma normata*).

The primary norm, the *norma normans,* that decides all other norms, is the primordial biblical testimony, which in the Catholic view of Vatican II must also be the "soul," the "principle of life," of any theology. Thus the theologian in the church community can appeal at all times to this primordial biblical testimony. In practice theologians have constantly mediated the immediacy of the primordial biblical testimony. Yet there have also been creative individuals and groups who have gone their own way and to whom the title of theologian could not be denied. (The criteria for discerning a genuine mediation of immediacy will be discussed later.) With an appeal to the primordial testimony, theologians have developed their own theological models away from the mainstream of theology: for instance, the Dutch and German mystics of the Middle Ages, or Pascal, Berulle, and the École Française of the seventeenth century. It is clear from all this what must be said in regard to thesis 2.

2. On thesis 2 on *crisis as a starting position*: In theology a crisis can be caused by certain contemporary socio-political factors in world history or by developments with the science (*Wissenschaft*) itself. In a particular historical situation, however, the crisis can also come to a head (as in the case of Luther and other "reformers" in antiquity, the Middle Ages, and modern times) mainly as a result of an immediate,

wholly personal, spiritual experience of the original Christian message itself.

The primordial Christian testimony, of which theology always falls short, has repeatedly developed an inspiring force that is both disturbing and surprising for theology. And in cases of far too great ecclesiastical and theological consolidation, it even has approached a veritably revolutionary, explosive force. Then occasionally even older, forgotten paradigms recurred, and backward glances opened up new vistas. We may recall the appeal of Augustine, Luther, and Karl Barth to Paul's Letter to the Romans, the consequent "theology of crisis" that each developed. We may also recall the rediscovery of Jesus' proclamation of the imminent advent of the kingdom of God by Johannes Weiss and Albert Schweitzer.

The gospel itself, which obviously and always is manifest in connection with a particular development in contemporary world history, appears here as a direct cause of the theological crisis, as ground of discontinuity in theology, as impetus to the new paradigm. This leads us to the third thesis.

3. On thesis 3 on *paradigmatic* changes: The same primordial Christian testimony is also the permanent, basic testimony for theology and the church. It can be the occasion not only for theology reaching a crisis, but also for the emergence of a new paradigm in the theological upheaval, but not simply for total replacement or total suppression of the old paradigm.

Even in natural science serious questions are raised about Kuhn's insistence that in scientific revolutions the new model — for example, Einsteinian mechanics after Newtonian — completely supplants, completely suppresses the old. In theology, anyway, the primordial and basic Christian testimony, which is common to the "old thinkers" and the "new thinkers," to the "puzzle solvers" of normal science and the "paradigm testers" who oppose them, ensures that the old paradigm is not completely suppressed. This means that, in principle, elements of the old paradigm can be taken up into a new one, as long as they do not contradict the primordial and basic testimony. From the very outset, then, there is an assurance that an upheaval will not lead to a total break, not only between Origen and Augustine, but also between Augustine and Aquinas and even between Aquinas and Luther. And from the outset there is an assurance that a certain theological solidarity will be maintained with a solidarity in Christian faith. We may recall, for instance, the affirmation of justification by faith alone not only in Luther's commentary on Romans but also in the commentaries of Aquinas, Augustine, and Origen.

Certainly, the Christian message (gospel, faith), on the one hand, and Christian theology (doctrine, science), on the other, must be distinguished. But for two reasons they cannot be completely separated. First of all, even the New Testament writings themselves always present the Christian message in definite and very diverse forms of theological language and systems. And second, the theological models after the New Testament were always intended to interpret one and the same Christian message. Hence it was not only opportunism but a completely serious objective reason that made great theologians, including Luther, always have inhibitions about completely rejecting the previous theology and speak of their new theological insights as they might speak of the new discovery of hitherto unknown stars. In this context, an aversion against even the world "revolution" in theology is understandable.

All this means that even a "paradigmatic change," a revolution in Christian theology — if it is to be and to remain Christian — can never take place except on the basis of and ultimately because of the gospel, and never against the gospel. As far as the truth is concerned, the gospel of Jesus Christ himself — however much the testimonies of him must be subjected to historical criticism — is not more at the disposal of the theologian than the history of the constitution is at the disposal of the historian or the constitutional lawyer. The gospel itself appears here as the ground, not only of discontinuity, but also of continuity in theology: on the basis of the paradigm change.

4. On thesis 4 on *conversion and extra-scientific factors:* This thesis becomes even more relevant when considered from a specifically theological standpoint. Something of this kind does indeed happen in natural science, but in theology there is always the danger that an academic decision for one paradigm or another will be turned into an existential decision for or against the reality of faith itself.

The "decision of faith" (in the non-religious sense) for or against a theological paradigm is then upgraded and turned into a decision of faith in the strictly religious sense for or against God and his Christ. And conversion to the "gospel" or to "Catholic teaching" is demanded by the Protestant fundamentalist of the Catholic traditionalist even when it is a question merely of conversion to a (perhaps long obsolete) theological paradigm. The theological opponent is then necessarily regarded as guilty of false belief or unbelief, as not truly Catholic or truly Protestant, as a heretic, even as potentially an anti-Christian or an atheist. In the light of all of this, thesis 5 also acquires a greater relevance.

5. On thesis 5 on the *three possible consequences* of a controversy: If in the theological community and in the church a particular model of understanding is rejected, rejection easily leads to condemnation, discussion to excommunication. Gospel and theology, content of faith and outward form of faith, are identified. And conversely, as a result of this identification, if a model of understanding is eventually accepted and innovation is turned into tradition, it is again easy to turn a theological interpretation into a truth of faith. A theologoumenon becomes a dogma, and tradition becomes traditionalism. If a model of understanding is shelved, this shelving can be a purely academic process. But particularly in theology and in the church, the shelving has frequently been established by compulsion and repression against all human rights and persecution of heretics, inquisition (physical and psychological burning of opponents), or simply suppression of discussion. Even the greatest theologians mentioned earlier — Origen, Augustine, Aquinas, Luther — did not, at least posthumously, escape blame or even condemnation.

(1) *Origen* was involved in a serious conflict with his bishop, Demetrius. As the church's teaching became increasingly consolidated after the Council of Nicea and after his death, he was charged with heresy by Epiphanus and Jerome, condemned by Pope Anastasius in the sixth century, disapproved by the Emperor Justinian (who had the greater part of his works burned), and eventually denounced by the fifth ecumenical council of Constantinople.

(2) Against *Augustine,* whose authority was not to be preferred to that of the magisterium, quite formal warnings were issued at an early date, in the Middle Ages, the time of Jansenism, and up to the present century. With reference to his doctrine of dual predestination and the irresistible efficacy of grace, the practical disappearance of later Augustinianism might not be unjust.

(3) The condemnation of *Aquinas* in 1277, three years after his death, by the bishops of the two leading universities of Christendom — Paris and Oxford — has been described (by van Steenberghen) as "the most serious condemnation of the middle ages," and for a long time it brought to a standstill any further free development of theology.

(4) And what the condemnation and excommunication of *Luther* has meant and does mean for Christendom is well known.

The question, however, can no longer be postponed: What paradigm, what model of understanding, is appropriate to present-day theology? I shall attempt, cautiously, to provide an outline of it, not as an all-embracing hermeneutics (with regard to Scripture, tradition, magisterium) but as a set of some guidelines with regard especially to the heuristic criteria, the historical presuppositions, and the theological constants of the new paradigm.

The New Theological Paradigm

1. *Heuristic criteria:* I mention here some decisive presuppositions of the new paradigm that are not only applicable to theology but that should be understood as the heuristic criteria informing all genuine human inquiry. These criteria are especially important in elucidating the mediation process whereby the primordial biblical testimony is actualized again and again in new situations throughout history. Precisely because these criteria inform all human inquiry, the paradigmatic approach cannot be used to legitimate a traditionalist or fundamentalist theological sectarianism. (We have another paradigm — "Christian," "biblical," "Catholic" — than that of the "world.")

I cannot here fully develop the heuristic character of these presuppositions. Instead, I will only briefly indicate the relevance of these very basic human attitudes for theology. (1) A *truthful* (not a conformist, opportunist) theology: An intellectually honest account of faith seeks and states Christian truth in truthfulness. All this is accomplished wholly at the service of the church's unity. For there cannot be a truthful church without a truthful theology. (2) A *free* (not an authoritarian, system-imminent) theology: A theology can pursue its task without being obstructed by administrative measures and sanctions and can express and publish its reasoned convictions to the best of its knowledge and belief. All this is accomplished wholly at the service of the church's community and authority. For there cannot be a free church without a free theology. (3) A *critical* (not a fundamentalist or traditionalist) theology: A theology, free and truthful, is bound by the ethos of scientific truth, by methodological discipline and the critical testing of the formulation of its problems, methods, and conclusions. All this is accomplished wholly at the service of the church's edification (building up?) in this society. For there cannot be a critical church in this society without a critical theology. (4) An *ecumenical* (not a denominationalist, confessionalist) theology: A theology sees in every other theology not its opponent but its partner. It also is intent on agreement instead of separation, on agreement in two directions: *ad intra,* inwardly, in the sphere of the *oikoumene* among the churches and within Christianity; and *ad extra,* outwardly, in the sphere of the world-*oikoumene* outside the churches and outside Christianity, with its different regions, religions, ideologies, and sciences. This kind of ecumenicity corresponds to the transcultural or universalist aspects of paradigm analysis in theology and in other disciplines. All this is accomplished wholly at the service of the church's mission in this society. For there cannot be an ecumenical church without an ecumenical theology.

2. *Historical presuppositions:* It would be a fundamental mistake to pretend that every new development in church and society were a new macroparadigm. Of course, they influence and modify the ripening process of the new paradigm that was initiated a long time ago. This paradigm of a truthful, free, and critical ecumenical theology has not been invented only today, nor has it only recently been suggested as something entirely new. Such an evaluation would be absurd in view of the important theological figures of the present century like Adolf Harnack, Albert Schweitzer, Karl Barth, Rudolf Bultmann, Dietrich Bonhoeffer, and Paul Tillich, to say nothing of living persons. Such a paradigm "ripens" (a term of which Kuhn also is aware in connection with the development of natural science) over a long period of time, and not least today it must take up the impulses of the theologians just named.

We should not think in too brief periods of time. The "wars of religion" and denominationalist thinking in the seventeenth and eighteenth centuries, for instance, ended at the same time as the rise of natural science, new philosophy, and a modern way of thought and life emerged with the Enlightenment and German Idealism. All this amounted to a great epoch-making break for theology that is not fully realized even today. From that time onward, an abundance of the most diverse experiences touched this theology of the modern age and often entered into it and utterly changed its understanding of the human person, society, history, and religion.

Briefly and schematically stated, theology has been changed by the permanent, corroborated conclusions and results: (1) of modern *natural science,* which, from Copernicus and Galileo to Darwin and Einstein, have thrown a completely new light on the position of the human being in the cosmos, the creation and evolution of the world, and consequently the Creator; (2) of modern *philosophy,* which, from Descartes, Hume, Kant, and Hegel to Heidegger, Whitehead, and Critical Theory, have given us a new understanding, not only of human reason, freedom, historicity, and sociability, but also of God's historicity and secularity; (3)

of modern *democracy,* which, beginning with the American declarations of independence and human fights and with the French Revolution, led to a new understanding of individual freedom — of conscience, speech, press, assembly, and religion — and thus to a new understanding of state, society, and so too the church; (4) of modern *criticism of religion,* which, beginning with the British and French Enlightenment, laid bare the ever-present possibility of the misuse of religion for anti-human alienation (Feuerbach), for stabilizing unjust socio-political structures (Marx), for the moral degradation of the human individual (Nietzsche), and for infantile regression (Freud); (5) of the modern *human and social sciences,* which, especially from the nineteenth century, have helped us to gain a concrete and discriminating understanding of the human being, his/her psyche (the conscious and the unconscious), behavior, sociological make-up, in a way quite different from what was possible at the times of Aristotle, Origen, Augustine, Aquinas, Martin Luther, and Protestant or Tridentine Orthodoxy; (6) of modern *exegesis and history,* which, from the time of Spinoza, Simon, and Bayle, from the time of Reimarus, Lessing, Semler, and Strauss, taught us to understand afresh in a critical light both the history of Israel, that of Jesus of Nazareth, and that of the history of the church and of dogma; (7) of modern *liberation movements,* which, already in the nineteenth century, fought against the purely formalistic freedom for the "bourgeois," against sexism, unjust social structures, racism, imperialism, and colonialism in order to give full justice to women, blacks, and the Third World.

We have now seen the heuristic criteria and the historical presuppositions of the new theological paradigm. The only theology that could provide a theology for our age is one that has entered critically and constructively into the historical and present-day experiences of humanity. And looking now in the midst of the flux of history for some constants of the new paradigm, we may summarize all that. The first constant of the new theological paradigm has to be the present world of experience. These then are some (but not all) of the historical elements and developments that have to be taken into account for a fully modern and ecumenical theological paradigm.

The First Constant: The Present World as Horizon

Here then is revealed one pole or, to be more exact, horizon of the paradigm of a critical ecumenical theology. Horizon can only mean our present world of human experience. All the historical and actual experiences that make up present-day reality in all its ambivalence and contingency delineate our horizon. But what does "reality" here signify? It is all that is real, all that is: all being, the totality of beings, existent being as a whole. What reality is, of course, cannot be closely analyzed here. Reality cannot be defined *a priori*. For the all-embracing, by its very nature, is not definable, not delimitable. Yet to avoid talking only in abstract terms, we shall briefly illustrate here a little of what is meant concretely by this complex and multi-dimensional concept.

The reality with which theology has to deal is primarily the *world* and all that constitutes the world in space and time: as macrocosm and microcosm; in its history — in the past, present, and future; with matter and energy, with nature and civilization, with all its marvels and horrors. Not an *heile Welt*, an "unbroken world," but the real world in all its uncertainty: with all its concrete conditions and natural disasters, with its social misery and all its pain; animals and human beings in their struggle for existence, rise and decline, "devouring" and "being devoured"; the whole world, so difficult to accept in its ambivalence.

Reality means especially *human beings* in the world: men and women of all groups and classes, of all colors and races, of all nations, regions, and religions. Human beings as individuals and in societies, often in unjust and inhumane conditions. Human beings who are the most distant aliens and particularly our neighbors, who often seem to us the most remote. Human beings who are indeed human, all too human. Not by any means ideal humanity, but humanity that includes all that we would prefer to exclude when we sing with Schiller and Beethoven: "You millions, I embrace you. This kiss is for all the world." Including, too, all those who can make life hell for us, on a grand or a small scale, as when we say with Sartre: *L'enfer, c'est les autres*: "Hell...is other people."

Reality means above all *myself,* I who as subject can become object to myself. I myself with mind and body, with disposition and behavior, with weaknesses and strengths. Certainly not an ideal human being, but a human being with heights and depths, with bright and seamy sides, with all that which C. G. Jung calls the "shadow" of the person, with all that we have pushed off, suppressed, repressed — what Freud with the aid of analysis tried to restore to consciousness and make acceptable. Also, a human being who is always splitting up into the various roles we have to play in society, who always has to fulfill particular social functions that society expects of us. We often accept the world more easily than ourselves, as we happen to be or as we are made by others.

One thing should now be clear. The reality of world, humanity, myself, is revealed in depth in its obvious *ambivalence,* its radical *contingency,* and its continual *change:* an ongoing history of success and suffering, justice and injustice, happiness and unhappiness, salvation and disaster, sense and nonsense. Nor does this mean making the world evil, so that theologians can more easily get their God involved; it means taking stock without prejudice of what is. Theology does not create any reality, but interprets it.

Summarizing these thoughts in a short first thesis, we can say: *The first constant, the first pole or the horizon of a critical ecumenical theology is our present world of experience in all its ambivalence, contingency, and change.*

Only a strictly scientific theology drawn against the background of present-day experience deserves a place today in the university in the midst of all the other disciplines. Such a theology must be open to the world and related to the present, not in a tacitly authoritarian way but, as we observed, in a way that is aware of being bound by the ethos of scientific truth, by methodological discipline, and by the critical testing of the formulations of its problems, its methods, and its conclusions. The critical ecumenical theology is one that has cast off all denominationalist ghetto mentality and is able to combine the utmost possible tolerance toward what is outside the church — toward what is religious in a general sense and toward the human as such — with working out what is specifically Christian. Thus we have reached the second pole of a new theological paradigm that has to move as it were elliptically from one pole to the other and back again. Not only is there tension between the two poles, but continuous movement in what Paul Tillich calls "critical correlation."

The Second Constant: The Christian Message as Standard

In view of the broad horizon of such an ecumenical theology, in view particularly of the inconsistencies of numerous individual and collective everyday and historical experiences, there arises the great question: In all this, by what is theology to abide? What is its criterion?

We have already given the fundamental criteriological answer: If ecumenical theology wants to be Christian theology, its other pole must be the Judeo-Christian tradition and its primary *norm* cannot be anything except the Christian message on which this tradition is constructed as on its ultimate ground. That is to say, the Christian primordial testimony, the gospel itself in the sense of the good news in its entirety, as recorded in the Old and New Testament Scriptures, is the basic norm of ecumenical theology. If the universal (spatial and temporal) horizon manifests the *catholic* dimension of such an ecumenical theology, then the orientation to the Christian primordial testimony — the gospel — manifests its *evangelical* or Protestant dimension; and only by combining the Catholic and Protestant dimensions, catholic breadth and evangelical depth, is a truly ecumenical theology possible.

In connection with the Old and New Testament witness, we do not hesitate to speak of God's world and revelation, appealing to the faith of the human being. This, however, must not be understood mythologically or in a fundamentalistic sense, but historically. For God's revelation does not drop down from heaven as the Koran (according to strict Muslim believers) is supposed to have been dictated by angels word for word to Mohammed and consequently must still be accepted, repeated, and applied literally even today, including the exact observation of the regulations of an archaic penal law. No, God's revelation takes place in and through the history of Israel and of Jesus of Nazareth and is perceived in and through the *experiences* that believers have had of their God in very varied ways in the course of this history. Even the Old and New Testament Scriptures, therefore, are not directly and immediately God's word in the sense that the Koran is claimed to be such. They are and remain human words, attesting the word of God and from the outset interpreting the latter in very individual ways. Speaking metaphorically, we may say that revelation comes "from above," from God, but not as a result of a miraculous, "supernatural" intervention. Revelation from above can be experienced and articulated only "from below," by the human being in the whole practice of one's life.

It is therefore a question of experiences from the history of Israel and experiences with Jesus that are always already interpreted by the biblical authors themselves, each in his own way, sometimes profoundly but sometimes also superficially. The common basic experience in Israel and with Jesus of a salvation coming from God is never presented purely and simply as such, but always through a variety of human interpretations, with the aid of different terminologies and figurative expressions, patterns, and paradigms. Terms like "Son of man" and "Son of God" are used, along with metaphors like "descent into hell" and "ascension into heaven," with individual patterns such as expiatory blood-sacrifice and the ransom of slaves in the doctrine of the redemption, and with complete paradigms like that of the apocalyptic-eschatological or eccle-sial salvation history (*Heilsgeshichte*).

All these stem from the world of experience and language of that time, and for the most part they are not directly accessible to us to-day. Consequently, all of them must be continually brought home to us in new ways, must be distinguished for the better understanding of the reality they are meant to convey, and sometimes must be replaced. In any case, through all the texts, the important thing is to enable the reality itself, the Christian message, the gospel, to be continually and freshly perceived *and* understood. Only when the Judeo-Christian tra-dition of experience, when even words like "God," "salvation," "grace," "redemption" are related to our present-day experiences, can we make the biblical experiences our own. In theology, therefore, it is not merely a question of the simple "application" of a supposedly perennial teach-ing. It is a question of *trans-lating,* of taking over a historical message from the world of experience of that time and placing it in the setting of our present world of experience — in theory and practice!

In that sense theology is faced with the great task of *critical correla-tion,* which frequently enough assumes the form of a critical confronta-tion. In it we interpret our own experiences in light of the history of the Judeo-Christian experience and even to correct them when a con-tradiction occurs. For if biblical and contemporary experiences are ba-sically opposed to one another, if contemporary "experiences" as in the Third Reich once more bestow on us on the right (or left) a *Fuhrer,* then what kind of political "salvation movement" or similar achievements in the decisive, ultimate, and primary questions should turn the scale? For Christians, clearly the standard must be the biblical experiences, the Christian message, the gospel, Jesus Christ himself. For this Jesus Christ is in person "the essence of Christianity," the "Christian message," the "gospel" itself, and indeed God's "Word" that is "made flesh."

We can summarize this section in a second thesis: *The second con-stant, the second pole or standard of a critical ecumenical theology is the Judeo-Christian tradition that is ultimately based on the Christian message, the gospel of Jesus Christ.*

These, it seems to me, are the essential structures of the new para-digm of theology: a theology in the horizon of the present world of expe-rience, but critically based on the Christian message. It is a theology that in a new age tries to be at the same time both: (1) *catholic,* concerned constantly for the "whole," the "universal" church, and *evangelical,* re-lated consistently to the Scriptures, to the gospel; (2) *traditional,* contin-

ually responsible to history, and *contemporary,* unhesitatingly taking up
the questions of the present day; (3) *Christocentric,* specifically and distinctively Christian, and *universalistic,* directed to the "ecumene," the
whole "inhabited orbis," all Christian churches, all religions, all societies; and (4) *theoretical-scholarly,* concerned with doctrine, with truth,
and *practical-pastoral,* concerned with life, with renewal.

In this essay I have attempted to sketch as closely as possible the outlines of a long ripened paradigm of a critical ecumenical theology. And
I am well aware that only practical theological implementation can decide the effectiveness, persuasive power, and truth content in such a new
paradigm. But, in the midst of all the problems and troubles of theology,
church, and society, I would like to hope that (despite all differences) a
way has been opened here toward a *basic consensus* in theology: not
one uninformed by the theological schools, not one all-embracing theory, not one exclusive method, but one theological paradigm that allows
different methods, theories, and schools.

NOTES

1. Karl Popper, *The Logic of Scientific Discovery* (New York: Harper and Row, 1965).

2. Thomas S. Kuhn, *The Structure of Scientific Revolutions,* 2nd enlarged ed. (Chicago: University of Chicago Press, 1970).

3. Kuhn, ibid., p. 175. Kuhn himself has recently attempted to avoid misunderstandings by speaking of a "disciplinary matrix," which, for him, includes "symbolical generalizations, models and classical examples" (cf. T. S. Kuhn, "Die Entstehung des Neuen," in L. Krüger, ed., *Studien zur Struktur der Wissenschaftsgeschichte,* 1978, pp. 392–393; cf. Kuhn, *The Structure of Scientific Revolutions,* pp. 182–187). I. Lakatos and A. Musgrave published a miscellany, *Criticism and the Growth of Knowledge* (London, 1970), on the discussion between Kuhn and the critics among Popper's followers. For the relevance of the new paradigm in the many diverse disciplines, see G. Gutting, *Paradigms and Revolutions* (Notre Dame: University of Notre Dame Press, 1980).

4. Stephen Toulmin, *Human Understanding,* vol. 1 (Princeton: Princeton University Press, 1972), p. 106.

5. Ibid., p. 116.

6. Kuhn, *The Structure of Scientific Revolutions,* p. 10.

7. Ibid., p. 181.

8. Cited in ibid., pp. 83–84.

9. Max Planck, *Scientific Autobiography and Other Papers,* with a memorial address on Max Planck by Max von Laue, trans. Frank Gaynor (New York: Philosophical Library, 1949), pp. 33–34.

10. Kuhn, *The Structure of Scientific Revolutions,* p. 85.

11. Ibid., p. 102.

12. Ibid., pp. 129–130.

13. Toulmin, *Human Understanding,* p. 105f.

14. Kuhn, *The Structure of Scientific Revolutions,* p. 169.

15. Ibid., p. 164.

16. Ibid., pp. 171, 173.

Chapter 4

Theological Reasoning: A Tillichian Perspective

DONALD W. MUSSER

No ONE HAS DOCUMENTED THE FAR-REACHING EFFECTS of science and technology on contemporary religion more than has Langdon Gilkey. He has devoted two of his ten books to this topic. In *Religion and the Scientific Future* (1970) he documented the relentless results of geology, biology, and historiography on nineteenth-century Christianity. He claimed with considerable force that "the most important change in the understanding of religious truth... has been caused more by the work of science than by any other factor."[1] He then proceeded to show how there is a "creative and necessary usage of the mythical symbolism of religion."[2] More recently in *Creationism on Trial: God and Evolution at Little Rock* (1985) he analyzed the stresses and ambiguities in our culture wrought by an advanced scientific culture dominated by science and technology. One of the chief influences has been the elevation of science to a "sacred status." Gilkey claims, for example, that frequently in our culture science represents the only way we know. Scientific explanations, moreover, often represent the total and solely relevant explanations of whatever is. He points out of course that this conclusion is erroneous. Nevertheless it represents a pervasive and influential cultural attitude. Gilkey unmasks this view of science as a "scientism" derived from an outmoded positivism. He further urges a more desirable relation between the humanities (especially religion) and science "respectful of the autonomy and yet the creative power of each."[3] At the same time, calling on the creative resources of philosophy of science and philosophy of religion, he desires a position in which scientific and theological speech are both related and distinguished. The chief question needing exploration is: "How are the many diverse ways of thinking in a culture... to find *unity,* that is, together to achieve coherence, mutual credibility, and effectiveness?"[4]

In this essay I will contribute to formulating an answer to this question, or at least providing a basis for an answer, by probing the complex area of the relationship between scientific and theological language. First, I will explore the criteria for an adequate view of reason proposed by John E. Smith. Assuming those criteria, I will argue that Paul Tillich's epistemology meets these criteria and provides a foundation for the enterprise that Gilkey has in mind when he proposes to unify science and theology and yet maintain their creative independence.

Thirty years ago, in her critique of Tillich's epistemology, Dorothy Emmet remarked that the "difficulty of justifying as meaningful any way of talking about God" was a central philosophical issue.[5] Still, Emmet saw Tillich's approach to the methods and criteria of theological assertions as relevant and promising, though not without problems.[6] I think it is fair to say that the promise seen by Professor Emmet has not been fulfilled. Tillich's view of reason is not widely accepted in our culture. Why is this the case? Is it because his view of reason is internally flawed beyond use? Or are there other reasons? While there may be other reasons, I think that the main reason has more to do with widely accepted philosophical assumptions about truth and knowing in our culture than it does with any question about the internal logic of Tillich's position.

The Anglo-American philosophical climate of the last fifty years has ignored or rejected out of hand an epistemological position such as Tillich's, one that favors speculative or ontological elements. John E. Smith makes this point with acute precision in a recent essay.[7] Smith argues that the rationality of religious belief is denied *a fortiori* because accepted epistemological assumptions rooted in an empiricism that demands observable facts are alien to religion, and that they are based on an ideal of rationality developed from natural science and common sense. He observes that in this situation the question of rational belief is moot.[8]

If Smith is correct, as I believe, one must find a basis for arguing for the potential rationality of theological claims on other epistemological grounds or else abandon the notion of cognitive claims for theology. Recognizing this, Smith plots a path toward conceptuality receptive to religious claims. The first step out of this situation, Smith argues, must begin by questioning the cherished assumptions of the philosophical establishment and by showing that religion raises legitimate rational claims. While Smith does not acknowledge Tillich overtly, he makes an assertion reminiscent of Tillich. Smith claims that "some form of religious concern is inescapable" in the sense that humans "raise the religious question of the ground and goal of [their] own existence."[9] The rationality of such claims cannot be based on science or common sense, which do not raise such questions, but, rather, on a "critical comparison...[of] beliefs within the universe of discourse established by the religions themselves and their secular counterparts."[10] Others have made this claim; and I believe that, while theologians and philosophers do not universally acknowledge it, they widely entertain it.[11] If one acknowledges it, one cannot rule out as meaningless the attempt to justify theological truth-claims as cognitive.

Granting the possibility of theological rationality, Smith further observes that metaphysics, ethics, history, and more recently the social sciences have provided this structure. Without opting for any of these particular frameworks, Smith believes that an appropriate theological method must come "to terms with the ontological dimension and the sort of reality to which religious insight points."[12] Such a framework will have, according to Smith, at least three characteristics. First, the classical conception of static and timeless Being must give way to dynamic concepts of life and spirit that imply "not only change and development but also relationality with a world of time and history."[13] Second, Smith holds that reason can no longer be conceived as the timeless surveyor of fixed forms, but must include a developmental and experiential dimension. Third, experience must become a reliable medium for understanding.

If one accepts Smith's conditions for an adequate theological epistemology, then the possibility of addressing the issue that worried Dorothy Emmet thirty years ago arises, namely, the issue of justifying God-talk as meaningful. When one surveys the landscape of contemporary theology, one finds that most, if not all, theologians provide some grounds for theological rationality. The grounds that they propose vary widely; several of these address adequately the particular problems and meet the criteria set out by Smith. I believe that Tillich's epistemology bears the characteristics that are required for an adequate view of reason in this sense. Moreover, Tillich enables one to distinguish and yet to relate science and theology creatively.

In order to argue that, I must first set out in bold strokes Tillich's view of the knowing process. Then, I will evaluate Tillich's view of reason in light of the criteria for an adequate conceptual framework set out by Professor Smith.

Tillich's Epistemology

One can analyze Tillich's epistemology by attending to two central concerns: (1) his view of the process of knowing and (2) his understanding of the grounds of knowing. In his *Systematic Theology* Tillich discusses both of these issues under the rubrics "the structure of reason" and "truth and verification."

The Process of Knowing: Tillich believes theology must always account for its path to knowledge. He chooses to do this by analyzing the term "reason." He distinguishes two concepts of reason: the ontological, which he identifies with the classical tradition, and the technical, which he relates to British empiricism. He defines ontological reason as "the structure of the mind which enables it to grasp and to shape reality."[14] By this he means that the knower (the structure of the mind) and the known (reality) are similarly structured (the *logos* structure). While explanations of this mutual, *logos* structure have varied in history (e.g., realism, idealism, dualism, and monism), Tillich claims that one must assume some structure between knower and known, else knowledge would be an impossibility. Within the structure of ontological reason he distinguishes between subjective and objective reason. Subjective reason "is the structure of the mind which enables it to grasp and shape reality on the basis of a corresponding structure of reality," whereas objective reason "is the rational structure of reality which the mind can grasp and according to which it can shape reality."[15]

Consequently, ontological reason has two functions: It grasps and shapes reality. "Grasping" refers to the mind's passive "receiving" what is given in the knowing process. "Shaping" refers to the mind's active reaction to what is received. With respect to grasping and shaping, then, Tillich concludes that "in every act of reasonable reaction an act of shaping is involved, and in every act of reasonable reaction an act of grasping is involved."[16]

In the grasping and shaping activities of reason, one can discern a basic polarity between them due to the presence of an emotional element. In receiving, one finds a polarity between the cognitive and aesthetic elements. In grasping, one encounters a polarity between organizational and organic elements. The element of the emotional or the personal is a part of every rational act, although with varying degrees of importance in different disciplines. In music, for instance, the aesthetic element far outweighs the cognitive whereas in chemistry the opposite is the case. Further, personal relationships emphasize the organic element whereas relations between nations emphasize the organizational element.[17]

Tillich claims that the introduction of an emotional element into the receiving and reacting functions of the knower does not make the knowing process "less rational." Each avenue of inquiry has its own rational structure that opens various dimensions of reality. Put within the language of one of the ontological polarities, "reason unites a dynamic with a static element in an indissoluble amalgam."[18]

Tillich next introduces the idea of the depth of reason with regard to ontological reason. The depth of reason is both the ground of reason, that from which reason proceeds, and the manifestation of reason. As such, the depth of reason is present in all inquiry. For example: "In the cognitive realm the depth of reason is its quality of pointing to truth-itself, namely, to the infinite power of being and of the ultimately real, through the relative truths in every field of knowledge. In the aesthetic realm the depth of reason is its quality of pointing to 'beauty-itself,' namely, to an infinite meaning and an ultimate significance, through the creations in every field of aesthetic intuition. In the legal realm the depth of reason is its quality of pointing to 'justice-itself,' namely, to an infinite seriousness and an ultimate dignity, through every structure of actualized justice. In the communal realm the depth of reason is its quality of pointing to 'love-itself,' namely, to an infinite richness and an ultimate unity, through every form of actualized love. This dimension of reason, the dimension of depth, is an essential quality of all rational functions."[19]

The depth of reason grounds ontological reason. Under the conditions of existence, however, the transparency of ontological or essential reason toward its depth becomes opaque because reason in existence is reason in conflict with itself. Thus, Tillich delineates existential reason (or actual reason or finite reason) and its ambiguities.

Finite reason is contradictory, ambiguous, and threatened by disruption and self-destruction.[20] He describes the conflict within actual reason in three ways: as the conflict between autonomy and heteronomy, as the conflict between relativism and absolutism, and as the conflict between formalism and emotionalism. One can chart these conflicts summarily:

1. The polarity of structure and depth produces a conflict between autonomous and heteronomous reason that results in a quest for theonomy.

2. The polarity of the static and dynamic produces a conflict between absolutism and relativism that results in a quest for the concrete-absolute.

3. The polarity of the formal and emotional produces a conflict between formalism and irrationalism that results in a quest for the union of form and mystery.

These conflicts provide the crucible in which reason is actualized. In the first conflict, that between autonomy and heteronomy, reason that affirms and actualizes its structure without regarding its depth is autonomous. Reason that claims to express the depth of reason, but does so on the basis of a power outside of reason, is heteronomous. Heteronomous reason emerges as a reaction against autonomous reason that has lost its depth. An autonomy that has given birth to a heteronomy results in the conflict of reason divided against itself. This conflict of reason separated within itself results in a quest for a reunion of the polarity of its structure and depth, a quest for a theonomy or an autonomous reason reunited with its own depth.[21]

Likewise, in the conflict between absolutism and relativism, reason that actualizes the static element without regarding the dynamic element results in two forms of absolutism. In one form, the absolutism of tradition, Tillich defends "the static side of reason against an exclusive emphasis on the dynamic side." In the other form, the absolutism of revolution, he sees the "dynamic structures of reason as static and elevate[d]...to absolute validity." On the other hand, reason that denies the static element and emphasizes the dynamic element results in two forms of relativism. The first form, positivistic relativism, "takes what is 'given' (posited) without applying absolute criteria to its valuation." The other form, cynical relativism, "is disbelief in the validity of any rational act" that results in a "vacuum into which new absolutisms pour."[22]

Tillich similarly explicates the third conflict in finite reason, that between formalism and irrationalism. "Formalism appears in the exclusive emphasis on the formal side" of reason to the denial of the emotional.[23] Reason is reduced to strict, technically correct thinking processes. Irrationalism, on the other hand, is a reaction against formalism from solely emotional reason. It is still reason, but a blind and fanatical reason.

A drive toward existential reason emerges from these three conflicts in actual reason, and existential reason, estranged from its ground, yearns to return to its essential ground. It quests for revelation or "the manifestation of the ground of being for human knowledge."[24] Tillich here correlates reason and revelation. The intersection is important because here Tillich distinguishes and defines the roles of philosophy and theology. At this point, however, we must focus on his view of reason.

Tillich also delineates ontological reason in terms of the more familiar language of subject and object or knower and known. He asserts that "knowledge is based on an original unity which involves a separation and a reunion of subject and object."[25] There is an original unity, necessary separation, and possible reunion. The ontological problem of knowledge is caused by the concomitant unity of the knower's separation from the known and the knower's participation with the known. By this strange-sounding paradox, he means that the knower must be detached from the object; that is, the knower must be separated and estranged from the object of inquiry. Still, knower and known remain united in the sense that objects of inquiry contain "essential structures with which the cognitive [knower] is essentially united."[26] In existence, knowing is the quest "which unites the certainty of existential union with the openness of cognitive detachment."[27]

The process of knowing therefore contains two fundamental elements, those of union and detachment. All cognitive reason contains both elements in different proportions. In "controlling knowledge," that associated with the sciences, the knower remains primarily detached from the subject and objectifies it. "Receiving knowledge," that associated with the humanities, including religion and theology, on the other hand, takes the object into itself. The aim of controlling knowledge is manipulation whereas the aim of receiving knowledge is understanding. Still, knowledge requires the presence of both elements.[28] When one side is disregarded, cognitive distortions occur.

The most typical distortion deals with technical reason, which is reason "reduced to the capacity for reasoning."[29] It eliminates the emotional element from the reasoning process and with it the polarities present in grasping and shaping, thus denying the aesthetic and organic sides of the polarities. Technical reason permits no emotive, personal, or subjective elements. As a result, it reduces the objects of its knowing to things. While technical reason is a legitimate element or companion of ontological reasoning, Tillich observes that it has a tendency, however, to separate itself from ontological reasoning.[30]

The Grounds of Knowing: My discussion of reason according to Tillich has thus far set out his analysis of how knowledge is possible within the structures and contours of the human mind. In epistemological terms one can describe this as the logic of discovery or context of discovery. The other major epistemological issue with which philosophers deal is the context or logic of justification. Here one seeks to specify criteria by which one measures the validity of a knowledge claim.

Tillich considers this topic in *Systematic Theology* briefly under the heading of "Truth and Verification." He asserts that every cognitive act strives for the truth, which has to do with the essence of things, or that which gives them the power of being. "Truth," he claims, "is the essence of things as well as the cognitive act in which their essence is grasped.... A judgment is true because it grasps and expresses true being; and the really real becomes truth if it is grasped and expressed in a true judgment."[31]

Tillich asks how one can discern if a judgment is true or false? He answers that every judgment must be tested. There are, according to Tillich, two methods of verification, which correspond to the two cognitive attitudes, the controlling and the receiving. One verifies controlling knowledge by repeatable experiments. One verifies receiving knowledge, on the other hand, by experience in the creative union of two natures. The proper objects of controlling knowledge are machines, things, and separable elements of life-processes, such as livers, kidneys, or prostate glands. Life-processes, however, are the objects of receiving knowledge. As one would expect, controlling knowledge is relatively certain; receiving knowledge, on the other hand, is necessarily indefinite, preliminary, and imprecise. Tillich observes that "controlling knowledge is safe but not ultimately significant, while receiving knowledge can be ultimately significant, but it cannot give certainty."[32]

An Assessment of Tillich's Epistemology

In the previous section I have attempted to describe Tillich's epistemology in two parts. The first part described his "logic of discovery" (the process of knowing). The second part treated his "logic of justification" (the grounds of knowing). I now wish to raise the question of the adequacy of Tillich's understanding of knowledge by applying to it Smith's analytical framework that I discussed in the introductory section.

Smith holds that a conceptual framework is necessary for religious belief. He further claims that a conceptual framework must be commensurate with and not alien to the nature of religious belief as empiricist frameworks are. Smith observes that a particularly appropriate match can be made between a philosophical ontology and theology. He states that "both construe reality in ultimate and comprehensive or holistic forms and this is their point of contact."[33] He then suggests three criteria for a modern ontology.

The first criterion is that a contemporary ontology must be dynamic and not static. Smith holds that concepts of Being must give way to concepts of life and spirit that take seriously change and temporality.[34] This criterion applies more directly to ontology than epistemology, and it does not bear specifically on the question of the adequacy of Tillich's theory of knowledge. Nevertheless, every epistemology implies an ontology; that is, an adequate understanding of the knowing process requires an adequate ontology. Thus, one must address the question of the adequacy of Tillich's ontology in the light of Smith's criterion. I believe one can make a case that Tillich's concept of Being has dynamic elements. His concept of Being is not static as is frequently alleged. Along with the Parmenidean "isness" of being is a polar opposite, a Heracletian "becoming." For Tillich there is a "given" that makes the world of becoming possible. "Being is the basic absolute";[35] being is not static, however, but is dynamic under the conditions of existence. In existence reason evidences a polar structure as we saw above. Further, Tillich's *Systematic Theology,* especially Parts IV and V on life, spirit, and history, aptly illustrates a dynamic structure. If this is the case, Tillich's ontology meets Smith's first criterion that an ontology appropriate for theology must be dynamic.

Smith's second criterion for judging the adequacy of a theological framework is that "reason can no longer be conceived as the timeless surveyor of fixed forms."[36] Rather it must take personal experience seriously. I take this criterion as the epistemological analog of the previous ontological criterion. Just as an ontology must be dynamic, so a modern epistemology must account for changes and shifts in what one claims as true. It must affirm the relativity of all truth-claims. And, just as Tillich's ontology includes a dynamic side, so also does his epistemology. To be sure, Tillich's notion of the depth of reason clearly implies an absolute. Tillich defines truth in terms of reason's ability to grasp the depth of an object. There are absolutes. Yet, every statement about the absolutes in knowledge is relative because in existence the transparency of essential reason toward its depth is opaque and ambiguous.[37] All knowledge claims are bound to finite space and time because they are relative to the conditions of a particular existence. Nevertheless, this degree of relativity does not imply a relativism that is devoid of an absolute. Tillich holds that absolute relativism is logically incoherent and practically impossible. On the one hand, the term "absolute relativism" is self-contradictory. On the other hand, life demands that one decide. There is no other choice. Practically one lives "as though" something is true. Tillich's dialectical view of the structure of reason therefore denies the possibility of absolute knowledge; he maintains, however, the necessity of the concept of an absolute ground for any knowing to occur. Thus, Tillich rejects any thoroughgoing relativism or dogmatic absolutism.[38]

Tillich's attempt to hold in polar tension subject/object or knower/known seems necessary as a criterion for any adequate epistemology. Recent work in the history and philosophy of science by Thomas Kuhn, Mary Hesse, Stephen Toulmin, Rom Harré, Michael Polanyi, and others has shown that in science itself a dynamic view of rational inquiry that affirms the historical relativity of scientific claims emerges from a phenomenology of the scientific process. Richard Bernstein, among others, has documented how both epistemological objectivism and subjectivism, and their cognates absolutism and relativism, are no longer live options in science. Recent philosophy of science, claims Bernstein, is "characterized by the increasing realization that when it comes to understanding questions about the rationality of scientific inquiry we must focus on the conflict of theories, paradigms, research programs, and research traditions in their historical development." Tradition and reason must be seen together, he claims, because "traditions...are the bearers of reason."[39] Tillich sensed this decades before the work of historians and philosophers of science opened the door to the possibility of a post-empirical epistemology that placed reason firmly within the traditions of historical process. Thus, Tillich's view of actual reason thoroughly immersed in the relativity, ambiguity, and contingency of the historical process meets Smith's second criterion.

The third criterion for an adequate theological firmament according to Smith is that theological inquiry must consider experience as "a reliable medium for understanding the religious belief which is an inter-

pretation of that experience."[40] From the foregoing discussion it is clear
that for Tillich the test of experience is the chief criterion by which one
judges the validity of receiving knowledge, although Tillich's notion of
experience needs more thorough explication. In Tillich, the experienc-
ing knower is never completely eliminated from controlling knowledge.
Tillich elucidates his view of the role of experience in knowing by the
concept of participation. By participation he refers to the element of
identity between knower and known within the polarity of individual-
ization and participation. "Subject and object meet in the situation of
knowledge."[41] All understanding depends upon participation. But how
does empathetic participation avoid wishful thinking or romantic idealization? Tillich answers that one must have "right" participation. By
this he means that true knowledge depends upon one being "detached
and involved at the same time," although he does not develop and clarify this demand for simultaneous detachment and involvement.[42] In the
final analysis the introduction of the criterion of experience or participation into the knowing process results in the inability to specify exactly
the criteria of truth or falsehood. But, can one have it any other way?
Can the subject be eliminated from the process? The answer is "no,"
and this is one of the chief accomplishments of recent history and philosophy of science. Tillich's own emphasis on participation would lead
him to be receptive toward this conclusion of historically sensitive epis-
temologies.

In conclusion, Tillich's view of reason has the structural framework to buttress an ontology and epistemology along the lines drawn
by Smith. If my analysis is accurate, then theologians who wish to construct belief-statements within the frame of post-empiricist epistemology
would profit from reading Tillich's view of the process of reason and the
grounds for knowing.

In his essay, "Faith, Belief, and the Problem of Rationality," Smith
himself supports neither Tillich nor any particular "constructive philosophy" as a candidate for providing an appropriate theological firmament. He speaks of "a program to be worked out."[43] He goes on to
suggest that recent studies of the history and philosophy of science hold
the greatest promise. Certainly, he is on the right track. The work of one
post-empiricist philosopher, namely Michael Polanyi, is quite promising in this regard. Polanyi, a first-rate physical chemist who turned to
philosophical reflection late in his career, studied the history of science
and developed an epistemology (the theory of personal knowledge) and
a correlative ontology (a stratified universe) that provide the beginnings

for a constructive philosophy that awaits development and application to theology.[44]

In Dorothy Emmet's analysis of Tillich's epistemology three decades ago, she raised the question of meaningful God-talk and saw hope for a positive answer in Tillich's view of reason and revelation. At the time of her essay, however, our understanding of reason was dominated by philosophies alien to religious truth-claims. Perhaps the time is upon us, a kairotic moment, when loosed from the fetters of a stifling empiricism that looked askance at theology, we can reappropriate Tillich's dynamic view of reason and find ground for justifying theological truth-claims. Moreover, we may be able to retrieve from Tillich's epistemology resources to forge a unity between science and theology that respects their autonomy and encourages their creativity in our culture.

NOTES

1. Langdon Gilkey, *Religion and the Scientific Future* (New York: Harper and Row, 1970), p. 4.

2. Ibid., p. 66.

3. Langdon Gilkey, *Creationism on Trial: God and Evolution at Little Rock* (Minneapolis: Winston, 1985), p. 206.

4. Ibid., p. 208.

5. Dorothy Emmet, "Epistemology and the Idea of Revelation," in *The Theology of Paul Tillich,* ed. Charles W. Kegley and Robert W. Bretall (New York: Macmillan, 1952), pp. 198–214.

6. Ibid., p. 199.

7. John E. Smith, "Faith, Belief, and the Problem of Rationality in Religion," in *Rationality and Religious Belief,* ed. C. F. DeLaney (Notre Dame: University of Notre Dame Press, 1979), pp. 42–64.

8. Ibid., pp. 48–49, 56. Happily, there is no longer a monolithic epistemological stance dominant among philosophers. The current status of the debate, along with a constructive proposal, can be found in Richard J. Bernstein, (Philadelphia: University of Pennsylvania Press, 1983).

9. Smith, ibid., p. 58.

10. Ibid., p. 57.

11. A cogent argument for the possible rationality of theological claims is in David Tracy, *A Blessed Rage for Order* (New York: Seabury Press, 1975), pp. 91–110.

12. Smith, "Faith, Belief, and the Problem of Rationality in Religion," p. 59.

13. Ibid., p. 59.

14. Paul Tillich, *Systematic Theology,* 3 vols. (Chicago: University of Chicago Press, 1951, 1957, 1963), 1:73.

15. Ibid., pp. 76–77.

16. Ibid., p. 76.

17. Ibid., p. 77.

18. Ibid., p. 78.

19. Ibid., pp. 79–80.

20. Ibid., pp. 80–83.
21. Ibid., pp. 83–85.
22. Ibid., pp. 87–88.
23. Ibid., p. 89.
24. Ibid., p. 94.
25. Tillich, *My Search for Absolutes* (New York: Simon and Schuster, 1967), p. 67.
26. Tillich, *Systematic Theology*, 1:95.
27. Ibid., p. 97.
28. Ibid., pp. 97–98. Tillich makes this point concisely in "Participation and Knowledge," in *Sociologica Frankfurter Beitrage zur Soziologie*, Band I (Europaische Verlagsanstalt, 1955) 201–209.
29. Tillich, *Systematic Theology*, 1:72–73.
30. Ibid., pp. 73–74.
31. Ibid., pp. 102.
32. Ibid., pp. 105.
33. Smith, "Faith, Belief, and the Problem of Rationality in Religion," p. 59.
34. Ibid., p. 59.
35. Tillich, *My Search for Absolutes*, p. 81.
36. Smith, "Faith, Belief, and the Problem of Rationality in Religion," p. 59.
37. Tillich, *My Search for Absolutes*, p. 80.
38. Ibid.,, pp. 65–66.
39. Bernstein, *Beyond Objectivism and Relativism*, p. 77.
40. Smith, "Faith, Belief, and the Problem of Rationality in Religion," pp. 59–60.
41. Tillich, "Participation and Knowledge," p. 202.
42. Ibid., p. 206.
43. Smith, "Faith, Belief, and the Problem of Rationality in Religion," p. 60.
44. There are, for example, striking similarities between the views of reason in Tillich and Polanyi. Tillich's idea of the depth of reason and Polanyi's notion of the tacit dimension suggest comparison. Or, to take a second example, Tillich's idea of participation and Polanyi's concept of indwelling merit exposition. Polanyi's seminal ideas are in *Personal Knowledge: Towards a Post-Critical Philosophy* (New York: Harper and Row, 1964) and *The Tacit Dimension* (Garden City, N.Y.: Doubleday and Co., 1966).

Chapter 5

Satan as the Messiah of Nature?

THOMAS J. J. ALTIZER

IF THEOLOGY IS TRULY TO UNDERGO A RADICAL TURN OR TURNING in our time, then not the least of its tasks will be a new encounter with the theological meaning of space, and with that meaning or those meanings of space that have dominated the modern consciousness. Even at this late date theology has yet to enter a genuine dialogue with modern science, a dialogue in which the scientific revolution of the modern world is accepted and affirmed, and accepted not as an exploration of a domain isolated from faith, but rather accepted as the unveiling of a world that is either inseparable from or identical with the world of faith. Recognizing the profound challenge to faith of the comprehensive mechanism of classical physics, many theologians hailed the advent of the twentieth-century revolutions in physics, but in doing so they commonly ignored the scientific testimony to the effect that there is a genuine continuity between classical and contemporary physics. Having yet to master the positive theological significance of the scientific revolution of the seventeenth century, it would seem audacious for theology to claim that it can absorb the revolutions of relativity and quantum physics, and most particularly so since those revolutions continue to be isolated in contemporary thinking from the other revolutions of the nineteenth and twentieth centuries. Our theological understanding here is just as fragmentary and problematic as it is in other areas, indeed, far more so, for here we cannot speak of a theological understanding that as such has entered a purely scientifically comprehended time and space.

Obviously the time has not yet arrived for a genuine dialogue between science and theology. Nevertheless, the moment may be propitious for theological questions that arise on the basis of a theological acceptance of the reality of the world or worlds of modern science. Here, we may not yet hope for critical or sophisticated theological questions, or even for questions that can be translated into a scientific language, for the worlds of science and theology remain divorced. But at the very least theologians can foreswear all attempts to an impotent rape of science, just as they can renounce all imperialistic claims that science is a consequence of what they know as faith. So far as I know there are no longer any major scientists who accept such claims, or even find them to be meaningful, and the claims themselves do little more than perpetuate the illusion that there is no chasm between science and faith. Voices that attempt to cross this chasm may do no more than meet with a vanishing echo of themselves, but nonetheless the very attempt itself may preserve the power of speech. But first we must seek some sense of a theological meaning of the chasm itself. Alexander Koyré, perhaps the most authoritative master of the intellectual significance of the scientific revolution of the seventeenth century, has characterized this revolution by two closely connected and complementary features: (1) the destruction of the classical idea of the cosmos, and (2) the geometrization of space. As he says, this characterization is very nearly equivalent to the mathematization (geometricization) of nature and therefore the mathematization (geometricization) of science.

> The disappearance — or destruction — of the cosmos means that the world of science, the real world is no more seen, or conceived, as a finite and hierarchically ordered, therefore qualitatively and ontologically differentiated, whole, but as an open, indefinite, and even infinite universe, united not by its immanent structure but only by the identity of its fundamental contents and laws; a universe in which, in contradistinction to the traditional conception with its separation and opposition of the two worlds of becoming and being, that is, of the heavens and the earth, all its components appear as placed on the same ontological level; a universe in which the *physica coelestis* and *physica terrestris* are identified and unified, in which astronomy and physics become interdependent and united because of their common subjection to geometry.[1]

The geometrization of space necessarily implies its infinitization; accordingly, the destruction of the cosmos can be characterized either as "the breaking of the circle" (Marjorie Nicolson) or "the bursting of the sphere" (Koyré). And the inevitable effect of this fundamental negation was the disappearance of all formal and final causes as modes of explanation in the new science.

As Nietzsche so forcefully declared, ever since Copernicus we have been falling into a mysterious X, an X testifying to the total estrangement of the worlds of objectivity and subjectivity. We cannot escape this X, as so many theologians have imagined, by following the turn of Heidegger in 1929, and maintaining that science does not seek the truth in itself, and therefore no matter where and however deeply science investigates what-is, it will never find Being ("Postscript" to *What Is Metaphysics?*). Let Christian thinkers resist the temptation of believing that science touches neither God nor Being, unless they are prepared to isolate totally faith from the world. Should not theologians far rather follow Pascal and be terrified by the eternal silence of infinite spaces? For, at least, a reaction of terror is an ultimate response, one taking with total seriousness a new space in which it is no longer possible to speak. Ironically enough, Newton, that profoundly Christian believer, whose own physics conceived the world as composed of the three elements of matter, motion, and space, identified space as the eternal realm of God's presence and action. Yet Newton created an idea of space that Pascal could not have known, and Newtonian space is an infinite *and* homogeneous void in which matter or particles move. Moreover, as Koyré insists, Newton's introduction of the void into physics was a stroke of genius and a step of decisive importance: "It is this step that enables Newton to oppose and unite at the same time — and to do it *really,* and not *seemingly,* like Descartes — the discontinuity of matter and the continuity of space."[2] The full reality and the ultimate meaning of matter is here made possible by an infinite and homogeneous void; and this void not only seals the dissolution of the heavens of the classical Christian cosmos, but that very dissolution itself makes manifest the mathematical order of the universe.

From the perspective of the twentieth century, what is most distinctive about seventeenth-century physics is that it could know a world that is at once mathematically or geometrically ordered and physically visualizable or intuitively coherent. If it geometricized nature and science, this was nevertheless a visualizable geometry, and it made possible a unification of the universe that it apprehended. That unity of the universe was lost in the scientific revolutions of the twentieth century, and ironically it was lost by more nearly pure and radical modes of mathematical thinking. Perhaps Pascal saw beyond Newton in being terrified by the eternal silence of infinite spaces, for twentieth-century physics has not only dissolved an absolute space and time, but it has thereby lost a homogeneous, a unified, and an integrably coherent world or universe. Indeed, it is precisely a universe that has disappeared from view, for no way has yet appeared of integrating, without mathematical inconsistencies, the quantum theory with the special theory of relativity. The revolution of quantum physics is to this day philosophically, as opposed to mathematically, unabsorbed; it might even be said to be *terra incognita* to a non-mathematical thinking. Nevertheless, we have some sense of the problems that it poses. Werner Heisenberg, in his Chicago lectures of 1929, described the indeterminacy principle, which he had discovered in 1925, as follows:

> There exists a body of exact mathematical laws, but these cannot be interpreted as expressing simple relationships between objects existing in space and time. The observable predictions of this theory can be approximately described in such terms, but not uniquely — the wave and the corpuscular pictures both possess the same approximate validity. This indeterminateness of the picture of the process is a direct result of the indeterminateness of the concept of "observation" — it is not possible to decide, other than arbitrarily, what objects are to be considered as part of the observed system and what is part of the observer's apparatus.[3]

Experimental evidence has shown that both matter and radiation possess a paradoxical duality of character, for sometimes they exhibit the properties of waves, at other times those of particles. Indeed, microcosmic phenomena can no longer be described coherently in a non-mathematical language, for the whole domain of atomic and sub-atomic processes can no longer be visualized by a physical schema, but only by the mathematical schema of quantum mechanics.

Following Niels Bohr's concept of complementarity, Heisenberg was led to believe that the resolution of the paradoxes of atomic physics can be accomplished only by recognizing that space-time relations and causal relations can no longer be coherently conjoined: "They represent complementary and mutually exclusive aspects of atomic phenomena."[4] This interpretation of quantum theory is incisively illustrated by the following diagramatic form from Bohr:[5]

CLASSICAL THEORY
CAUSAL RELATIONSHIPS OF PHENOMENA
DESCRIBED IN TERMS OF SPACE AND TIME

QUANTUM THEORY

Either		*Or*
Phenomena described in	Alternatives	Causal relationship expressed
terms of space and time	related	by mathematical laws
But	statistically	*But*
Uncertainty principle		Physical description of
		phenomena in space-time
		impossible

Forty years later the Danish philosopher of quantum physics, Aage Petersen, could declare that we are still unable to state clearly the difference between classical and quantum physics and to judge the significance of the distinction between the "physical" and the "symbolic."[6] Nevertheless, the distinction is real, so real that theories in physics may now be completely unvisualizable and inaccessible to intuitive understanding. As Petersen says:

> Unlike the account of classical physical process, the analysis of a quantum phenomenon treats instrument and system behavior in essentially different ways. The experimental setup and the characteristics of the object are described by means of ordinary physical concepts; the "behavior" of the object when the object is placed in the given experimental situation is described by means of the quantal formalism. Since the phenomenon's interior is not representable as a sequence of well-defined physical steps, the quantum algorithm is a logical procedure that is not open to physical description. In a classical physical process each infinitesimal step is "closed," *i.e.* it is a definite physical event. The event may be unknown, but it is decided or well defined. In quantum physics the object's "behavior" is not a sequence of "closed" steps. In the quantum domain the observations are still described in ordinary physical terms but they are linked together by a symbolic or physically inscrutable algorithm.[7]

Here, the very word "symbolic" bears the meaning of physically indescribable and inscrutable, as quantum mechanics has evolved a mathematical formalism existing at a seemingly infinite distance from the ordinary world of common experience.

The correspondence idea of the Copenhagen school of quantum physics was fundamentally directed to the problem of the relation between quantum and classical physics. Bohr became persuaded that there is an intimate formal analogy between the classical and the quantum scheme, and his correspondence principle was intended to utilize in the development of quantum theory every feature of the classical theories in a rational transcription appropriate to the fundamental contrast between the quantum postulates and the classical theories. Mathematically, the idea of correspondence suggested that the quantal formalism ought to emerge as a generalization of classical mechanism. As Bohr declared, "quantum physics is in every respect a generalization of the classical physical theories."[8] Bohr even believed that the language of Newton and Maxwell will remain the language of physicists for all time, just as he believed that "common sense" judges the correct usage of words. Accordingly, no scientific revolution of conceptual frameworks is possible. Initially, Heisenberg accepted Bohr's idea of correspondence or complementarity, but he was gradually led to break with this idea. Patrick A. Heelan, in his recent study of the quantum mechanics of Heisenberg, asserts that the Gifford lectures of 1955–56 marked a turning point in Heisenberg's philosophy, directing it to a more rational interpretation of complementarity.[9] Here, Heisenberg identifies a traditional metaphysical or dogmatic realism as the deepest obstacle to a new scientific breakthrough, a realism arising from the Cartesian partition between *res cogitans* and *res extensa*.

Heisenberg notes that the Cartesian partition between subject and object or mind and body was extremely successful for several centuries. Classical mechanics started from the assumption that one can describe the world without speaking about God or ourselves; but with the advent of quantum mechanics the observed no longer appears or is real apart from the instruments and framework of the observer. And here there appears to be an essential union between the observer and the observed.

It has been pointed out before that in the Copenhagen interpretation of quantum theory we can indeed proceed without mentioning ourselves as individuals, but we cannot disregard the fact that natural science is formed by men. Natural science does not simply describe and explain nature; it is a part of the interplay between nature and ourselves. This was a possibility of which Descartes could not have thought, but it makes the sharp distinction between the world and the I impossible.[10]

Significantly enough, Heisenberg says nothing in his Gifford lectures about the possible end of the sharp distinction between God and the world. Nonetheless, it is instructive to set the above words of Heisenberg beside the parallel although opposing words of Koyré:

> Yet there is something for which Newton — or better to say not Newton alone, but modern science in general — can still be made responsible: it is the splitting of our world in two. I have been saying that modern science broke down the barriers that separated the heavens and the earth, and that it united and unified the universe. And that is true. But, as I have said, too, it did this by substituting for our world of quality and sense perception, the world in which we live, and love, and die, another world — the world of quantity, of reified geometry, a world in which, though there is a place for everything, there is no place for man. Thus the world of science — the real world — became estranged and utterly divorced from the world of life, which science has been unable to explain — not even to explain by calling it "subjective."[11]

Upon reflection, one realizes that there is no necessary difference between these statements of Heisenberg and Koyré. For what is the "I" of which Heisenberg speaks? Is it not quite simply the "I" as purely empirical observer or purely mathematical thinker? The most striking thing about Heisenberg's oft-quoted statement is that it so spontaneously and innocently assumes that the totally quantitative "I" is identical with the "individual"!

Heelan is persuaded that Heisenberg realized, or is realizing, his original goal of giving an objective and ontological account of nature or physical reality by his adoption of the Aristotelian notion of *potentia,* which he proposed in his Gifford lectures to describe the kind of reality represented in quantum mechanics by the wave function. This significant shift is clearly presented by Heelan as follows:

> Antecedently to observation, a quantum mechanical system is described by a wave function. What is the ontological status of that which a wave function purports to describe? In the complemen-

tarity interpretation, the wave function was just one of the mathematical tools used by quantum mechanics: it was a mere mental construct and not part of a description of nature. This was the view which Bohr held and which Heisenberg agreed to in 1927. But in his Gifford lectures of 1955-56, Heisenberg adopted for it the Aristotelian term "potency," or *"potentia"* or *"Potentialität,"* a translation of Aristotle's *dynamis*. He also used as synonyms, "Possibility" (*"Möglichkeit"*), "objective tendency" (*"objektiv Tendenz"*), and "probability" (*"Wahrscheinlichkeit"*). A potency, in Aristotle's philosophy, is a metaphysical principle of being ordained to its corresponding act. It is either a passive desire for its act (a passive potency), or a power to perform its act (an active potency). In either case it gets its meaning and definition from the goal it envisages, a goal passively envisaged for the passive potency and actively envisaged for the active potency. *Potency* then is denominated (gets its definition) from *act* and not *act* from *potency*. Both forms of potency achieve their completion and fulfillment with the actualization of their act.[12]

Are we to imagine, then, that Heisenberg is effecting a revolutionary conceptual breakthrough in physics by resurrecting the classical cosmos? Is the wave-function as "reality-in-potency" a ground of a new teleological universe? Does the quantum mechanical wave function represent the "form" (in Aristotle's sense) of some fundamental matter or substance, which Heisenberg names as energy?

Heelan is careful to point out that here the wave function represents a qualified kind of reality that is not reality-in-actuality, but reality-in-potency; or, in Aristotelian philosophy, it is a metaphysical principle of being, like a substantial or accidental form constituted by its natural tendency towards its proper act or goal. Yet, the quantum mechanical potency is not fully specified with regard to its goal. Part of the specification of its goal comes from the observer, and given a fixed observer, it is specified only to a set of possible goals, and only to a schedule of probabilities for the actualization of these goals. One wonders if in an Aristotelian or classical sense it can have any goal or end at all. One also wonders if an Aristotelian language can be renewed in modern physics because modern science has long since brought classical metaphysics to an end, and if an Aristotelian language can function without any Aristotelian metaphysical overtones. Heisenberg himself affirms that the goal of physics is to reach a complete understanding of the unity of matter: "The term 'complete understanding' would mean that the forms of matter in the sense of Aristotelian philosophy would appear as results, as solutions of a closed mathematical scheme representing the natural laws for matter."[13] How ironic that Aristotelian forms could be conceived as results of a closed mathematical scheme, for Aristotle's own forms, unlike Plato's, could have no possible mathematical ground. Is not Heisenberg the conceptual thinker a pure example of the scientific thinker who is liberated even from the memory of the classical cosmos and the Christian God?

Perhaps the decisive difference, at least from a theological point of view, between modern physics and classical physics is that modern physics is liberated even from the shadow or the reflection of a teleological universe and its final cause or cosmological origin and end. It would be misleading to say that the classical Christian heaven is missing from modern physics and astronomy, or even to speak of an identification and unification of the *physica coelestis* and the *physica terrestris,* for all meaning of either an ontological or a religious transcendence has simply vanished without leaving a trace. Who, in our day, can even shudder in the presence of a scientifically comprehended time and space? So far from failing to give signs of a transcendent ground or sources, the space that is manifest upon our horizon is a space-time continuum, which while it may be finite is also unbounded; and thereby all sense of a beyond is simply dissolved. There is no "up" or "down" in our space, and while there would appear to be a chasm between the macrocosmic and the microcosmic domains, this is a chasm created by their respective theoretical foundations (relativity theory and quantum theory), which have yet to be integrated by the discovery of a unified field theory. The pious may rejoice in response to Einstein's declaration that the cosmic religious experience is the strongest and noblest mainspring of scientific research; but Einstein identified the center of true religiousness as the knowledge or feeling that what is impenetrable to us really exists. Who could imagine a Christian Newton in the twentieth century?

Einstein, who for many years questioned and opposed quantum mechanics with all his power, finally acknowledged the beauty and the validity of quantum theory. But he continued until his death to insist that it could not be the last word. For him the wave function could provide only a description of ensembles and not of the "real state" of an individual system. As he declared in a famous letter to Hedwig and Max Born:

> Quantum mechanics is very impressive. But an inner voice tells
> me that this is not the real Jacob. The theory has much to offer,
> but it does not bring us closer to the secret of the Old One. I am
> convinced that He does not throw dice.[14]

Can contemporary theologians join Einstein and believe that God does
not throw dice? Or should they join Nietzsche and believe that God now
seems incapable of communicating clearly? Nietzsche, who if nothing
else is the supreme master of the meaning of religious cruelty, conceived
of three primary rungs of a great ladder of religious cruelty. The first
is the sacrifice of human beings to one's God, and the second is the
sacrifice to one's deity of one's strongest instincts, one's "natural man."

> And finally — what remains that could be sacrificed? Don't we
> in the end have to sacrifice everything consolatory, holy, and heal-
> ing: all hope, all belief in invisible harmony, in future blessedness
> and justice? Don't we have to sacrifice God himself and idolize
> a rock, the forces of stupidity, of gravity, fate, nothingness — all
> in order to be sufficiently cruel to ourselves? To sacrifice God for
> nothingness — this is the paradoxical mystery of ultimate cruelty
> that remained in store for the generation now growing up. All of
> us know something about it already.[15]

While theologians may be impelled to a quest for a "non-objective"
or transcendental theology that effects an absolute boundary between
faith's knowledge of God and human knowledge of the world, they
should recognize that modern science has already sacrificed the God
of faith to make manifest the full meaning and reality of the world.
From the perspective of faith, that meaning may well be the idolization
of gravity, fate, and nothingness, but it is such "idolization" that has un-
locked the deepest secrets of nature thus far, and so much so, that any
effort now to integrate or even associate the God of faith with the world
we know can only appear as a hopelessly anachronistic act. Unless,
perhaps, faith limits itself to the God who has sacrificed Himself, the
God who has wholly disappeared from out space-time continuum, and
can only appear in the language of those such as Einstein, Whitehead,
and Teilhard, who are driven to resist the revolutionary consequences
of modern science. We may well respect and even venerate those scientists and thinkers who resist the revolutionary momentum of science
in the name of the clarity and coherence of an earlier worldview, but

should not the theologian be open to the frontiers of thinking with the hope that the establishment of these frontiers may well make possible a new form and language of faith? Above all, should we not now finally recognize that it is no longer possible to speak of God in a classical theological language, or any form thereof, and this means that God can no longer be conceived as transcendent or immanent, either as "above" or "below," in the "heights" or in the "depths," and certainly not as a cosmic power or force of any sort, to say nothing of speaking of God as the cosmological origin or teleological end of the world?

If we no longer can speak of God in a classical theological language, can we truly speak of God in any language at all? In the visionary world of William Blake, deity, humanity, and nature are originally or eternally identical, and the primary symbolic names of this identity are "Jesus" and the "Imagination." Yet Imagination has all but been destroyed by "imitation of Nature's Images drawn from Remembrance" (*Milton* 41:24) as humankind now sleeps a sleep of eternal death. We *see* what we *are,* proclaims the seer; the forms of existence create the forms of perception. But a Fall from the original unity has inverted the original harmony of the senses, shattering their initial unity, so that the senses become isolated and estranged from one another, with the result that we actually perceive an alien "Goddess Nature." In the eternal cycle of the fallen cosmos, human beings perceive themselves and their world as mutually alien others, yet so likewise do they themselves actually become an alien other; hence, the haunting refrain of *Jerusalem,* "they become what they beheld." However, this deepest darkness is an apocalyptic sign of the imminence of the coming Day:

> Will you suffer this Satan, this Body of Doubt that
>   Seems but is Not,
> To occupy the very threshold of Eternal Life? If Bacon,
>   Newton, Locke
> Deny a Conscience in Man and the Communion of Saints and
>   Angels,
> Contemning the Divine Vision and Fruition, Worshipping
>   the Deus
> Of the Heathen, the God of this World, and the Goddess
>   Nature,
> Mystery, Babylon the Great, The Druid Dragon and
>   hidden Harlot,
> Is it not that Signal of the Morning which was told

us in the Beginning?   (*Jerusalem* 93:20–26)

Here, the full meaning of a fallen cosmos cannot become manifest until the cosmos has become most deeply alienated from humankind and can now truly appear as the apocalyptic "Mystery."

It is not insignificant that Blake chose Newton as a spiritual enemy, and that he imagined Satan in his Urizenic form as a geometrical reasoner with Newton's compasses, for Blake saw Newton-Urizen as the creator of a purely autonomous nature, a nature eternally binding human beings by wholly enclosing them within their solitary and isolated "Selfhood." Already in *The Marriage of Heaven and Hell,* one of Blake's proverbs of Hell states that "Where man is not, nature is barren." Nature is barren apart from humanity because nature does not and cannot exist apart from humanity; the idea of an autonomous nature ("the delusive Goddess Nature") is the product of a fallen humanity estranged from its own eternal being. Blake's clearest evocation of his vision of nature is present in the first book of Milton:

> The nature of infinity is this: That every thing has its
> Own Vortex, and when once a traveller thro' Eternity
> Has pass'd that Vortex, he perceives it roll backward behind.
> His path, into a globe itself unfolding like a sun,
> Or like a moon, or like a universe of starry majesty,
> While he keeps onwards in his wondrous journey on the earth,
> Or like a human form, a friend with whom he lived benevolent.
> As the eye of man views both the east and west encompassing
> Its vortex, and the North & South with all their starry host,
> Also the rising sun & setting moon he views surrounding
> His corn-fields and his valleys of five hundred acres square,
> Thus is the earth one infinite plane, and not as apparent
> To the weak traveller confin'd beneath the moony shade.
> Thus is the heaven a vortex passed already, and the earth
> A vortex not yet pass'd by the traveller thro' Eternity.
>
>   (15:21–35)

What we know as natural objects are vortexes, reflections of the past movements of humankind. Likewise, nature itself is a reflection of the human "traveller"; its form is always a response to a particular human state; hence the vast distances of the starry heavens give witness to the vast time separating us from our ancient and original form, just as the compelling immediacy of the earth arises from a particular and present human condition, a condition not yet "pass'd."

May we also affirm that the compelling immediacy of our space-time continuum arises from a wholly alien human condition, a condition in which interior subjects or individuals are wholly estranged from the space they can know, and therefore a condition in which the ultimate ground of space is humanly unnameable? But Blake named that ground by employing an apocalyptic imagery to speak of "the God of this World" and "the Goddess Nature" as "Mystery, Babylon the Great, the Druid Dragon and hidden Harlot." By naming our darkness, Blake gave it a human face, a face that progressively assumed the form of Satan in his visionary world. But in the climax of that world, on the penultimate plate of *Jerusalem,* Satan passes into his own contrary or opposite, Jerusalem or the cosmic and apocalyptic Christ. Such an apocalyptic transformation cannot occur so long as the full darkness and human emptiness of an alien nature of space is resisted and refused, for the epiphany of Satan is the "signal of the Morning." We *see* what we *are,* yes, and we become what we behold; but we will not pass that space which is our "Vortex" until we travel *through* its dark abyss. Is not every effort to name or conceive a God of our space a refusal or resistance of its compelling immediacy, an evasion of a darkness that dissolves all previous forms of speech, and therewith a refusal of a fullness or epiphany of the world itself? Our apocalyptic seers may name our space as Satan, and so name it because it is totally alien to everything that we can know or experience as an interior or within, but it is precisely the appearance of the manifestation of the total darkness of the world that is the decisive sign of the dawning or epiphany of Jerusalem. Therefore faith must know that darkness as light, as the "Signal of the Morning." Must not theology, too, be prepared to accept a space that dissolves every image of God as a new ground for the epiphany or actualization of Christ?

Satan as the Messiah of nature? Grossly absurd as such an image may appear in our existing theological language, it may not be so absurd from the perspective of contemporary physics. The laws of physics had always shown complete symmetry between the left and the right (mirror symmetry); and this symmetry can also be formulated in quantum mechanics as a conservation law called the conservation of parity, which is completely identical to the principle of right-left symmetry.[16] But, in the summer of 1956, T. D. Lee and C. N. Yang examined the then existing experimental foundation of this concept and came to the conclusion that, contrary to generally held belief, no experimental evidence of right-left symmetry actually existed for weak interactions, such as are, for example, responsible for radioactive phenomena. Soon thereafter Madame Wu's experiments demonstrated quite clearly that radioactive beta decay is accompanied by deviations from mirror symmetry. As Heisenberg noted: "It looked very much as if the weightless particles emitted during beta decay — the so-called neutrinos — existed in only one form, let us call it the left-hand form, while antineutrinos occurred only in the right-hand form."[17] Wolfgang Pauli had predicted the existence of neutrinos twenty years earlier, and now he and Heisenberg, in response to the suspicion that mirror symmetry is not a primary aspect of the fundamental laws of nature, embarked upon the construction of a unified field theory or a self-consistent relativistic quantum field theory. Perhaps the observed reduction in symmetry might be the result of a cosmic asymmetry. Pauli, who was a great mathematician and who had the reputation of having the most brilliantly critical mind in modern physics, became persuaded that the concept of division or doubling might introduce new symmetries. On this basis he and Heisenberg developed a field equation that promised to be the "golden key to the gate that had hitherto barred access to the world of elementary particles."[18]

Contrary to his usual nature, Pauli became elated (Heisenberg reports that never before or after had he seen him so excited about physics), and shortly before Christmas in 1957 he declared in a letter to Heisenberg:

> ... Division and reduction of symmetry, this then the kernel of the brute! The former is an ancient attribute of the devil (they tell me that the original meaning of *"Zweifel"* [doubt] was *"Zweiteilung"* [dichotomy]. A bishop in a play by Bernard Shaw says: "A fair play for the devil, please." So let him join us for Christmas. If only the two divine contenders — Christ and the devil — could notice that they had grown so much more symmetrical![19]

A week after he wrote Heisenberg: "The cat is out of the bag, and has shown its claws: division and symmetry reduction. I have gone to meet it with my antisymmetry — I gave it fair play — whereupon it made its quietus."[20] A few weeks later Pauli went to the United States for a three month's stay, and while there he presented the ideas that he and Heisenberg had developed to a New York audience of physicists that included Niels Bohr. Many of the physicists found fault with the new theory, and when the discussion was over, Bohr summed it up in terms of the lessons physicists had learned from quantum theory about common sense:

> We are all agreed that your theory is crazy. The question which divides us is whether it is crazy enough to have a chance of being correct. My own feeling is that it is not crazy enough.[21]

Whatever may have been Pauli's response to this reaction, he suddenly withdrew from the work with Heisenberg and died that year of an illness whose advent coincided with his loss of faith in the unified field theory that he and Heisenberg were attempting. No unified field theory has yet triumphed in physics, perhaps because none of the attempts have been crazy enough. May we not accept this as a parabolic lesson for theology?

NOTES

1. Alexander Koyré, "The Significance of the Newtonian Synthesis," *Newtonian Studies* (Chicago: University of Chicago Press, 1965), p. 7.

2. Ibid., p. 13.

3. Werner Heisenberg, *The Physical Principles of the Quantum Theory* (New York: Dover Publications, 1949), p. 64.

4. Ibid.

5. Ibid., p. 65.

6. Aage Petersen, *Quantum Physics and the Philosophical Tradition* (Cambridge: MIT Press, 1968), p. 177.

7. Ibid., pp. 173f.

8. Niels Bohr, *Atomic Theory and the Description of Nature* (Cambridge, 1934), p. 4.

9. Patrick A. Heelan, *The Observable, Observation, Description, and Ontology in the Quantum Mechanics of Werner Heisenberg* (Chicago: University of Chicago Press, 1972), chap. 13.

10. Werner Heisenberg, *Physics and Philosophy* (New York: Harper and Row, 1958), p. 81.

11. Koyré, "The Significance of the Newtonian Synthesis," p. 23.

12. Heelan, *The Observable, Observation, Description, and Ontology in the Quantum Mechanics of Werner Heisenberg,* chapter 13.

13. Heisenberg, *Physics and Philosophy,* p. 166.

14. Quoted and translated by Boyce S. Dewitt and R. Neill Graham, "Resource Letter IQ-M-1 on the Interpretation of Quantum Physics," *American Journal of Physics* 39:7 (July 1971), p. 731.

15. Friedrich Nietzsche, *Beyond Good and Evil,* no. 55, translated by Marianne Cowan (Chicago: Henry Regnery, 1955), p. 63.

16. Chen Ning Yang, *Elementary Particles* (Princeton: Princeton University Press, 1961), p. 54.

17. Werner Heisenberg, *Physics and Beyond: Encounters and Conversations,* trans. Arnold J. Pomerans (New York: Harper and Row, 1971), p. 230.

18. Ibid., p. 233.

19. Ibid., p. 234.

20. Ibid.

21. William H. Cropper, *The Quantum Physicists* (New York: Oxford University Press, 1970), p. 57. Cf. Barbara Lovett Cline, *Men Who Made a New Physics* (New York: Signet, 1969), p. 205.

Chapter 6

Theology and Economics

JOHN B. COBB, JR.

CHRISTIANS HAVE WRITTEN MUCH on the economic order, and Christians believe that they have a major stake in economic policies. They have written little, however, on the relation of theology to economic theory. An exception is an essay of Kenneth Boulding originally published in 1950.[1] In this essay Boulding discusses the importance of the influence of religion on the economic order and the importance of the influences of the economic order on religion. But he sharply distinguishes from this the question of the relation of theology as a discipline to economics as a discipline. Some years later (1957) he wrote another essay, "Some Contributions of Economics to Theology and Religion," showing thereby that he does not exclude all influence between disciplines, although in the 1950 essay he asserts that economic theory developed in almost complete separation from theology.[2] In addition to this historical point he makes a strong systematic statement. He states:

> There is no more reason to suppose a "Christian" economic theory...than there is a "Christian" mathematics. Theory is essentially a tool, and should not be even a highly specialized tool. Tools or instruments can only be given moral or religious attributes as they are specialized. There is no such thing as a Christian screwdriver, for screwdrivers may be used either for good or for evil ends quite indiscriminately.[3]

Boulding also proceeds to exclude Christian considerations from the description of present-day economic institutions and the study of economic history. It is only in relation to the application of theory in policy that the door is open to theology, for there "the *ends* of society cannot be left out of the picture."

The exclusion of theology from economic theory and description does not come from one who is indifferent to Christianity or opposed to it. Kenneth Boulding is a life-long Christian and an active churchman. Since he is also a highly respected professional economist, one can hardly doubt his credentials for speaking on this relationship.

Boulding recognizes a certain paradox. On the one hand, religion and the economic order are deeply intertwined. On the other hand, "in thought and theory they are quite distinct and have very little contact. Both theology and economics — along with all other theoretical frameworks — represent *abstractions* from reality, and hence we should not expect them to cover much of the same material. It is as if economic theory looks only at the black threads, and religious theory (i.e., theology, in its broad sense) only at the gold threads of a great and complex tapestry."[4]

Despite Boulding's consistent insistence on the separateness of theology from economics as such, there are three topics in the article that open the door to a different view. In my opinion, each should be pursued. They have to do with the specialization of theory, with Adam Smith, and with the relation of economic abstractions to ordinary people.

I

In the first quotation from Boulding above, he implies that theories lose their scientific neutrality with respect to religious concerns when they become too specialized. He then acknowledges that "historically economic theory developed as a rather specialized instrument for the interpretation of early industrial capitalism."[5] He sees that this would open it to criticism from the religious community, since the merits of early industrial capitalism are debatable. Hence he proceeds: "This limitation however has been steadily relaxed, and the progress of theory is towards greater and greater generality: the most significant techniques of economic theory, for instance, are as applicable to socialist or to primitive economies as they are to capitalism. This is particularly true of what may be called 'equilibrium economics'; it is less true of the theory of economic change and development, where purely economic abstractions are less useful and a broad interpretation of history is necessary."[6]

The logic of Boulding's argument implies that theology could have almost nothing to say with respect to equilibrium economics but might be able to make contributions in the fields of economic change and development. Boulding does not draw this conclusion. His point is that a core of pure economic theory is independent of any particular purpose to which it is put. He has this in mind when he speaks of economic theory as a neutral tool like a screwdriver, but he knows too much about economics and is too honest a writer to pretend that nothing else goes on in the teaching of economic theory. Allegedly neutral economic theories, developed for particular purposes, are subject to evaluation by persons other than economists.

Whether there exists in fact any pure economic theory, any wholly neutral tool, I doubt. But that question is not the one I want to press here. My point is that much of economic theory, and indeed that part of greatest interest to the Christian, *is* specialized in Boulding's sense. Boulding saw this as an element of imperfection in the theory and probably hoped it would disappear as the discipline advanced; so he made nothing of it. But viewing the contemporary scene, one can hardly suppose that this specialization of economic theory has become less important. It ill behooves theologians to wait patiently on one side while economists purify their discipline of specialization. We will always need specialized economics. The question is: What specialization is desirable?

To see the contemporary relevance of this question, let us consider the issue of free trade. When lower priced goods from other countries undercut the sale of American textiles and heavy industries, there is always a cry for protection. At times the political pressures are so strong that tariffs are imposed or raised. But right-thinking people of both political parties typically view this at best as a necessary evil. The goal is almost always to move toward as much freedom of trade as possible. To interfere with the international market is believed to be inherently undesirable.

Let us now ask: Why? A few people might answer that tariffs would hurt the poor of the world and that it is our duty to help them by buying from them. But this is not the argument that counts or that has shaped our deep seated attitudes. Most of our purchases are from the rich. The effective argument is that free trade contributes to economic growth, and tariffs inhibit it. Free trade rewards efficient producers and encourages people everywhere to produce what they can produce most efficiently or cheaply. As a result, total production increases the quantity of goods for all. Economic theory spells this out in detail. Almost all economists are persuaded of this.

Certain relationships exist between free trade and economic development patterns, and it is entirely appropriate for economists to point out these and describe them. But we do not have another comparable body of theory that indicates the human and social values that may be preserved and strengthened through protectionism. France, for example, is seeking to preserve the family farm and farming communities through protection of its produce from competition from global agribusiness. But to the best of my knowledge there is no economic theory in the United States explaining this procedure. It is viewed only as a restraint of trade. Why? Because economic theory is specialized to economic growth rather than to the values of community.

For at least a generation this specialization has been so strong that it has become difficult to think of any other possibility. The economic system itself depends upon growth. That it is better to have more is a virtually unquestioned axiom. And for that reason we can assume that economists and all who seek their advice will promote free trade.

Some economists have long noted the social costs involved in economic growth. A few have argued that there should be an economic theory specialized to steady-state. In the past such respected economists as John Stuart Mill have held this idea although today it is almost entirely ignored by the community of economists. Why? Not, I think, because no one has shown that there are no serious problems connected with growth. It is because almost all the economic theory of the past generation is so specialized to growth that there is very little left of that pure and neutral theory to draw upon. The attack on growth is perceived to be an attack on economics as such rather than a proposal to develop new and interesting supplementary theories.

William Nordhaus and James Tobin present an important exception to the general neglect of critics of growth economics in their article "Is Growth Obsolete?"[7] By "growth" they mean increase of the Gross National Product. They pay close attention to those who point out how much of what is included in that product fails to contribute to human welfare. They also note contributions to human welfare not included in the GNP. Working carefully with these data they produce a different measure, which they call the Measure of Economic Welfare, or MEW. Although they make no claims for the perfection of this instrument, they rightly hold that it more directly measures the contribution of the economy to human welfare than does the GNP. They understand the question in the title — "Is growth obsolete? — to mean, "Does growth of the GNP correlate positively with MEW?" They find that there is a positive correlation, and from this they conclude that, indeed, growth is far from obsolete. So far as I can find, this conclusion was so decisive for them that they have not kept continuing records on the MEW or proposed any modifications of growth economics.

If the correlation they showed between GNP and MEW had been consistently high, their conclusions and subsequent actions might be warranted. But this was not the case. From 1929 to 1947 per capita GNP grew around 30 percent, and MEW, 33 percent. Such a close correlation, if continued, might well render MEW figures superfluous. Between 1947 and 1965, however, the latest year for which calculations were made, per capita GNP grew 47 percent while MEW grew only 6 percent. This drastic decline in the correlation suggests the need for further work. It does not warrant the conclusion that whole-hearted commitment to increasing GNP has been justified once and for all. Again, why did excellent economists who invested a great deal of time and energy in developing a new and better measure of economic welfare abandon interest in it on such flimsy grounds? One can only assume that loyalty to the discipline of growth economics runs deep!

I stated that Nordhaus and Tobin were remarkably sensitive and responsive to critics of growth. This does not apply, however, to those who criticize growth because of its contribution to resource depletion, pollution, and other negative changes in the environment. MEW excludes these considerations as fully as does the GNP. Nordhaus and Tobin do propose that the price of commodities could include the cost of cleaning up pollution so that consumers pay the full cost of what they consume. But this afterthought is in no way reflected in their statistics. That is, they subtract nothing from the GNP to indicate what it would have cost to clean up pollution in the years covered. Further, they ignore the depletion of resources on the typically economic grounds that "reproducible capital is a near-perfect substitute for land and other exhaustible resources."[8] Hence they do not subtract the vast loss of topsoil, to take one example, from the GNP in calculating MEW. Americans are, apparently, as well off with eroded farms as fertile ones. The authors do acknowledge that the possibility that continued industrial development will change the weather gives them pause. They suggest further study. But the MEW figures do not reflect any such concern.

It seems clear that if one approaches matters with a different understanding of reality, subtractions from welfare would be needed for all

of these. Those who agree to the economic importance of the physical condition of the nation would almost certainly find that there was
no growth of MEW between 1947 and 1965, even while GNP rose by
nearly half. The case for growth, so convincing to Nordhaus and Tobin,
seems very weak to one not already convinced.

Mainstream economists have also largely ignored another level of
questioning growth. Studies have shown that within any country at a
given time, the rich appraise themselves as somewhat happier than do
the poor. One might suppose that this means that economic growth
makes everyone happier. But this is not the case. Studies of happiness
do not show that those in wealthy countries are happier than those in
poorer ones. Also, no change accompanies growth of GNP within a
single country. Although more study is needed, one doubts that even
an increase in MEW increases the average happiness of the people who
benefit from it. If the value of growth of the GNP lies in its contribution
to human welfare, then there is no evidence of its success.

Of course, we are all intuitively convinced that sufficient food, cloth-
ing, and shelter contribute to human well-being. The statistics about
happiness did not include starving people. If growth is the only way to
meet basic needs, then the argument in its favor remains strong. But
this is not the case. On the contrary, the main argument against legislation in our country that would permanently insure the basic needs of
all is that such legislation would inhibit growth. Of course, many prejudices against welfare payments must be overcome, but if we were not
committed to growth, there would be no economic objections to dealing with these needs. Granted, the situation is different in some very
poor and overpopulated countries where there is simply not enough
to go around. There, indeed, a measure of growth is crucial. But
growth economics as it now exists does not have such situations in
view.

From a theological point of view one sees clearly an idolatrous element attached to growth economics. Such idolatries can be found in
all disciplines, including theology itself. Economists are not worse than
others, but because so much suffering and danger result from this particular idolatry, theologians do have reason to name it.

II

I have said enough to indicate why I think Boulding's concession that
theologians may criticize a specialized tool is important enough to em-

phasize. I turn now to the question of whether theology has in fact played any role in the development of economic theory.

Boulding correctly concludes that economists have done little direct borrowing from theologians. But I doubt that he would believe that economists have had no opinions on questions of importance to theologians or that these opinions had no effect on their theories. Boulding's comments on Adam Smith are instructive in this regard, especially because they form part of his explanation of the complete independence of economics from theology. "Economics... sprang at least half-grown from the head of Adam Smith, who may very properly be regarded as the founder of economics as a *unified* abstract realm of discourse, and it still, almost without knowing it, breathes a good deal of the air of eighteenth-century rationalism and Deism."[9]

Far from indicating that theologians should stay away from economics, as Boulding intended, this statement seems to invite their intrusion. If economic theory today still breathes the air of eighteenth-century rationalism, and if theologians believe that rationalism is inadequate to an adequate understanding of the human being, of human community, and of the natural world besides, why should theologians not say so? But, of course, generalized criticism of rationalistic tendencies are useless or worse than useless. What is needed is a clear analysis of assumptions that became imbedded in economic theory and of their effects. This is a large and important task.

In this essay one example will have to suffice. The eighteenth-century rationalist, Adam Smith, shared in the atomistic individualism of the epoch. He thought that nature consisted of discrete material atoms and that human society consisted of discrete individuals. Both atoms and humans are related to one another externally; that is, their relations do not enter into the description of what they are. In the case of the human individuals, he viewed them as essentially free, rational wills. As they come together in the market, each makes a rational choice about what is to her or his economic advantage. No other factor counts in the decision.

Smith himself knew that sympathy binds society together. This society tacitly provides the context within which the market functions so well. But it plays no role in his description of the market.

This rationalistic, voluntaristic, individualistic understanding has pervaded economic thinking to this day. Contemporary markets are vastly more complex than those of Smith's day, but the models by which they are explained are even more explicitly individualistic. Robinson

Crusoe became, long ago, the paradigm of the individual unit. His man
Friday constitutes his household and does not figure separately in the
market. Clearly, ties of sympathy do not bind Crusoe to those with
whom he does business in the market. He enters the market purely out
of self-interest and encounters there others who have no other motive.
But all are assumed to understand well enough the goods they buy and
sell so that no one is cheated and all gain through the transactions. And
all are assumed to have the wherewithal to enter the market, that is, to
have something to offer in exchange.

Everyone knows that many of the most important actors in today's
economy are not individuals or households. One views General Motors
and ITT nevertheless on the Crusoe model. One sees the individual
person as engaged in market exchange with them in the same way as with
other individuals. One even assumes that the involuntarily unemployed
poor are free actors in the market.

Of course, economists know that they must introduce many quali-
fications into this model in order to take account of reality. Galbraith
has shown that the relation of large corporations to the public and to
government is, and must be, of a quite different sort. Others have noted
how advertising alters the nature of our market choices, not by providing us with information, but by associating goods with objects of desire,
and by generating artificial wants. But as Boulding says, the economics
community still breathes a good deal of the air of eighteenth-century
rationalism. The model of free rational wills, acting in the market for
their own (or their household's) interests, still dominates.

Since this model has proved very fruitful and illuminating of much
that transpires, we might smile benignly at the naiveté of its anthropology and sociology and admire the economic theory it has generated.
The model, however, also describes processes that take place indepen-
dently of the theory. From the beginning it was prescriptive as well.
Economists should make the actual economic process to conform as
much as possible to this model. Hence they should see all customs and
traditions that inhibit people from functioning in this way as obsta-
cles to freedom and progress. Economic progress destroys traditional
communities. The accepted theory discourages values that do not correspond with rational self-interest. It weakens the bonds of sympathy
presupposed by Smith.

Individualism shows up also in the important economic idea of productivity. One finds in the nineteenth century that the way in which
production could be increased as fast or faster than need was by increas-

ing the amount of product per worker. Economic thought has guided technology, and more and more mechanical and chemical energy has been used in production per worker. Thus workers have become more productive and, as they become more productive, they increased their real wages.

On first glance this seems harmless and even desirable. But even if we ignore environmental matters, it has serious negative effects with which economists have struggled. The chief one is unemployment. Quite obviously, if each worker produces more, the production of a given quantity requires fewer workers. There may be some increase in demand, but productivity has risen faster than demand in most established businesses. Notably true of agriculture, this has led to vast migrations to the cities. In heavy industry as well, fewer and fewer workers are needed. The economists have hoped that the prosperity generated by productivity will call into being new jobs, and this has occurred to some extent. Nevertheless, unemployment is chronic in many industrial societies. In the Third World it is now on a scale so large that one despairs of responding. On the whole it increases in the process of economic development.

Yet the commitment to productivity is so great that even in the midst of vast unemployment economists call for improved productivity. In the United States the research on the mechanical cotton picker went on during the Depression. Economists even now envision highly automated factories in Third World countries.

The point here is a simple one. Suppose that instead of asking about the productivity per worker, one asked about the productivity of the entire work force, employed and unemployed. That would correlate better with human welfare. Or, suppose one asked about the quality of work, the enjoyment of the worker, instead of productivity. Then one would see as problematic many of the simplifications involved in increasing productivity. The emphasis on productivity often makes interesting work dull and breaks up community within the workforce. The individualistic starting point seems to predetermine which questions will be asked and how progress will be measured.

At this point we can tie the discussion of individual productivity to that of growth discussed in Section I. One argument for growth not mentioned there is that it is the only way of combatting unemployment. The argument is ironical. The substitution of energy for labor for the sake of productivity and growth largely causes unemployment. It is true that at this point only the generation of new employment opportunities by the economy can help. And in the context of present practice that entails growth. In short, in this system only growth can solve the problems caused by working for growth. But if we cease substituting energy for labor, especially where this makes work boring, we will reduce the cause of unemployment. As Amory B. Lovins has shown, if we shift from hard energy to soft energy paths, we will employ more people at less cost in more enjoyable roles as well as giving communities more control over their destinies.[10] If agriculture moves from energy-intensive agribusiness to moderately labor-intensive family farming, many more workers will find useful and satisfying roles in the economy while pressures on the environment will be reduced and human communities will become more stable. Similar changes are possible in some business and industrial situations. I am convinced that by such developments true economic welfare would rise as the GNP fell.

Theologians know that we are not individual persons except in relation to one another. Bargains in the market place or voluntary association of autonomous rational wills do not constitute real community. We are social beings through and through. If an economic theory that denies this affects economic practice, it is our task to call it to account.

III

The third point of contact for theology and economics suggested in Boulding's essay concerns the relation of the abstract to the concrete. No one disputes that economic theory is abstract. All theory is. That is no criticism. The question is whether the abstractions are adequate and fruitful for the task at hand and whether those who use them take their abstractness into account. As Boulding notes, "In any field which involves the *application* of economic principles there is great danger of confounding abstraction with reality, and of drawing unwarranted conclusions from abstract logic."[11]

One could take the discussion in the preceding section as an illustration of this. Having, for purposes of analysis of the market, abstracted the free rational will from the total human being and the individual from the matrix of community, economists forgot about what they had left out. Some economists have argued as if no abstraction were involved. Most have failed to revert to concreteness as they made application of their theories. I have suggested that this abstraction is no longer fruitful for the task at hand.

Boulding here has a different question in mind. He writes, "Economics is not...primarily interested in human behavior as such: it is interested in the 'behavior of commodities.' The world of commodities is something which is regarded as following its own laws of motion, like the planets of the solar system."[12] Where we are dealing with human behavior in the mass, it is sufficiently predictable, he thinks, to be ignored. He proceeds to his example: "A good example of both the necessity and the danger of economic abstraction is found in the study of labor; unless we understand clearly that labor is a commodity, in spite of pious pronouncements to the contrary, we shall never understand the phenomenon of industrial relations. But we shall also not understand industrial relations unless we realize that labor is much *more* than a commodity, and that the labor-bargain involves a complex set of psychological, sociological, and theological relationships out of which the commodity aspect is abstracted."[13]

In many ways one can illustrate the failure to recognize the abstract character of the elements constituting the theory. In Section I, I quoted Nordhaus and Tobin as denying the importance of loss of land for economics on the ground that capital could replace it. Outside of economic thought the statement sounds odd. It means, of course, that by sufficient expenditure of capital the agricultural production lost be erosion can be made up. Presumably this might be by rebuilding the soil on this particular land, by increasing production on other land, or by bringing new land into production through irrigation. How it is done does not interest economists. The problems physically encountered in all these solutions as the world runs out of arable land are outside their province. They test their knowledge that capital can substitute for land not in the real world but on computers. Nordhaus and Tobin tell us that their confidence rests on "simulations." As in many contemporary sciences, empirical study becomes rare as computer models generate information. This thereby reduces chances for checking abstractions against reality.

Jan Tinbergen affirms the promise of econometrics for empirical research, but ruefully notes in an article entitled "More Empirical Research" that within it "there appeared a further tendency to concentrate too strongly on methods of verification or testing of assumptions and too weakly on the collection of well-devised new statistical material."[14] Theory repeatedly triumphs over evidence. Even more important in his view would be empirical research about the basic concepts of the science, such as utility or welfare.

Another economist, Tibor Scitovsky, reports on extensive empirical research of just this sort in *The Joyless Economy*.[15] He believes, rightly, that if economists would take his results seriously, important consequences would result for economic theory. He notes, for example, that the organism needs both the satisfaction of its wants, or comforts, and the stimulus of novelty. Economic theory has taken the former as normative in understanding its function. But at a certain point in economic development, the latter becomes more important. What is required for stimulation differs from what is needed for comfort.

These matters, too, are important to the theologian. Even if Boulding correctly claims that labor must be considered a commodity in economic theory, theologians must share his concern to see that this abstraction not dominate the way we conceive labor when we formulate policy. One who believes that the earth is the Lord's and the fullness thereof cannot accept the view that land, with all its biota, is simply a commodity for which capital will substitute. Indeed, one may question whether a theory that treats both labor and land as commodities and loses sight of the abstraction involved is not profoundly dangerous.

The theologian must also challenge the view that beyond meeting basic needs the primary purpose of the economic order is to make people comfortable. As Scitovsky shows, human well-being does not consist primarily in comfort. He begins the formulation of a more adequate view. There is no reason for theologians to remain silent.

IV

Thus far in this essay I have dealt only with one early article by Boulding. I selected it because here an eminently qualified thinker gave expression to what I take to be the standard view of the relation of theology to economic theory. This view reflects the organization of the university into *Wissenschaften,* or disciplines. Each has its separate subject matter and develops the proper methods for analysis and prediction. At least at its core each is independent of all the others. Whereas once philosophy might have undertaken either to unite the disciplines or criticize their assumptions, philosophy is now re-defined as one discipline among others. And theology, once the queen of the sciences, is lucky if it is accepted as a discipline at all. In any case it tries hard to be one. That requires that it mind its own business and not bother the others.

My *Auseinandersetzung* with Boulding has been for the purpose of proposing a quite different view of the relation of theology and economic theory. This presupposes that neither one exemplifies the ideal of the university discipline, which, indeed, provides a misleading and damaging ideal from which both have suffered. In all fairness to Boulding, however, we must note that he, too, expressed more radical ideas.

So far as I know he never took up again thematically the relation of theology to economic theory. But implicitly, at least, he moved far beyond the view of the self-contained autonomy of economic theory. And specifically with respect to the environmental concerns that have played a considerable role in my formulations above, he took the lead among economists. I refer especially to his now classic 1966 essay, "The Economics of the Coming Spaceship Earth."[16]

In this essay he characterizes the past and present economy as the "cowboy economy." It has acted as though resources for consumption and disposal sinks for waste were inexhaustible. Although the resources are not yet exhausted, it is time for economists to think in very different terms, those of a "spaceman economy" in which almost everything is recycled.

He proposes a fundamental shift here in economy theory. In the earlier essay he had stated that economics is about the exchange, production, consumption, and accumulation of commodities. This is standard economic theory. In 1966, however, he writes: "I would argue strongly...that our obsession with production and consumption to the exclusion of the 'state' aspects of human welfare distorts the process of technological change in a most undesirable way."[17] By the "state" aspects of human welfare, Boulding refers to wealth over against consumption. Instead of aiming at maximum production and consumption, he proposes that economics focus on "capital stock, that is, the set of all objects, people, organizations and so on, which are interesting from the point of view of the system of exchange."[18] Material inputs into the economy come from the physical world and material outputs go back into the physical world, which contains limited supplies of inputs and possesses limited ability to absorb outputs.

This leads Boulding to a profound shift:

> In the cowboy economy, consumption is regarded as a good thing and production likewise; and the success of the economy is measured by the amount of the throughput from the "factors of production," a part of which, at any rate, is extracted from the reservoirs of raw materials and non-economic objects, and another part of which is output into the reservoirs of pollution.... The gross national product is a rough measure of this total throughput....

By contrast, in the spaceman economy, throughput is by no
means a desideratum, and is indeed to be regarded as something
to be minimized rather than maximized. The essential measure
of the success of the economy is not production and consumption
at all, but the nature, extent, quality, and complexity of the total
capital stock, including in this the state of the human bodies and
minds included in the system.[19]

This idea is still largely ignored by economists; one exception is Herman
Daly who has richly developed it in his *Steady-State Economics*.[20]

These contrasting economic theories emerge from two quite different
worldviews. In one, the world, including the human ingenuity that is
part of it, is virtually infinite in its capacity to satisfy human desires for
goods and services. In the other, the world is finite, and human beings
need to adjust to that finitude. The strength of the view of the world's
practical infinity in this respect can be seen in standard economic textbooks. For example, one remarks: "After all, there is an absolute maximum to the world's land area; there is an upper limit to the number of
workers; there is only so much sand and gravel, coal, oil, copper, and
iron ore in the earth. In none of these cases, however, are we near the
upper limits. The *effective* supplies of land, labor, and natural resources
are thus not fixed in any meaningful sense."[21] The economic theories appropriate to these worldviews markedly differ. The policy implications
are often diametrically opposed. Empirical evidence cannot settle the
question. Is the decision one that economists are particularly competent to make? Surely not. If it belonged to *any* "discipline," it would be
to one that reflected on the merits of competing worldviews. Theology
would be the best candidate.

V

Thus far I have proposed a variety of points at which theological concerns impinge on economic theory. I have selected ones where my own
theology leads me to be critical of the dominant theory.

Is random criticism of the sort offered above the limit of theology's
role in relation to economic theory? It may be the most that theologians
are currently equipped to do. But it is not enough. Merely to complain
cannot exhaust the Christian's responsibility.

For this reason I propose as a goal just what Boulding in 1950 declared to be absurd: a Christian economic theory. Such a theory need

not be unique to Christians. The assumptions out of which it develops may be shared by people of other faiths and indeed by many who do not think of themselves as believers at all. In assembling support from economists for various points above, I have not inquired as to whether they are Christians! For many purposes the theory should be formulated without any specific reference to Christianity. Yet, without apology, it is appropriate for Christians to bring their faith to bear in determining the assumptions on the basis of which an economic theory is to be developed. Whether we call it so or not, the theory that develops from those assumptions will be Christian.

Since no effort has been made to cover all relevant points, any conclusions about the nature of a Christian economic theory must be tentative and random. Nevertheless, I do draw some scattered conclusions from these investigations. An economic theory should posit a finite earth in which capital stock is more important than consumption. The primary function of the economic order should be to provide basic necessities for all. Beyond that, the values of community are greater than those of consumption and possession. Human well-being is not correlated highly to consumption, and the quality of work is more important than the quantity of production. All creatures have intrinsic value, and none should be considered merely as commodities. Every theory should be tested against the facts as far as that is possible. In particular, theory about corporations should be developed empirically rather than by adapting an individualistic, voluntaristic model.

These are meager conclusions, but in relation to dominant economic practice and theory they are very radical indeed. It is time Christians individually and collectively decided what they believe and express their convictions. We could hope that many others would join us. The intellectual task of developing theory on these assumptions is enormous. The practical task of implementing appropriate policies is daunting. But much is at stake. Perhaps even human survival.

NOTES

1. Kenneth Boulding, "Religious Perspectives in Economics," in *Beyond Economics* (Ann Arbor, Mich.: University of Michigan Press, 1968), pp. 179–97.

2. In ibid., pp. 219–226.

3. Ibid., p. 192.

4. Ibid., p. 187.

5. Ibid., p. 192.

6. Ibid., p. 192.

7. William Nordhaus and James Tobin, "Is Growth Obsolete?" in *Economic Growth* (New York: National Bureau of Economic Research, 1972).

8. Ibid., p. 14.

9. Boulding, "Religious Perspectives in Economics," p. 187.

10. Amory B. Lovins, *Soft Energy Paths* (New York: Harper and Row, 1979).

11. Boulding, "Religious Perspectives in Economics," p. 192.

12. Ibid., p. 193.

13. Ibid., p. 194.

14. Jan Tinbergen, *Economics in the Future,* ed. Kurt Dopfer (Boulder, Co.: Westview Press, 1976), p. 45.

15. Tibor Scitovsky, *The Joyless Economy* (Oxford: Oxford University Press, 1976).

16. "The Economics of the Coming Spaceship Earth," in *Beyond Economics.*

17. Ibid., p. 285.

18. Ibid., p. 277.

19. Ibid., pp. 281–282.

20. Herman Daly, *Steady-State Economics* (San Francisco: W. H. Freeman, 1977).

21. Richard G. Lipsey, Peter O. Steiner, Douglas D. Purvis, *Economics,* 7th ed. (New York: Harper and Row, 1984), p. 345.

Chapter 7

Cosmicization and Legitimation: Religious Dimensions of Aesthetic Worlds

JOSEPH L. PRICE

ONE OF THE SIGNAL CONTRIBUTIONS OF LANGDON GILKEY to the modern theological enterprise has been his ability to traverse traditional disciplinary boundaries, appreciating the methods and conclusions of scientific and social scientific studies and appropriating them into his own theological method and reflection. In *Naming the Whirlwind,* for instance, Gilkey frequently utilizes the work of historian of religions Mircea Eliade to inform his own theological methodology. In *Religion and the Scientific Future* Gilkey turns to biologists and geologists and finds in their works the stimulation for dialogue. And in *Reaping the Whirlwind* he engages the modern social theorist Karl Marx and economic theorist Robert Heilbroner.

By design, then, I seek to pay tribute to the pioneering spirit of Langdon Gilkey by turning to the social sciences to inform constructive reflection on religious dimensions of literature. Building upon social scientific understandings of human worlds and their religious dimensions, I construct a framework for exploring the religious dimensions of aesthetic worlds germinated by imaginary (literary) texts. Throughout the essay, I focus on the outline of a foundational theory rather than upon a developed interpretation of a single text. Nevertheless, at several points I suggest ways in which the theory might be exemplified by or applied to a variety of specific literary works.

151

Before explicating the social scientific understandings of worlds and their religious dimensions, I will identify some of the constraints imposed by previous analyses of religious dimensions of literature. Then, examining Peter Berger's *The Sacred Canopy*, I will look at what constitutes, comprises, and continues the existence of a world, especially as worlds relate to persons as world-makers, world-meaners, and world-maintainers. Following this, I will survey how the processes of world-making and world-maintaining facilitate an aesthetic orientation, not only in terms of artistic production but also in terms of aesthetic perception. Finally, I will explore the ways in which the world-making and world-maintaining processes indicate fundamentally religious dimensions of human and aesthetic experience, and I will briefly suggest how this framework might be applied.

I

In recent years arguments and articles about the relations between religion and literature have taken on a "meta-critical" character, moving away from a focus on the religious dimensions of particular literary works or the religious vision of an author and turning toward a conceptualization of the network of connections among religious experience, the nature of narrative, the disclosive power of metaphor, hermeneutics, and toward deconstructionistic projects about expressions of faith.[1] To a certain extent, I want to continue the "meta-critical" discussion, but I want to enter the conversation with a different voice, one that includes religious tonalities that have been excluded by two of the more dominant modes of reflecting on the religious dimensions of literature. Thus far, the "meta-critical" discourse has been dominated by voices from the disciplines in the humanities, which, traditionally, have dealt with that which is exceptional, that which emphasizes large conceptions of reality. But because I want to include the possibility of appreciating the religious dimensions of the ordinary (indeed, of the profane), I shift the focus to a social scientific perspective that customarily deals with the typical, with particular cases and instances.

Before the recent turn to "meta" theorizing, reflections on the relations between religion and literature had often been conceived in explicitly theological terms based on interpretations and applications of Paul Tillich's understanding of religion as "ultimate concern." In exploring and explicating the religious dimensions of a literary work, theologically oriented literary critics often identified ultimate concern with the dominant conflict or the controlling vision of a fictive or artistic "world." Although the interpretations have proved illuminating for literary criticism and theological discourse, they have not provided an inclusive basis for examining the religious dimensions of all literary works. Their limitations have become apparent at two major points.

First of all, the concept of ultimate implies that which is Other. (Even the capitalization of this word signifies its separateness — its otherness — from ordinary usage and its specific context.) The ultimate, although it might have connections with the penultimate and the antepenultimate by virtue of being at the infinite reach of the scale by which they are measured, is a unique, non-comparative category. The ultimate is different not only in degree but also in kind. Ultimate is finally and fully Other. It is absolute, while all degrees and manifestations of antepenultimate and penultimate are relative.

Because of the identification of the ultimate with alterity, the application of the category of "ultimate" to literary interpretations has proved fruitful for both theological and literary reflection. For the works often analyzed are those that come out of monotheistic cultures and those that deal with the more general religious recognition of Otherness. In fact, a characteristic common to classic texts is that they somehow engage the reader with that which is Other: as a sense of power whose Otherness evades full comprehension (e.g., the worlds of *Wieland* and *Moby Dick*), as a suspension of the simplicities of mundane moralistic systems (e.g., the worlds of the novels of Nathaniel Hawthorne and Henry James), as a mystery whose complexities derive from events and relations that seem larger than life (e.g., the dark worlds of Joseph Conrad's works). In each of these, a sense of awe and fascination pervade the events. Yet popular literature — if for the moment we can consider it to be a contrapuntal opposite to classic literature — often depicts the ordinary events in life, or the ordinary events swelled large. Unlike the classics, popular literature does not usually evoke a sense of fascination or disclose the mysterious dimension of that which is holy, that which is the *mysterium tremendum et fascinans.*

Yet the familiar routines and pleasures expressed, exemplified, and represented in popular literature can be understood in religious terms, because it is possible for there to be religious dimensions or uses of the profane. Too often, religious significance is identified exclusively with that which is sacred; but one of the insights of social scientific analyses of religion is that the profane and mundane often provide the structures of meaning and destiny for persons. In his monumental study of religion from a sociological perspective, Emile Durkheim makes this very distinction:

> For religious conceptions have as their object, before everything else, to express and explain, not that which is exceptional and abnormal in things, but, on the contrary, that which is constant and regular. Very frequently, the gods serve less to account for the monstrosities, fantasies and anomalies than for the regular march of the universe, for the movement of the stars, the rhythm of the seasons, the unusual growth of vegetation, the perpetuation of species, etc. It is far from being true, then, that the notion of the religious coincides with that of the extraordinary or the unforeseen.[2]

Even as Durkheim allows, the Other and the sacred are significant dimensions of religion. Yet the familiar and the ordinary are also the subject and substance of much that is neglected in the study of religion.

Tillichian interpretations that rely on the category of ultimacy to define that which is religious adequately treat the sacred character of the Other (as encountered or experienced in monotheistic traditions), but they fail to include the prospects for dealing with the religious functions of the familiar. Not even the development of Tillich's understanding of $\mu\varepsilon$ $o\nu$ addresses the issue, for the power of the abyss, of the threat of non-being, and manifestations of the demonic are radically Other, even as the holy is radically Other. Because the negative pull of non-being comes from the Otherness of the abyss, it also excludes the familiar from significant contribution to the understanding of that which is religious.

A second limitation of a Tillichian sort of interpretation is that the category of "ultimate concern" is implicitly monotheistic. Tillich conceived "utlimate concern" as being in direct relation with Being. For him, there could be only one genuine or authentic ultimate concern, only one beyond which no other concerns could exist, only one which could be labelled as "truly" ultimate. In contrast to the one real or true ultimate concern, then, all other concerns would carry the stigma or implicit critique of monotheism, that is, that the standard by which they are measured is that of ultimacy — one god — while they as incomplete are imperfect, penultimate approximations of that standard. Although this way of connecting ultimacy with the religious dimensions of a literary work might be appropriate for much of the literature of Western monotheistic traditions, it fails to account for the possibility that there might be a genuine plurality of voices, worlds, or concerns that co-exist in a single work and that do not exemplify, presuppose, or imply a single, absolute category like that of "ultimacy." Although one might expect to encounter such a multiplicity of perspectives in an aesthetic work from a culture espousing a plurality of gods, one finds, as Mikhail Bakhtin has so perceptively noted, that very sort of pluralism pervading Dosto-evsky's novels,[3] and one can identify the same plurivocity in much of Faulkner's fiction, particularly *The Sound and the Fury* and *As I Lay Dying*.

A common problem that undergirds both of the shortcomings of a Tillichian sort of interpretation is that the religious dimensions of a literary work have often been identified with that which, according to monotheistic categories, is concerned exclusively with the sacred and its Otherness. Beginning to address this problem, one can ask how the re-ligious character of a literary work might be explored by using language that is not specifically and theologically oriented to a transcendent (or Other) force. In this respect, Giles Gunn has clearly formulated the ba-sic question: "how does one discuss the religious elements, motifs, or characteristics of any given work of literature without either turning lit-erature into a surrogate for philosophy or theology, or reducing religion to any and every work's dimension of seriousness or depth?"[4]

To chart the course demanded, Gunn turns away from traditional theology and its related modes of discourse to literary criticism and its unconcern for theologically laden language. As such, he locates the re-ligious dimension of a literary work in its evocation or presentation of Otherness. Gunn thus accurately specifies the religious dimension of many literary works whose ritualistic and affective dimensions are in-adequately considered, if not altogether neglected, by even an expanded theological approach like that suggested by Tillich. Yet the emphasis on Otherness still fundamentally identifies the religious with the sacred and its secular supplantations. It does not include ways that the religious can also be ordinary and profane.

The focus of a religious appreciation of a literary work, however, should not be restricted to the category of alterity. At this point, one of Langdon Gilkey's contributions to the analysis of the modern religious situation is relevant. He has recognized that the religious moments of life often involve the ordinary, not as a vehicle for that which is totally other, but as an exemplification or expression of the meaningfulness that emerges from the routine character of the familiar. One does not need to defamiliarize that which is ordinary, exploring its depths and encountering its disclosive dimensions, in order to identify it as gen-

uinely religious. In *Shantung Compound,* for instance, Gilkey exposes
and examines the ways in which the familiarity of family relationships,
communal meals, and ordinary living space orient religious affections
and allegiances.

Other literary works, like W. H. Auden's *About the House,* also convey a sense of religious order not by their articulation of encounter with
alterity but by their fondness for familiarity, by their celebrations of the
mundane or trivial things and events of day-to-day life, by their realization as structures that establish and maintain both meaning and being.
For Western readers these celebrations of the quotidian often evoke a
sense of meaningfulness, security, comfort, and enduring pleasure not
because of their evocation of Otherness but because of the familiar —
often homely — position that the particular items or events assume. In
addition, the rhythms of familiarity often provoke and evoke religious
affections and affiliations by means of ritual regularity.

II

One way to incorporate the insight of Gunn's emphasis on Otherness
and to include the possibility of the religious being found in the familiar is to interpret literary works using the concepts of world-making,
world-meaning, and world-maintaining. Peter Berger identifies these
three processes respectively as cosmicization, nomization, and legitimation, and he understands them as constituting fundamental dimensions
of religion. The association of "worlds" with the basic character of religion, however, is not a theme unique to Berger. Before him and with
him, Durkheim, Mircea Eliade,[5] Clifford Geertz,[6] and Ninian Smart,[7]
to name only a few, have also focused on the world-envisioning and
world-making character of religion. Yet two elementary questions arise
with respect to the world-construing character of religion: (1) What constitutes a world? And (2) what is the specific character of a world that
makes it religious?

At the very least, a world comprises a social matrix of meanings.
As such, it is a human experience and a human expression, and it is an
experience that is subject to articulation if not inscription. The situation
is much like that described by Paul Ricoeur: "For me," he writes,

> the world is the ensemble of references opened up by every kind of
> text, descriptive or poetic, that I have read, understood, and loved.
> And to understand a text is to interpolate among the predicates

of our situation all the signification that make a *Welt* out of our *Umwelt*. It is this enlarging of our horizon of existence that permits us to speak of the references opened up by the text or of the world opened up by the referential claims of most texts.[8]

For Ricoeur, literacy is fundamental to the ways in which he responds to and formulates his worlds. He goes on to add that in the world of a written text one is freed from the constraints of speaker (author) and hearer (audience) of the original dialogical situation. In such a manner a written text reveals the "destination of discourse as projecting a world," as disclosing a new way of being in the world.[9]

Ricoeur's definition of "world" provides an adequate starting point for us to describe the aesthetic dimension of world-making, for he emphasizes the literate character of the world, and he describes the world as opening up and enlarging the set of references that one has. In other words, a world enables one to expand the repertoire of one's references and thereby to enlarge the horizons of one's understanding, an interpretation of one's experiences, a construal of meaning *in* life if not the meaning *of* life. The meaning is not just the congealment of one's hopes, actions, and values; it is the structure by which one accounts for the set of things that have gone right and establishes continuity if not coherence with the things that have gone wrong. Even the voices, then, that proclaim and protest the meaninglessness or absurdity of existence manifest a paradoxical and fundamental appreciation for the meaningfulness of their own voice crying in the wilderness and, thereby, the meaningfulness (at least in a rudimentary, articulated way) of life itself.

A world cannot exist where there is no language, no exchange of signs, for if there were such a situation, meaning would not exist. In this regard, a world is social because of the social character of language. Once a person starts to use language, one finds that one's speaking and thinking are dominated by the syntax and semantics of the language. According to Berger, the linguistic basis for world-making is so crucial that "the subjective reality of the world hangs on the thin thread of conversation." And, he continues, "The reason why most of us are unaware of this precariousness most of the time is grounded in the continuity of our conversation with significant others."[10]

The process of world-making, however, is not merely one activity among others that persons are free to engage or ignore. Persons find that they are born into a world that antedates their appearance. But unlike other animals, human beings are not simply thrust into an inflexible, traditional order. After being born into a physical world, persons must construct their worlds of meaning, not because of some genetic causality, but because, for lack of better terminology, of having been thrust into the existential and biological conditions of the human community. The sensible worlds that persons construct are open worlds, dynamic worlds, worlds pregnant with disclosive power. In the process of world-making, Berger continues, a person develops a specialization of one's own drives and establishes a stability for one's own activity. Simply put, the worlds that persons produce constitute culture, which is forever alive and forever requiring support, alteration, restitution, and invigoration.

The world-making activity of humans includes and exceeds the act of ascribing meaning to objective reality, personal relationships, and historical events. By constructing a world, a person not only establishes the order of relationships that are governed by the world; one also produces oneself by establishing one's own relationship with the world and within the world.

Although it is an individual who thus apparently creates his or her own world, the process of world-making is never an isolated affair; it is, instead, inexorably and inevitably a collective affair. For groups of persons devise, comprise, and revise institutions, languages, values, and implements that constantly impinge upon and orient personal attitudes and affections. Society as such, then, is not merely a product of culture; it is also its precondition. And the social character of the world-making process is accentuated in the process of legitimation, or that of world-maintaining.

In addition to the process of world-making or "cosmicization," the process of world-maintaining is necessary to keep alive the structures of meaning that have been germinated in the act of cosmicization. At the personal level, this means that one seeks to retain the ties of belonging. Berger uses the term "legitimation" to identify the process of maintaining world order. By this designation, he indicates the process whereby "socially objectivated knowledge...serves to explain and justify the social order."[11] In and of itself, the process of legitimation is larger than, yet inclusive of, religion, but there is a significant connection between legitimation and religion. All legitimation seeks to maintain the meaningful structures of reality, but only a religious orientation locates and maintains the power or source of the meaningful structures themselves within "a cosmic frame of reference." By grounding the reality of the structure of meaning in reality as such, by granting them some form of ontological status, the institutions, practices, and values that are legitimated are, as Berger concludes, "thus given a semblance of inevitability, firmness, and durability that is analogous to these qualities as ascribed to the gods themselves."[12] Significant processes of legitimation thus tend toward concern for institutions and values customarily recognized as religious.

For one to live in a world and to live with a world, one must maintain the world by ordering meaningful structures of the world, not only in some objective sense as in participation in its institutions, but also in a subjective sense, whereby a person's consciousness is structured by the grammar and rhetoric of the world's language. "It is for this reason," Berger writes,

> that radical separation from the world, or anomy, constitutes such a powerful threat to the individual. It is not only that the individual loses emotionally satisfying ties in such cases. He loses his orientation in experience. In extreme cases, he loses his sense of reality and identity. He becomes anomic in the sense of becoming world-less. Just as an individual's nomos is constructed and sustained in conversation with significant others, so is the individual plunged toward anomy when such conversation is radically interrupted.[13]

Anomy (Berger's spelling of Durkheim's designation *"anomie"*), which is the threat of disintegration and chaos, is the threat to every constructed world, since the nomic structures are constantly confronted with the human perplexities of disease, disorder, decay, and death. When conversation with significant others ceases to be voiced about these liminal experiences of life, one becomes alienated from the nomic structures that render life meaningful, and one may even seek death in preference to the haunting threat of continuing anomy.

With the suggestion that a world is the structure of meaning that one constructs for one's life, the cognitive or reflective dimension of religion again seems to assert dominance over affective and active levels of religion. But the structures of meaning are established for the purpose of acknowledging and including the affections rather than denying them or minimizing them. For the feelings of hate and love, of disgust and joy, and of all species of attractive and repulsive feelings do not become a part of one's world until they are identified, until they are named, until the structure of meaning is extended to them. Berger calls this process of establishing meaning by ordering and naming "nomization." The "nomos" is the structure of meaning, the common knowledge of human relatedness with the world, that all persons in that world share.

III

Persons are, as we have seen in the previous section, fundamentally world-makers, world-maintainers, and world-revisers. But persons are not world-makers only in the arena of their social contacts. They also express and perceive worlds in the relations implied by and enacted within their literary and other artistic works.

Although Berger writes about social groups in everyday life, his insights into the structures of meaning and the human drive for meaningfulness can be extended to the similar processes represented, depicted, exemplified, or annulled in imaginative worlds. If one takes aesthetics to include systems of reference, then the processes of world-making and world-maintaining include an aesthetic dimension because of their drive to establish and preserve realms of reference.

The aesthetic process of world-making and its relation to ways of meaning have comprised one of the major concerns of Nelson Goodman, long-time philosopher at Harvard and himself an avid lover of aesthetic objects and their worlds. Two of his most recent works, *Languages of Art* and *Ways of Worldmaking,* directly address the issue. Although Goodman is most interested in the process of creating artistic works, his thought also illuminates reflection on the process of aesthetic perception.

According to Goodman, a writer or an artist can utilize five variant processes or means for creating the places, persons, and perspectives that give a world its particularity. The first, "composition and decomposition," is the process of "taking apart and putting together." Often the two tasks are conjointly brought about: While one analyzes and classifies the complexities of composite configurations, one also connects disparate elements and composes new combinations. Yet, Goodman cautions, the mere act of taking something apart and reassembling or reconfiguring it does not create a new world. "Though we make worlds by making versions," Goodman avers, "we no more make a world by putting symbols together at random than a carpenter makes a chair by putting pieces of wood together at random."[14] Worlds are constituted not merely by constructing an object but also by providing the context for the object and perspective to perceive its placement.

The second process of aesthetic world-making is that of "weighting," which deals with tone and accent, density and thickness. To distinguish one world from another, this process emphasizes a particular feature or features, thus adding "weight" to one portion rather than another. Goodman notes that "a difference between two versions that consists primarily or even solely in their relative weighting of the same entities may be striking and consequential."[15] The Victorian worlds of Charles Dickens, for instance, differ from those devised by Thomas Hardy in the density of soot that pervades the British cities and their factories. By contrast, Hardy intensifies the symbolic soot in the lives of his characters, like Tess and Richard Henchard.

Goodman's third process of world-making is "ordering," which generates its worlds by positioning and repositioning persons and their perspectives in both time and space. And the final two processes are "deletion and supplementation" and "deformation," both of which are *explicitly* world-remaking since both derive their distinctions by revising previously existing worlds. Yet for Goodman, all world-making is based on the ability to make new versions of the stuff and ideas of old worlds: For him, there is no artistic analogue to the Christian idea of *creatio ex nihilo.*

In the end, world-making, as an act either of artistic creation or artistic perception, cannot be accomplished alone by any one of the five processes identified by Goodman. The establishment of a world requires a combination of some of these aesthetic functions.

Although Goodman writes specifically about the creation of aesthetic worlds, the processes that he identifies are not unique to artistic creation. Indeed, his analysis of the functional components in the process of creating aesthetic worlds amplifies one's understanding of the processes of cosmicization, nomization, and legitimation that have been the concerns of social scientists. For the same premise underlies both: Worlds are realms of reference. Because of their referential underpinnings, social worlds have an aesthetic core, one which not only enables and sustains the possibilities of physical existence, but also one which reveals alternative ways of construing meaning and being.

IV

Having described the world-making dimensions of cosmicization, nomization, and legitimation, and having suggested the increased understanding of these processes afforded through an aesthetic analysis like that of Goodman, I need now to explore how worlds can be understood as religious. For the most part, the theorists of religion who have identified world-making, world-viewing, and world-meaning as distinctly religious functions or dimensions of experience have based their recognition of the religious character of the "worlding" processes on the ways in which worlds reflect or disclose the Other. Although my final purpose also includes the recognition of the genuine religious character or potential of that which is familiar, I will begin my analysis of the religious significance of the "worlding" processes by looking at their conceptions of the religious significance of worlds.

With regard to religious persons, Mircea Eliade remarks that their worlds are sacred because they perceive the design of and orientation to the Other in everything that they encounter. Religious persons thus express the nostalgic desire "to live in a pure and holy cosmos, as it was at the beginning, when it came fresh from the Creator's hands."[16] For them, all worlds are religious; for them, the sacred ontologically grounds all world foundings. Religious persons, then, think that which is not a part of a sacred world is not a world, but chaos.

For those who think of themselves as having matured beyond the necessity of religious beliefs, who think of themselves as having desacralized their worlds, Eliade notes that they are, nevertheless, the descendants of *homo religiosus* and that, like it or not, they "still behave religiously," even though they might be unaware of their religious actions. The modern secular person who feels and believes that he or she is "nonreligious still retains a large stock of camouflaged myths and degenerated rituals."[17] All persons, therefore, whether self-consciously acting out of religious motives or ignorant of or antagonistic toward them, behave religiously. For religious behavior is not a stage or phase of human development; it is a structure of human consciousness.[18] Religious activity emerges out of human responsiveness to issues and ideas of being, meaning, and truth. The inescapable religious behavior of persons with respect to their worlds does not result from the fact that they have not developed or degenerated sufficiently to escape the far reaches of religion.

As examples of desacralized religious rituals, Eliade identifies several activities that relate to symbols of a world. For one, the settlement of a territory is reminiscent of the primeval creation, for settlement establishes order and relationships where there had been chaos. Moving to a new house also reflects the paradigmatic primordial creative act of the gods, for by moving into a house a person settles space, ordering it and constructing a world out of it. To organize any space — even to make a microcosm out of one's room — reflects the divine ordering that characterized the beginning creation by the gods. "And every beginning," Eliade concludes, "repeats the primordial beginning, when the universe first saw the light of day. Even in modern societies, with their high degree of desacralization, the festivity and rejoicing that accompany settling in a new house still preserve the memory of the festival exuberance that, long ago, marked the *incipit vita nova.*"[19] Another example indicates that the erection of all sorts of territorial barriers or defenses — from trenches and ramparts common in medieval times to the more contemporary cinder block and chain-link fences that surround suburban properties — reflect the mythical attempts to protect one's world against demonic or military forces, both of which religiously threaten one's world with disintegration and death.

Knowingly or naively, every act of world-making thus reflects cosmogonic creation by the gods. For Eliade, the act of cosmicization is religious because it, acknowledgedly or not, indicates a realm of transcendence, the Otherness of the gods. Even the fully secularized rituals involving the primordially sacred symbols of the cosmos — such as body, house, temple, city — are religious by virtue of their repetition that seeks some reference beyond the daily realm of reality. "A religious symbol conveys its message even if it is no longer *consciously* understood in every part," Eliade concludes. "For a symbol speaks to the whole human being and not only to the intelligence."[20]

Following Eliade, Berger understands religion as the human process by which a sacred cosmos is founded, and he identifies the character of sacred as being that "quality of mysterious and awesome power, other than man and yet related to him, which is believed to reside in certain objects of experience."[21] Basically, for Berger, the sacred is that which is extraordinary, that which sticks out of the quotidian, that power which, unharnessed for application to everyday circumstances, is threatening and "potentially dangerous." For him, then, the sacred character of the cosmos stems from its origin in and relation to Otherness. "The cosmos posited by religion," he writes, "thus both transcends and includes man. The sacred cosmos is confronted by man as an immensely powerful reality other than himself. Yet this reality addresses itself to him and locates his life in an ultimately meaningful order."[22] In the final analysis, cosmicization is a religious process because it seeks to establish a completely comprehensive basis for meaning in life and, perhaps, the meaning of life.

In addition to the fundamental religious character of the cosmicization as identified by both Eliade and Berger, the process of legitimation is religious in ways other than those of established religions seeking to legitimate their attitudes and actions. The arena in which a religious perspective performs perhaps its most significant legitimating function is that which concerns marginal situations, such as the confrontation with disease, decay, destruction, disorder, and death. In the face of each of these potentially disruptive forces within a world, the process of legitimation seeks to maintain the structures of meaning that thwart tendencies to dissipate and dissolve the life of the world. Through its legitimating process, a religious perspective maintains the structures of meaning of a community by incorporating these marginal or liminal situations and threats into a fully inclusive cosmic reality. As a result, the individual who confronts these marginal situations continues to exist in his or her world despite the fragmentation, frustration, and failure often associated with treks through liminal regions. The person who maintains such a worldview does not ignore or forget the suffering that he or she has survived; rather, the religious orientation takes account of the problems, incorporating the experiences into the cosmos of which sense then must be made and maintained, even if it is merely to ascribe the apparent structure of senselessness to it. The power and efficacity of religion thus depend upon the structures of meaning that religion embraces and endorses as all persons march toward a meeting with the final marginal situation, that of death.

Although Eliade bases the religious character of cosmicization on its mythological connection with the gods, and although Berger defines the religious character of legitimation in terms of its reference to liminal experiences and their nearness to that which is Other, the religious character of nomization does not derive so specifically — if at all — from its reference to alterity. Nomization is religious because it posits particularity and place. First and foremost, the process of nomization appreciates creation itself, the thing being named. The very process of nomization takes that which was unfamiliar, extraordinary, unknown, and by naming it makes it known and accessible to the realms of the ordinary. Because the process of nomization attempts to clarify the meaning and truth implicit in the larger, unknown cosmos, nomization is also a religious process. And by maintaining the distinctive character of a particular name, the process of nomization continues to function in a religious way, sustaining the particularity of an object, idea, person, or event in the larger language and world of which the particular item is a part.

Even as the processes of cosmicization, legitimation, and nomization suggest religious interpretation, so too do the aesthetic functions of world-making (composition and decomposition, weighting, ordering, deletion and supplementation, and deformation) provoke similar realization of the religious character of worlds. But the aesthetic functions of the world-making process are religious in ways distinct from those suggested by Eliade and Berger. The aesthetic functions of world-making are religious, in part, because of their potential to restructure and revise that which is already given. With the stuff of familiarity, then, they fashion new worlds, arenas that address and exemplify human concerns about being, meaning, and truth. The aesthetic functions often express and address the issues of being and meaning in the context of the ordinary, not by reference to the realm of alterity. Recalling Durkheim's criticism, we find indeed that the aesthetic world-making functions can attempt to explain "the regular march of the universe" rather than to account for the monstrosities, fantasies, and anomalies that manifest the lure of the Other.

V

An analysis of world-making provides a framework for interpreting how imaginative literary works can express or exemplify a religious dimension that is not determined exclusively and specifically by reference to that which is Other. The process of exploring the worlds of the works as ways to appreciate their affective and ritualistically religious character means that a religious dimension need not be conceived explicitly in supernaturalistic, subconscious, or transcultural terms of Otherness but as the particularity and placement of persons, things, and events within a familiar cosmos — their "ordering" and "weighting," to use Goodman's terms. The recognition that the religious dimension(s) of literary worlds might be found (also) in engagement with the familiar rather than only in encounters with the Other also alleviates the second of the problems with a Tillichian perspective, that it is implicitly monotheistic because of the uniqueness of the category of ultimacy. A perspective that begins with the world or worlds disclosed by a literary work can be applied effectively to the literatures of Western monotheistic cultures and to the literary works of pluralistic cultures that manifest a sense of "divine ordinariness," as Charles Winquist suggests in his essay in this volume.

Like Paul Ricoeur, who approaches a literary work through the world disclosed by or through the text, I also want to identify the world or worlds of a work of literature as being the locus of the surplus of meaning that the text affords. And like the social scientists who have analyzed the religious character of worlds, identifying the fundamental religious character of the process of cosmicization and the religious tendency of the process of legitimation, I want to explore the religious dimensions of the profane in ways that do not require a theologically laden lexicon but do emphasize the religious dimensions of the literary worlds.

In this regard, popular literature perhaps would be most often subject to interpretation of the religious dimensions of the profane because the style and appeal of popular literature frequently emerge out of and press toward that which is familiar, not that which is radically Other. Examples of how this method might offer a religious interpretation (in contrast to former theologically oriented perspectives) abound in the genres of popular literature — in Westerns, detective stories, and romances. For instance, the religious interpretation of a Western novel about the conflict of the worlds between frontier settlers and Native Americans need not be framed in terms of the rather American Protestant notion of Manifest Destiny but can be conceived in terms of the cosmogonic settlement of territory by one people in conflict with another people for whom portions of the territory are already thought to be "sacred." Such an interpretation would recognize the possibility of a plurality of worlds disclosed in a work, and it would avoid the necessity of judging a Native American world in terms of the Protestant category of Manifest Destiny while recognizing its fundamental religious character.

The religious dimensions of detective fiction and murder mysteries also can be explored thoroughly because they need not be tied to the puzzle of the mystery that gets resolved or to the murderer who gets discovered by a detective who might be seen as a secular "hound of heaven," pursuing relentlessly and overwhelming others with "righteousness." In place of such implicitly theological approaches, a religious interpretation based on world-making and world-maintaining would turn to the worldview and rituals exemplified and dramatized by detectives, criminals, and even by-standers. In popular romances, too, the religious significance need not be identified with the lure of passion as it might relate to "*the* Passion,"[23] but the religious significance can be explored through the world-making and world-maintaining character of the familiarity of sensuality expressed in the sentimental world of popular lovers.

Obviously, the application of such an interpretative framework need not be restricted to popular fiction but can be extended to works in which religious significance might have been identified exclusively with encounters with Otherness. In this regard, one example might be provided by the way that one would approach Graham Greene's novel, *The End of the Affair.* Instead of focusing on the Catholicity of the novel and the specific Christian themes (such as those related to sacrificial suffering and its sacramental efficacy) that get portrayed and dramatized in the events and personalities of the novel, one could focus on the more universal and fundamental religious theme of the way in which the worlds of Henry, Bendrix, and Sarah deal with suffering, as it separates and occasions liminal situations. And a second example of this type could be provided by an interpretation of the poetry of the Puritan Anne Bradstreet. The religious interpretation of her work would not be required to deal with the way in which her poems challenged or exemplified the Otherness of Puritan values. Rather, a genuinely religious interpretation could focus on the ways in which the familiarity of home and family provide the metaphorical underpinnings for the making and maintaining of her poetic world.

The advantage and advancement of interpreting the religious dimension of literary works by focusing on the disclosive character of their worlds lies in the inclusiveness of the approach. For the focus on aesthetic worlds recognizes the religious character and radical significance of that which is Other, and it allows for the prospect of understanding how the routines and commonplace concerns of the ordinary life of the world might also constitute or comprise the religious significance of the literary work.

NOTES

1. See, for example, Paul Ricoeur, *The Rule of Metaphor: Multi-disciplinary Studies of the Creation of Meaning and Language,* trans. Robert Czerny, with Kathleen McLaughlin and John Costello (Toronto and Buffalo: University of Toronto Press, 1977); Paul Ricoeur, *Interpretation Theory: Discourse and the Surplus of Meaning* (Fort Worth: Texas Christian University Press, 1976); Paul Ricoeur, *Time and Narrative,* vols. 1 & 2, trans. Kathleen McLaughlin and David Pellauer (Chicago: University of Chicago Press, 1984, 1985); Mary Gerhart and Allan Russell, with intro. by Paul Ricoeur, *Metaphoric Process: The Creation of Scientific and Religious Understanding* (Fort Worth: The Texas Christian University Press, 1984); Gary Comstock, "Truth of Meaning: Ricoeur versus Frei on Biblical Narrative," *The Journal of Religion* 66:2 (April 1986), pp. 117–140; Thomas J.J. Altizer, "History as Apocalypse," in Altizer *et. al., Deconstruction and Theology* (New

York: Crossroad, 1982), pp. 147–177; Charles E. Winquist, "Body, Text, and Imagination," in Altizer *et al., Deconstruction and Theology,* pp. 34–57; Nathan A. Scott, Jr., "The New *Trahison des Clercs*: Reflections on the Present Crisis in Humanistic Studies," *The Viriginia Quarterly Review* 62:3 (Summer 1986), pp. 402–421; and Nathan A. Scott, Jr., *The Poetics of Belief: Studies in Coleridge, Arnold, Pater, Santayana, Stevens, and Heidegger* (Chapel Hill: University of North Carolina Press, 1985). A notable exception to this recent trend in the "meta-critical" character of the discourse in religion and literature is Robert W. Brinkmeyer, Jr., *Three Catholic Writers of the Modern South: Allen Tate, Caroline Gordon, Walker Percy* (Jackson: University of Mississippi Press, 1985).

2. Emile Durkheim, *The Elementary Forms of the Religious Life,* trans. Joseph Ward Stein (New York: Collier Books, 1961 [reprint of the Macmillan edition, 1915]), p. 43.

3. See Mikhail Bakhtin, *Problems of Dostoevsky's Poetics,* ed. and trans. Caryl Emerson, with intro. by Wayne Booth, "Theory and History of Literature," vol. 8 (Minneapolis: University of Minnesota Press, 1984).

4. Giles Gunn, *The Interpretation of Otherness: Literature, Religion, and the American Imagination* (New York: Oxford University Press, 1979), p. 67.

5. Mircea Eliade, *The Sacred and the Profane: The Nature of Religion,* trans. Willard R. Trask (New York: Harcourt, Brace and Company, 1959).

6. Clifford Geertz, "Religion as a Cultural System," in his *The Interpretation of Cultures: Selected Essays* (New York: Basic Books, 1973), pp. 87–125.

7. Ninian Smart, *Worldviews: Crosscultural Explorations in Human Belief* (New York: Charles Scribner's Sons, 1983).

8. Ricoeur, *Interpretation Theory,* p. 37.

9. Ricoeur, Ibid., p. 37.

10. Peter Berger, *The Sacred Canopy: Elements of a Sociological Theory of Religion* (New York: Anchor Books, 1969), p. 17.

11. Ibid., p. 29.

12. Ibid., p. 36.

13. Ibid., p. 21.

14. Nelson Goodman, *Ways of Worldmaking* (Indianapolis: Hackett Publishing Company, 1978), p. 94.

15. Ibid., p. 11.

16. Eliade, *The Sacred and Profane,* p. 65 (original in italics, which are here deleted).

17. Ibid., p. 204.

18. See Mircea Eliade, "Preface," in his *The Quest: History and Meaning in Religion* (Chicago: University of Chicago Press, 1969).

19. Eliade, *The Sacred and Profane,* p. 57.

20. Ibid., p. 129.

21. Berger, *The Sacred Canopy,* p. 25.

22. Ibid., p. 26.

23. Cf. Francis L. Kunkel, *Passion and the Passion: Sex and Religion in Modern Literature* (Philadelphia: Westminster Press, 1975).

PART II

THEOLOGY ENGAGES
THE WHIRLWIND

Chapter 8

Providence, God, and Eschatology

WOLFHART PANNENBERG

MODERN PROTESTANT THEOLOGY HAS BEEN CONCERNED with the theological interpretation of history for more than two centuries. Today it owes gratitude to Langdon Gilkey for his reminder that such a discussion should take due notice of the doctrine on providence, of the problems inherent in its classical presentations, and of its need for contemporary reinterpretation. As Gilkey has successfully demonstrated, the doctrine of providence offers opportunities for taking a fresh look at the problems of history and of its theological interpretation. One could be tempted, indeed, to cover by the notion of providence everything that modern theology has discussed in terms of a theology of history: the biblical history of salvation and revelation, including the incarnation of Christ, the history of the church, and the eschatological completion of all human history. In principle, it could be argued that the notion of the divine government of created reality, in spite of the presence of sin and evil in the midst of it, comprises all those issues.

Langdon Gilkey decided to work with a more restricted concept of providence in line with the traditional notion of providence as God's preservation and government of creatures. Therefore, in his judgment, providence "must be supplemented by incarnation and atonement, and ultimately by eschatology."[1] On the other hand, it is precisely such a restricted notion of providence that serves as an instrument of correction in relation to the one-sided emphases of neo-orthodox theology on christology and "contemporary eschatological theology" on the eschatological future. Gilkey does not want to deny the importance of any

171

of these other emphases, but he wants to supplement them by the issues of providence and thereby to correct the dangerous consequences of their exclusivism. In the case of neo-orthodoxy, Gilkey identifies its shortcoming in the fact that it leaves the world of social and historical reality to itself.[2] In the case of eschatological theology, he shows that the liberal concern for history was restored, but that the developmental view of history as progressively approaching the kingdom of God was replaced by a prospectus of "radical social change in the name of a historical kingdom to come," with the acute danger of overlooking the ambiguities inherent in radical social change. In turn, the radical social change can produce new forms of injustice, since sin is not a prerogative of clinging to the past, but lurks in the corruption of human freedom itself.[3] In both cases — of Neo-orthodoxy and of the contemporary theology of hope — the category of providence is seen to be vanishing from the theological agenda.[4] Gilkey, to the contrary, considers providence as providing the necessary presuppositions for the doctrines of christology and atonement as well as of eschatology.

One may perhaps wonder whether the negative attitude toward social and historical reality, which Gilkey attributes to neo-orthodoxy, was really characteristic of all its forms. It certainly was characteristic of Bultmann's thought; and his individualism may have been the main reason for the sudden decline of Bultmannianism in the early days of the students' movement in the late 1960s. But the case of Barthianism has been different, since by analogical reasoning from christology Barth reached quite definite conclusions concerning the political reconstruction of society. His sympathies for socialism, Marxist or otherwise, help to explain the resurgence of Barthianism in Germany, precisely during the years of the students' revolution. For the same reason, there is a line of continuity from Barth through the earlier Moltmann to Latin American liberation theologies, while there was no such connection on the side of other theologians whose concern was focused on eschatology.

Since in characterizing eschatological theology Gilkey deals at some length with my own arguments in favor of a futurist perspective in theology, and especially in the doctrine of God,[5] I may be forgiven to comment on his remarks. While the reality of God, in my argument, is indeed bound up with God's kingdom so that God's activity in creation is seen as the ultimate future impinging upon everything present, this does not entail a "radical negation of the present order of the world."[6] I rather emphasized that as the power of an ultimate future, God has been the future of all past events as much as of those still ahead of us, and I explicitly added that "we can now understand even our past as the creation of the coming God,"[7] since God's faithfulness grants continuity to creation. It is true that some theologians used the idea of the futurity of God in such as way as to oppose the future to the past and present, while overlooking the ambiguities of a future to be produced by human freedom, especially by political action. But that is by no means an inevitable consequence of the idea of God's futurity. It is rather a dualistic attitude, reminding one of the gnostics of the ancient world. As long as the idea of one God as creative origin of the world is not surrendered, the futurity of God has to be understood as origin of the past and the present no less than of things to come, and the unity of God inevitably imposes a measure of continuity upon the transition from any past or present to the future. Therefore, the traditional issues of the doctrine of providence cannot be excluded from the concerns of such a theology.

When Gilkey argues against unlimited secularism regarding the interpretation of present and past human reality, every Christian who adheres to the belief in the one God, creator of heaven and earth, should applaud him. There is indeed "a dimension of ultimacy on every level of our being."[8] To substantiate this claim was the rationale of my endeavors in the field of anthropology as early as 1962 and again in 1983.[9] I fully agree with Gilkey's warning that "if God be solely the future, and not also the God of our present, this 'religious' dimension of social and political experience fundamental to that experience — as well as the mythical and demonic elements of politics itself — become[s] unintelligible and irrelevant...."[10] Therefore I also share his criticism of Barth and Bultmann concerning the surprising fact that they accepted the "ontology" of the secular historical consciousness rather than trying to transform it.[11] It is not enough to relate a Christian interpretation of human life, personal and social, to contemporary experience in a merely extrinsic fashion, be it even by way of protest. Rather, theology has to enter into a dispute with purely secular interpretations of society and of personal life. The same applies to the interpretation of nature. A detailed argument concerning the "religious" or "ultimate" dimension in nature as well as in human life is indispensable, and it has to move on the same level as other philosophical reflections on the work of the relevant disciplines. Only on the basis of such an argument can theology hope for any degree of plausibility when it comes to statements concerning God's action in history.

While this level of general agreement concerns specifically the Tillichian heritage in Gilkey's thought, I find myself also in broad agreement

with what he says in the line of Reinhold Niebuhr's analysis of the ambiguities of human freedom and its exercise in history. If I am not
mistaken, Gilkey moves at this point beyond Tillich's language of estrangement toward Niebuhr's more Augustinian account of the human
situation. Niebuhr's Christian realism seems particularly important
in Gilkey's pointed criticism of the "apparent *identification* of liberation and especially of social and political liberation with the salvation
promised in the gospel." Gilkey hits the decisive point when he comments on this position: "It is the *corruption* of freedom in ourselves,
not the enslavement of our freedom to others that represents the most
basic issue of history." Therefore, "greater self-determination does not
guarantee greater freedom from sin. After all, present oppressors are
precisely those who have in the past been 'liberated.'"[12] If there are
some futurist theologies where such criticism applies, they certainly do
not represent my way of arguing from eschatology.[13] Our bondage to
the past consists precisely in the vigorous activity of the "old Adam"
in our lives and in what we call our freedom, rather than following
the spirit of the "new Adam" in ourselves. For this reason I could not
avoid disappointing some of my theological friends by refraining from
revolutionary conclusions from the primacy of the kingdom. After all,
Jesus did not join the zelotic dream of establishing the kingdom of God
on earth by way of political liberation. Because of human sinfulness,
no human society is possible without civil government; for the same
reason the noble task of civil government, the establishment of peace
and justice, will not be perfectly realized by human administrators, but
only in the event of the transcendent kingdom of God. This need not
rule out the possibility that human political action as well as political
institutions may be inspired by the vision of the eschatological kingdom. But as soon as the condition of human sinfulness in this world
is forgotten or, worse, attributed exclusively to the political opponent,
the political activist no longer honors God and the kingdom as distinct from human efforts; and the vision of the kingdom gets distorted
and perverted into the kingdom of one who puts himself in place of
God.

Thus I agree with Langdon Gilkey that eschatology must transcend
the conditions of the present world and the possibilities of human action.
Precisely in this transcendent quality the eschatological hope serves as
a criterion for evaluating the present situation, but it also provides a
source for illuminating and directing our ways through the history of
this world. According to a famous dictum of Ernst Troeltsch, the tran-

scendent empowers us to live our lives in the relativities of this world of finite existence.

But what end does it serve, then, to reformulate the doctrine of God on the basis of eschatology? Why talk of God in terms of "the power of future"? The main reason for doing so is, at least in my mind, the need for a new ontological basis for Christian theology. This is another concern that I share with Langdon Gilkey.[14] Theology needs an ontological basis not only for its assertions on human nature and history but also and especially for the task of reformulating the Christian doctrine on God in view of the arguments of modern critics of traditional philosophical theology and, in this context, also of modern atheism. With Gilkey's fine account of Augustine's doctrine of providence and its underlying concept of God (as opposed to basic concerns of the modern mind that are expressed in modern science as well as in modern history and philosophy), my judgment converges that the classical Christian concept of God, if rigorously developed, could result in unacceptable, deterministic consequences. This insight occurred to me when I studied the medieval doctrine on predestination and divine prescience in order to prepare my doctoral thesis in the early fifties. There are, of course, many other problems with the traditional doctrine of God's essence and attributes, some of which are connected with the more general problems of the traditional metaphysics of substance. But neither the reformulations of the concept of God by the philosophies of German idealism, especially by Hegel, nor the attempts of process philosophers, especially Whitehead's doctrine of God, can serve as an acceptable substitute for the traditional concept of God in Christian theology. I share Gilkey's reservations with regard to Whitehead's and Alexander's concepts of God, because Christian theology has to conceive the reality of God as "the source of our *total* existence."[15] On the other hand, the process philosophers' criticism of the traditional ontology of substance has to be taken seriously, especially in its convergence with the call of other thinkers like Heidegger or Bloch[16] for revising the separation of being from time. But as there is no generally accepted or theologically satisfactory solution of the ontological problem available, theologians themselves have to enter into the philosophical dispute at this point, although they may not be in a position to work out a comprehensive and detailed treatise on metaphysics. Such was my situation when I wrote the first chapter of *Theology and the Kingdom of God,* trying to reformulate the concept of God from the point of view of Jesus' eschatological message and his emphasis on the priority of the kingdom over any other concern.

This attempt was located in the context of the discussions on being and time and was related to their impact on the foundations of the traditional doctrine of God. It was not possible, of course, to discuss in that connection the whole range of the related problems of ontology, although a hint in that direction was given by the essay on appearance that was added as an appendix to that volume. Meanwhile, in connection with the development of my own systematic account of the doctrine of God, I obtained more clarity on a number of related issues in the context of the history of metaphysics; and during last year an invitation from the Institute for Philosophical Studies at Naples provided an opportunity to write down a series of lectures on metaphysical questions involved in the reformulation of the concept of God.

While Gilkey and I do not disagree about the basic requirement of ontological reconstruction for the task of theology, the direction that we envisage for that reconstruction may be somewhat different. In his assessment of the contrast of modern historical consciousness to the presuppositions of traditional Christian doctrines on providence, Gilkey starts with the new sense of historical and cultural relativity that characterizes the modern mind. He goes on to describe the new views of human creativity and freedom and then considers the "temporalization of being" as "indebted more to the developing themes of historicity and autonomy than to that of law in the modern historical consciousness."[17] Of course, I agree that the sense of historical and cultural relativity is distinctively modern, but I do not think that the emphasis on autonomy arose as a consequence of this, nor do I see the temporalization of being arising as a corollary to the modern conception of freedom. To consider time primarily in terms of actuality and possibility of decision, as Gilkey does,[18] occurs to me as a somewhat unsatisfactory account of the nature of time, although I grant that in relation to the human awareness of freedom the difference between present and future may appear in such a fashion. Gilkey himself says that temporal passage is to be conceived as "the ground of creativity." But how, then, can it "become this as a consequence of entities and events being self-creative?[19] Does it not have to be the other way around, if temporal passage is to be conceived as the *ground* of finite creativity? But then the nature of time itself has to be described in different terms, unless we end up with a circular definition.

In fact, the temporalization of being developed from different roots than the autonomy of decision. The Kantian doctrine described time as a subjective form of experience in relation to self-awareness rather than to autonomy. Later on, Heidegger could even refer to Kant's doctrine on time as the basis for his criticism of modern subjectivism. Bergson's analysis of time focussed on the experience of "duration," not autonomous decision. He used his philosophy of time as a starting point for a redefinition of freedom, not the other way around. In Dilthey's analysis of historical experience, time was conceived not in terms of decisions, but of occurrences, a sequence of contingent events which continuously change the frame of reference in our awareness of meaning and significance. It was only in Whitehead's metaphysics that the ideas of subjectivity and decision became ontologically basic in the description of time and that, therefore, the future became a mere possibility. Gilkey's description of time as "the movement of events from possibility to actuality" makes sense only on the basis of Whitehead's concept of creativity. But the description is circular, since it identifies *time* only in terms of the word "movement, which already presupposes the idea of time. The insight that time cannot be reduced to movement resulted already from the discussion on the nature of time in classical antiquity.

Moreover, Gilkey criticized Whitehead's doctrine of creativity on theological grounds, and at least to me his objections seem valid and theologically decisive. But if creativity is to be reconceived in terms of God's activity as creator and preserver (see note 15 above), then it does not seem consistent to use Whitehead's idea of self-determination of events as a basis for describing the nature of time. Rather, it will be inevitable to conceive the mode of God's being as constitutive of everything created, including time. That is to say, Christian theology cannot and should not try to avoid the notion of eternity as constituting the nature of time. This does not preclude a redefinition of eternity itself, especially a revision of the concept of eternity as fundamentally opposed to time. It may be that Augustine's idea of eternity was deficient in this respect. But if so, it was deficient at his own time already, since Plotinus had developed a theory of time and eternity that conceived of eternity in terms of the totality of life that in the perspective of time appears as a sequence of separate moments. The unity of time itself, according to Plotinus, depends on the idea of eternity. Only the future can recover the wholeness of life in the sequence of temporal moments. Unfortunately, Augustine did not recognize the potential of this coincidence of eternity and the future of time for a Christian eschatology and for his own theology of history. Nevertheless, the fault does not lie with his idea that everything is present to God's eternity.[20] Time and space are bound up with finite entities, and from every finite point of view they are different. But God, in his eternity, does not exist under the limitations of time and space. When I speak of God as the power of the future, I mean that the future of finite entities is the point where time and eternity coincide, the "place" also for that eternal presence that ancient Greek thought conceived as timeless, but that, in fact, in the course of time and history is available only by anticipation. This is not a simple spatialization of time, because the future of every finite entity occurs as contingent. The difference between a contingent future and the present seems to provide the main reason for the irreducible difference between time and space. But Bergson has been justly criticized for his almost complete separation and opposition of time and space. No satisfactory philosophy of nature is possible that does not also account for the interconnection of time and space.

If there was no fault in the traditional assertion that everything finite is present to God in eternity, the case is different with purposive action that can be attributed to God only metaphorically, because in the instance of eternity there is no separation between goal and execution. This applies also to predestination. The metaphor of purposive action pictures God at the beginning of the world process as looking ahead and determining everything from the outset. This anthropomorphic image of God's relation to the world, taken literally, was mainly responsible for the clash of the traditional doctrine of providence and predestination with the experience and intuition of human freedom, the point where Gilkey rightfully identifies one of the basic differences between modern historical consciousness and the traditional doctrine on providence. Those difficulties do not occur when God is understood to act from the eschatological future, because the notion of finite freedom is opposed only to the idea of determining forces that arise from the past. Admittedly, the ontology underlying and substantiating the argument of eschatological theology has not been worked out in detail, and the amazement that Langdon Gilkey shares with others in relation to talk about God as acting from the future[21] is understandable. But such language expresses a way of dealing with the ontological question of how the action of God in relation to contingency in general and to human freedom in particular can possibly be understood. One should expect similar ontological proposals from Gilkey himself, if his rejection of Whitehead's assumption of a principle of creativity besides God would be followed through consistently. All creativity then is to be attributed to or derived from the creator God, and at the same time the deterministic tendency of the traditional doctrine of providence is to be avoided.

I agree with Gilkey that the very act of creation involves some "self-limitation" on the part of the creator God in the sense that creation means that an existence of their own is granted to the creatures. Since this is a logical requirement inherent in the idea of creation, it applies to all conceivable ontological models of God's relation to a world of God's creation. For the same reason, to be sure, I am not happy with the *word* "self-limitation," because the act of creation with everything it implies is to be considered as an expression of God's sovereign will. But that may be a purely terminological problem. It seems more important that we agree concerning the ontological requirement of some autonomous existence of the creature as entailed in the idea of creation. But, of course, this does not relieve the theologian from the task of accounting for the kind of causality that is bound up with any idea of a sovereign creator God, nor does it actually limit the responsibility of the creator God for the world God created.

I understand Gilkey's argument that the question of theodicy is not yet solved simply by moving the conception of God's determinative influence upon creation from its beginning in the past to its future. Such an operation indeed does not solve the problem of theodicy. But it seems to me a precondition for any acceptable answer to that question. The idea of divine self-limitation as entailed in granting the creatures some existence of their own does not itself answer the question whether it was worthwhile or even responsible to create a world that would involve so much perversion and suffering. It does not even provide a basis for answering that question. Only the Christian belief in the reconciliation of the world in Jesus Christ and the hope for its final eschatological consummation can do justice to this complaint, because it points to a future when God will "wipe away every tear from their eyes" and put an end to mourning, crying, and pain (Rev. 21:4).

The ontological basis that Langdon Gilkey postulates for a reformulation of the doctrine of providence is particularly important in reinterpreting the notion of preservation. Gilkey does not go into much detail here, but it seems obvious that this issue requires a great deal of work, because since the introduction of the principle of inertia in seventeenth-century physics, the old doctrine that each creature needs a continuous action of God to preserve its existence has lost its plausibility. Such an external preservation became superfluous. To my knowledge, the Christian doctrine of providence never recovered from this blow, and very rarely has the issue been faced. Here the dialogue with science, especially physics, seems indispensable for any hope to overcome this impasse.

There is one other issue that I miss in Gilkey's treatment of providence. That is the notion of election. It can be argued, of course, that the doctrine of providence is not the proper place to deal with election. In my own systematic theology, election will be treated in connection with ecclesiology, because a Christian doctrine of election seems to require a concept of the church. But in the history of the doctrine of providence the issues of election and predestination were closely connected with providence. Even if in the present situation the doctrine of election and predestination have to be revised in terms of a continuous action of God in history,[22] one might contemplate whether some more general treatment of this subject would be appropriate in connection with God's governance of the course of history. Gilkey deals with these matters in terms of the tension between destiny and freedom and especially in relation to how destiny becomes fate. He made many pertinent observations on this matter. But his development of the doctrine of providence into a theology of history could profit from including also some general consideration on election. Is not the notion of election related to the issues of creative possibility that is provided by God to creatures and that has been deservedly emphasized by Gilkey?[23] If possibility is conceived not only in terms of formal alternatives, but in terms of a lure or of some special calling that is accompanied by a corresponding element of responsibility, then the notions of vocation and election seem rather close at hand. Their inclusion could also serve to broaden Gilkey's concept of "destiny," which he relates primarily to the "given" in personal and social life that is inherited from the past.[24] But if destiny is also related to our identity, as Gilkey affirms, does it not then include a relation to future possibilities, to a future completion of our identity? Is our identity not constituted by what we feel ourselves "meant" to be? If so, some notion of election should be included in the awareness of destiny. This would also be coherent with the fact that the transformation of destiny into fate, which Gilkey so eloquently addresses in many places, corresponds to the traditional notion of judgment.

Langdon Gilkey's work in theology gave me the rare pleasure of reassurance that there is a broad basis that theologians of different opinions can share in the assessment of the rich tradition that modern theology inherited from the past together with a clarification of the intricate problems inherent in the traditional doctrines. On this basis, there can be a high degree of convergence in the evaluation of the challenges that modernity poses both to traditional doctrines and to the contemporary work of theology. It is this sort of framework that allows for serious discussion of different opinions and for the development of a culture of theological discourse.

NOTES

1. Langdon Gilkey, *Reaping the Whirlwind: A Christian Interpretation of History* (New York: Crossroad, 1981), p. 266.

2. Ibid., pp. 216ff., especially 225f.

3. Ibid., pp. 226, 236f., and 258.

4. Ibid., p. 231.

5. Ibid., pp. 229ff. Cf. my *Theology and the Kingdom of God* (Philadelphia: Westminster Press, 1969), pp. 51ff., especially 55ff.

6. Gilkey, *Reaping the Whirlwind,* p. 229.

7. Pannenberg, *Theology and the Kingdom of God,* p. 61, cf. p. 63. See also the critical remark on p. 126 addressing the tendency of modern revolutions to disdain and destroy the values of the past, together with what is terms there conversion "to the present in the hope of fulfillment."

8. Gilkey, *Reaping the Whirlwind,* p. 247.

9. See Wolfhart Pannenberg, *What Is Man?* (Philadelphia: Westminster Press, 1970), and idem, *Anthropology in Theological Perspective* (Philadelphia: Westminster Press, 1985).

10. Gilkey, *Reaping the Whirlwind,* p. 234.

11. Ibid., pp. 219ff.

12. Ibid., pp. 236f.

13. Cf. especially my little book *Human Nature, Election, and History* (Philadelphia: Westminster Press, 1977), and the critical discussion of liberation theology in my *Christian Spirituality* (Philadelphia: Westminster Press, 1983), particularly chap. 3, "Sanctification and Politics."

14. The first chapter of *Theology and the Kingdom of God* alone would be enough to document the extent of my agreement with Gilkey on this requirement as he formulates it in *Reaping the Whirlwind,* pp. 135f., and on many subsequent occasions. I only wonder why he thinks that I did not explicitly draw this consequence. I always thought I had done so since 1959. However, I never found it possible to adopt some metaphysical design as it is offered in the philosophical tradition or by contemporary philosophers, for the purpose of theology, because none of them meets the specific requirement for a Christian doctrine of God as it has to be developed today.

15. Gilkey, *Reaping the Whirlwind,* p. 249. Creativity must not be treated as a separate ontological principle, as in Whitehead, but "as the divine power of being, as the activity of God as creator and preserver" (p. 414, n. 34).

16. By mentioning the process thinkers, Heidegger, and Bloch side by side, I do not want to suggest that the level of conceptual analysis in those cases is comparable. In the case of Heidegger, on the one hand, and the process thinkers on the other, there is a considerable degree of conceptual rigor, although in quite different ways; there is much less in the more imaginative language of Bloch. In distinction from Moltmann, I have never been as deeply influenced by Bloch's thought as Gilkey in some places seems to assume.

17. Gilkey, *Reaping the Whirlwind*, pp. 199f.; cf. pp. 188ff.

18. Ibid., p. 200, defines temporal passage as "the movement of events from possibility to actuality."

19. "If entities and the event in which they participate in time are *self*-creative, then temporal passage becomes the prime locus of being and the ground of activity" (Gilkey, *Reaping the Whirlwind*, p. 200).

20. Here my judgment differs from Gilkey's as presented in *Reaping the Whirlwind*, pp. 168 and 384 n. 40.

21. Gilkey, *Reaping the Whirlwind*, pp. 234f.

22. On this question see my *Human Nature, Election, and History*, especially chaps. 3 and 5.

23. Gilkey, *Reaping the Whirlwind*, pp. 250ff.

24. Ibid., p. 49.

Chapter 9

Narrating Creation

PATRICIA L. WISMER

W HEN THE GREAT RABBI ISRAEL BAAL SHEM-TOV saw misfortune threatening the Jews it was his custom to go into a certain part of the forest to meditate. There he would light a fire, say a special prayer, and the miracle would be accomplished and the misfortune averted.

Later, when his disciple, the celebrated Magid of Mazeritch, had occasion, for the same reason, to intercede with heaven, he would go to the same place in the forest and say, "Master of the Universe, listen! I do not know how to light the fire, but I am still able to say the prayer." And again the miracle would be accomplished.

Still later, Rabbi Moshe-Leib of Sassov, in order to save his people once more, would go into the forest and say: "I do not know how to light the fire; I do not know the prayer, but I know the place and this must be sufficient." It was sufficient and the miracle was accomplished.

Then it fell to Rabbi Israel of Rizhin to overcome misfortune. Sitting in his armchair, his head in his hands, he spoke to God: "I am unable to light the fire and I do not know the prayer; I cannot even find the place in the forest. All I can do is to tell the story, and this must be sufficient." And it was sufficient.

God made human beings because God loves stories.[1]

On the face of it, Elie Wiesel's story has little to do with the Christian doctrine of creation. It makes no mention of any of the traditional indicators of the "the beginning": the seven days, the garden, the first woman and man, or the two special trees. Instead, the story seems to focus on two very modern phenomena: the rise of secularization and the concomitant loss of the traditional avenues to God. But in this case, as so often happens in stories, appearances may be deceiving. The last line of this story suggests some connection between the experiences of the four rabbis and creation. In fact it goes far beyond any of the biblical stories of creation and asserts the specific motivation for creating humanity: God's love of stories. Human beings are the only creatures able to live in, tell, and appreciate stories. Without humankind God would be forever deprived of stories to hear and enjoy. So indispensable are stories, Wiesel's narrative implies, that they are more important to God than prayer or ritual.

Of course, Wiesel's story presents an imaginative anthropocentric picture of God, suitable to bring a smile to our faces but not to be taken literally. The most profound Christian theological reflection concludes that God's goodness is the motivation for creation.[2] At least, that is as close as we can come to understanding God's motivation, which ultimately lies shrouded in inscrutable mystery. Or so we should hope. If Wiesel is right, Christian theology may be in big trouble. For that discipline has by and large ignored the story form that lies at the heart of the Jewish and Christian traditions. If God really does love stories, then God has undoubtedly been rather bored by the state of Christian theology for the past fifteen hundred years or so.

But there may be hope in sight for Christian theology. Since the late 1960s an increasing interest has developed in recovering narrative for Christian theology.[3] To date, the resources of narrative language have been applied to various aspects of the theological task: interpretations of biblical narratives, descriptions of religion and Christian faith, statements of Christian identity, theological ethics, and foundational theological anthropology. While all these approaches show much theological promise, this essay treats only the first. It will reflect on one specific biblical narrative (Gen. 2: 4b–3:24) in order to discern its significance for a theology of creation.

Creation has been the subject of Langdon Gilkey's concentrated theological reflection twice during his professional career: early with *Maker of Heaven and Earth* and more recently with *Creationism on Trial,* a volume based on his participation in the 1981 Arkansas creationism trial.[4] Although none of his work falls specifically in the area of narrative theology, Gilkey has a knack for storytelling, as anyone can attest who ever read *Shantung Compound,*[5] heard one of his public lectures, or took one of his courses. Through his stories, usually drawn from his own life-experience and his vivid portrayals of the human condition, Gilkey has succeeded in reflecting on the whole range of theological topics without ever boring God or the lowliest neophyte theology student. But Gilkey never joined his interest in creation with explicitly narrative techniques of interpretation, preferring instead to focus on the mythic and symbolic character of the story. This essay, written in his honor, will attempt the experiment he left untried.

Taking a hint from Elie Wiesel's story, I will assert that there is an intimate connection between creation and narrative. Since this essay is not itself a story, I cannot claim the storyteller's privilege of seeing into the mind of God. Therefore my argument will be much more circumspect, claiming only that narrative language is a necessary part of theological reflection on creation because it is essential to the "event" of creation. It may be more than a historical accident that the earliest biblical reflection on creation (Gen. 2-3) is in the form of a narrative. It may be that narrative form is intrinsically well-suited to expressing the meaning of creation. These possibilities cannot be definitively established here, but we can discuss one indication of their validity. The key term in this two-stage discussion is "tension." "Tension" is used here primarily as a literary critical term. In this sense, tension occurs when two opposite ideas are held together in a metaphor or a fictional text. This results in a complex "stereoscopic vision" of reality that cannot be matched by literal language. In the first stage we will look at Genesis 2-3 and focus on the importance of narrative in conveying tension. Then, we will investigate four implications of this narrative approach that diverge from the traditional doctrine of creation.

Tensions in the Garden

Our study of Genesis 2-3 is based upon two unusual presuppositions derived from understanding Gen. 2:4b-3:24 as the *"story of creation."*[6] The first presupposition views this text as a *story* that can be analyzed by using the tools of narrative criticism. This approach differs from most contemporary theological reflections, which discuss the story's mythical character or pursue a symbolic interpretation. The predominant approach, while correct, is incomplete. To be sure, Genesis 2-3 is a myth, and the characteristics it shares with other myths must be recognized in any interpretation. But, as myth, it also belongs to the larger category of narrative texts. Thus, the characteristics it shares with other narratives must be recognized as well. This realization opens up a vast body of narrative theory for theological appropriation. The usefulness of this first presupposition will become evident as the interpretation unfolds.

According to the second presupposition, the entire text of Genesis 2–3 should be viewed as a story of *creation* (rather than of creation and fall). This more controversial presupposition is more difficult to justify than the first, and its implications are far-reaching. It goes against the broad stream of Christian tradition that has asserted, at least since the time of Augustine, that Genesis 3 recounts the fall, rather than the final phase of creation. It raises the question whether God is responsible for the existence of evil in the world, thus creating an apparently insurmountable theodicy problem. Nonetheless, the second presupposition remains a cornerstone of this discussion. A complete defense of this premise would lead far beyond the bounds of this essay, but we will attempt to show that its adoption does not make more difficult the theodicy problem and may generate some additional insight on the question.

These two presuppositions will help us to interpret the tensions present in Genesis 2–3. Although these tensions might be described in various ways, three different types are central to theological reflection on creation: tensions *between good and evil* in the created order (with the two terms intended here in their most general sense rather than in an exclusively moral one); tensions *within human beings* in their relation to God; and tensions *within God* in relation to humanity. Each of these will be investigated in turn, using the techniques of narrative analysis to ascertain how the tension is conveyed and what its implications are.

Although narrative theory has become sophisticated, one can easily comprehend the basic elements of narrative form. As Robert Scholes and Robert Kellogg state, a narrative requires only two things: "the presence of a story and a storyteller."[7] The story, for its part, requires characters whose actions and interactions constitute the plot. The other aspect of narrative, the story-teller or narrator, subtly guides the reader's understanding of the meaning of the story by providing an additional perspective (in the case of biblical narrative, an omniscient perspective[8]) on the characters and the action. As we will see, plot, characters, and narrator are all essential means of portraying the tensions in the garden.

"Plot," says Aristotle, "is the soul of narrative."[9] And plot is the key to understanding the first kind of tension in Genesis 2–3 — that *between good and evil* in the created order. The story opens with Yahweh Elohim creating a world filled with good things: a fertile garden, animals, and a man and a woman. The humans are meaningfully related to both nature and the animals. In addition they receive a command from Yahweh Elohim, thus initiating a relationship of obedience to the divine. But *somehow* evil erupts from within this goodness. This evil has both physical (or natural) and moral forms, affecting humans, animals, and the earth. In the end, Yahweh Elohim expels the man and the woman from the garden.

What remains to be understood is the "somehow" that connects the good and evil. Traditional theology has given a simple explanation: the man and the woman are at fault because they allowed themselves to be misled by the serpent and thereby disobeyed God's command. It may be, however, that this explanation is too simple to fit the complexity of the story. Narrative theory provides an alternative way of understanding this "somehow" through analyzing the structure and function of the plot.

Any plot has, according to Paul Ricoeur, two distinct dimensions: the "episodic" dimension, which builds up the story out of individual events, and the "configurational" dimension, which pulls together the individual events into a unity, transforming their bare succession into a meaningful whole.[10] The episodic dimension stacks up the various actions sequentially: first the good, then the evil. The configurational dimension, however, provides the link between good and evil; it enables us to see the pattern of how evil emerges out of good. Through configuration plots include tensions within a larger harmony.[11]

Related to the configurational dimension of plots is the ability of readers to "follow the story." Ricoeur explicates this relationship between the configurational dimension and the reader:

To follow a story is to move forward in the midst of contingencies and peripeteia under the guidance of an expectation that finds its fulfillment in the "conclusion" of the story. This conclusion is not logically implied by some previous premises. It gives the story an "end point," which, in turn, furnishes the point of view from which the story can be perceived as forming a whole. To understand the story is to understand how and why the successive episodes led to this conclusion, which, far from being foreseeable, must finally be acceptable, as congruent with the episodes brought together by the story."[12]

The concluding episode of Genesis 2–3, the expulsion from the garden — which represents here all the evil that erupted in the story — is
not directly caused by any one or two actions in the story. But it appears
acceptable because various earlier actions have prepared for it. Looking
back from the perspective of the end point, one can see all the episodes
transformed into a meaningful whole. Discovering exactly which earlier
actions prepare for the conclusion, and how they do so, will require an
investigation of the other two levels of tension in the story and, with
them, an analysis of the characterization of both the human couple and
Yahweh Elohim.

The second kind of tension exists *within the humans* in their relation to God. Specifically it is the tension between their dependence
on God and their autonomy. I use the word "autonomy" here rather
than "freedom" to sharpen the contrast with dependence. My intended
meaning is similar to that affirmed by Gilkey in *Naming the Whirlwind:
The Renewal of God-Language.*[13] If kept in tension with dependence,
autonomy is compatible with a full relationship with God. It demands
more independence, however, than the traditional understanding of this
relationship will allow.

In the beginning of the story, the man and the woman totally depend
upon the God who created them. At the same time the creator God
gives them a certain degree of autonomy within the created order. As
autonomous, they decide how to cultivate the garden, what to name the
animals, and how to relate to each other. In addition, Yahweh Elohim
allows them to choose their food from the many wonderful trees in the
garden, except from the explicitly forbidden tree of the knowledge of
good and evil.

This prohibition inserts an unsettling note into the human sphere,
bringing forth the latent conflict between dependence and autonomy.
The limitation arouses their freedom to desire what they have been told
they cannot have.[14] In addition the serpent continues the process begun
by Yahweh Elohim by providing a different and contradictory interpretation of the prohibition. The subtle serpent asserts that Yahweh Elohim
wants to keep the humans from gaining full autonomy in order to preserve the knowledge of good and evil for Yahweh Elohim alone. And so
the humans eat. The remainder of the story recounts the effects of the
humans' choice of autonomy at the price of disobeying the God upon
whom they are dependent for their very existence.

Was this choice beneficial or harmful, necessary or avoidable? The
traditional interpretation of the story responds with a resounding con-

demnation of the act. The humans fell prey to hubris by striving to make themselves gods and attempting to transcend the uncrossable barrier between human and divine. By obstinately refusing to obey their loving Creator who had only their welfare at heart, they committed the "original" sin, the effects of which corrupted the entire human race. There may be more ambiguities in the story than this interpretation recognizes, and, I would argue, these render the interpretation inadequate. The main ambiguities concern the effects of the forbidden fruit (which we will consider here) and Yahweh's role in the process (which we will consider in our discussion of the third tension of the story).

One cannot deny that eating the forbidden fruit results in negative and harmful effects. Our discussion of the first tension has already mentioned these. This does not present the whole picture, though, for certain beneficial consequences follow as well, such as the humans' first attempt to make clothes (3:7), an ending to the sufferings of life (3:19), and the continuation of life with procreation (3:20). Most important, however, are the immediate effects of the eating of the fruit, which are closer to those foretold by the serpent (3:4–5) than to Yahweh Elohim's dire prediction (2:17). The couple *did not die* "in the day" of their eating; in fact immortality remained a possibility for them afterwards (3:22). Their *eyes were opened,* although what they first saw was their nakedness (3:7) and not the knowledge of good and evil. Surprisingly, Yahweh Elohim's final statement confirms the serpent's prediction: "Behold, the man has become like one of us, knowing good and evil" (3:22). In some sense, then, the humans have become *like God;* they have indeed gained autonomy through disobeying the divine precept. Thus, their choice was both harmful and beneficial. To borrow an image from a later biblical story (Gen. 32), they wrestled with God and were not overcome, but they left the scene with a limp, bearing the marks of their struggle.

As characters in the story, the man and the woman must experience tension and conflict. Without these experiences, they would not come alive to the reader. Characters add to the tension already present in a story's plot and they are also one of the means by which narrative makes sense of tension. By providing "human interest" and "enlisting certain peculiarly human feelings," characters play a crucial role in convincing readers to accept discontinuities, tensions, or extreme contingencies in their act of following the story.[15] W. B. Gallie describes the process in this way:

> But exactly what discontinuities we are willing to accept or able
> to follow depends partly upon the set or orientation of our sympa-
> thy for some particular character as established so far, and partly
> upon the intrinsic nature of the kind of sympathy that has been
> established.... The main conclusion is not simply the goal of our
> following and understanding; it must also be, from the point of
> our emotional response, some kind of culmination.... More sim-
> ply, unless we were in some degree emotionally involved in a story,
> the point, nay the very existence of its climax would escape us.[16]

In reading the story in Genesis 2–3 our primary identification and sympathy lie with the human couple. We all have some experience of the
tension between dependence and autonomy and of the unstable situation inaugurated by any prohibition. We also know that the only way
to become fully ourselves is to reconcile that tension on the far side of
a transgression. Thus, viewed from human perspective, the story is, at
least in part, about the experience of becoming a fully human person
with the gains and losses that this process involves.[17]

If one is not fully convinced by this proposed interpretation, it may
be because of one's preconceptions about the role of God in the story.
One may ask, "Is not God the Caring Creator of human beings, their
Just Judge and Merciful Healer after their transgressions? How could
such a God set up a world in which one can become a fully human
person only after a transgression? Should it not have been possible to
achieve full autonomy without unleashing the evil recounted in Genesis
3?" These are questions posed by the traditional doctrine of God. But
they are not questions appropriately asked of the actual story recounted
in Genesis 2–3. The narrative does not portray God as a doctrinal construct nor does it supply a literal description of the actual, living God.
Like every character in every story, Yahweh Elohim is a person with
internal tensions and conflicts. As Stephen Crites states: "A story, by
its very form, can tolerate neither mindless bodies nor bodiless minds,
since narrative action presupposes a personal unity that is prior to any
of the factors into which interpretation can analyze its characters.... To
be drawn into a story [as a character] is to be personified, someone who
can be addressed, who remembers and responds, who is underway in
action."[18] To underline this special status required by the story, we will
refer to the God portrayed in Genesis 2–3 as God-as-character. This
God-as-character is the source of the third kind of tension in the story,
that *within God* in relation to human beings. The tension here lies be-

tween the positive side of God-as-character (composed of the Caring
Creator, Just Judge, and Merciful Healer) and a more negative side
(which we might term the Evil Designer).[19] One easily recognizes the
positive side in the story, especially because the traditional interpretation has concentrated its emphasis on this dimension. For the opposite
reason, the negative side requires some analysis of the story before its
presence becomes evident.

The term Evil Designer can mean either "designer of the possibility
of evil within creation" or, more radically, "one who has evil designs on
creation." There are elements of both these meanings in Genesis 2-3.
The first is suggested by three factors: (1) Yahweh Elohim's creation
of the tree of the knowledge of good and evil, the existence of which
is the first prerequisite for the transgression; (2) the prohibition which,
human nature being what it is, makes the forbidden more desirable; and
(3) Yahweh Elohim's creation of the serpent, "more subtle than any other
wild creature that the Lord God had made" (3:1), whose temptation of
the woman provides the immediate occasion of the disobedience. Had
any of these three factors been omitted, this particular story would have
taken a different turn.

The second meaning of Evil Designer is even more troublesome than
the first. It focuses on the serpent's allegation about Yahweh Elohim's
motivation in promulgating the prohibition. The serpent implies that
God-as-character's motivation is a self-serving, jealous one designed to
preserve the divine prerogative of the knowledge of good and evil and
to keep the humans perpetually dependent. The serpent thus represents
Yahweh Elohim as a liar, or at best a deceiver who threatens the humans
with a punishment (immediate death) with no intention of carrying it
out. But, having been warned by the narrator about the serpent's "subtlety," why should one give credence to its words rather than to Yahweh
Elohim's? The main reason is to be found in Gen. 3:22–23. Here, in
a highly reliable interior monologue, Yahweh Elohim confirms the serpent's prediction of the effects of the fruit on the humans. In the second
part of that statement Yahweh Elohim also supports the serpent's insin-
uation that jealousy is part of the divine motivation. Afraid that the
humans might gain immortality, Yahweh Elohim banishes them from
the garden.

Although there are major differences between the two possible meanings of Evil Designer, both agree that God-as-character bears some responsibility for the existence of evil in the world. The story portrays
God, and not just the humans, as participating in the creation of the

first tension, the eruption of evil out of good. But even in the story, this is not the whole picture, for the positive side of God's relation to humanity remains predominant. The initial goodness in creation (Gen. 2:4b–25) is solely the product of God-as-character's loving action.

It may be that this third tension (that within the portrayal of God) is the most theologically significant feature of the narrative analysis of Genesis 2–3. When this text is discussed as a story, a fictional story at that, it becomes evident that what is said and done by God-as-character does not accurately represent God's actual creative activity. Modern Christian theology has admitted this in principle by distinguishing between scientific and religious statements about creation. But it has not yet applied this principle exhaustively to its understanding of God. Theology still generally assumes that, as revelation, scripture must give a fairly reliable descriptive picture of God, excluding of course obvious anthropomorphisms. But treating God-as-character *as* a character in a story allows us to go much farther in analyzing the picture of God presented in certain biblical texts. Other biblical texts that could benefit from this kind of interpretation are Cain and Abel, the Flood, the Tower of Babel, and Job. These are all stories where God is portrayed as intervening directly in action and speech.

If God is to be a character in a narrative, then God-as-character must be subject to the same strategies of interpretation as any other personage in the story. This means God-as-character's actions and speeches must be evaluated over against the speeches and actions of all other characters as well as those of the narrator. Robert Alter provides a helpful schema for such an evaluation by listing six stages of characterization, ranging from least reliable to most reliable.

> Character can be revealed through the report of actions; through appearance, gestures, posture, costume; through one character's comments on another; through direct speech by the character; through inward speech, either summarized or quoted as interior monologue; or through statements by the narrator about the attitudes and intentions of the personages, which may come either as flat assertions or motivated explanations.[20]

Following this list, Gen. 3:22–23, comprised of Yahweh Elohim's interior monologue and the narrator's inside look at Yahweh Elohim's motivation for banishing the human couple from the garden, contains two of the four most reliable statements of the entire story. (The other two other examples are Yahweh Elohim's interior monologue preceding the creation of the woman (2:18) and the narrator's description of the woman's motivation for eating the fruit (3:6). But, as we have seen, Gen. 3:22–23 contains precisely the major support for the Evil Designer aspect of Yahweh Elohim's character. Although this support is not strong enough to overthrow the many positive aspects of Yahweh Elohim's portrayal, it is strong enough to establish the tension between the positive and negative sides of God's characterization in this story.

This third tension provides problems for theological reflection. What is one to do with such a God-as-character? Even when one respects the threefold distinction between God-as-character, the God of theological reflection, and the living God, there still remains too great a gap between the God-as-character of Genesis 2–3 and the God presented in widely influential theologies of creation. If we were to begin with God-as-character in the story and then move to theological reflection, we would end up with a quite different picture than the traditional one. In fact, a similar situation exists for all three levels of tension in the story. Thus, the present interpretation has far-reaching implications that challenge the traditional doctrine at four important points. These points, to be discussed in the following section, form the core of a revisionist theology of creation.

Tensions in the Theology of Creation

The three levels of tension portrayed in Genesis 2–3 in large part constitute the "world"[21] of that particular text. Ambiguity and the coincidence of opposites characterize this world that mediates between the text itself and the theology of creation. The characteristics of this text and its world impose some restrictions on the nature of the resulting theological reflection. On the one hand, clear and distinct, monovalent propositions cannot adequately convey the tensions found in the story. On the other hand, constructive theology cannot simply repeat the story, for then it would cease to be second-order reflection. Instead, constructive theology must attain a higher degree of generality and systematization, while also representing the ambiguities and tensions found in its fictional source. Rather than describing abstractly how such a task might be accomplished, I will look specifically at the theological ramifications of the three levels of tension portrayed in Genesis 2–3. Our discussion intends to be suggestive and not comprehensive. All that one can attempt here is a brief foray into the theology of creation, investigating only those aspects where this enterprise intersects with Genesis 2–3.

The first level of tension portrayed in the narrative, that between good and evil in the created order, necessitates the reinterpretation of the idea of the *goodness of creation*. Genesis 2–3 suggests that the goodness of the created order is not one of static perfection with neither challenge nor disruption to taint its purity. Rather, goodness precedes and encompasses the evil that is present. It may be that goodness also will overcome evil. This is the message of other biblical texts, but it is not suggested in Genesis 2–3. These ideas require some additional comment.

Goodness precedes evil, but not in any temporal order. As many theologians already recognize, theology can no longer hold onto the notion of an actual primeval state, even if it is interpreted in the most realistic terms available. A drastic change in the state of physical or human nature as a result of some human action is incompatible with the findings of modern science. Rather, the use of "precedes" refers to the order of priority. Goodness is more fundamental than evil. In the narrative language of Genesis 2–3 the initial goodness of creation is solely the product of God's activity. The created order does not produce its own basic goodness; God gives it that goodness.

Further, goodness encompasses the evil that is present from the first moment of creation. Humans suffer and die because they are made from "dust" (cf. Gen. 2–7; 3:19), not because of some specific primordial "sin" on their part. Yet, the emergence of new life always surrounds that death (cf. Gen. 3:20; 4:1). We are left with the impression that disruption is part of the created order, not a logically necessary part, but one that can be judged "acceptable after all."[22] As we have seen, narrative analysis reaches this judgment via the configurational dimension of the plot. Constructive theology can reach it by placing the disruption within the twofold encompassing goodness of creation and, ultimately, of God (a point to which we will return below).

The second tension portrayed in the story, that within human beings in relation to God, suggests two important implications. In the first place the coincidence of dependence on God and human autonomy calls for a shift from a child-parent to an *adult-adult model of humanity's relation to God* like that suggested by some feminist theologians.[23] A truly adult relationship of love includes both aspects of that tension. Free to be oneself, one chooses to become vulnerable to another. Conversely, only by being dependent on another can one find the strength to deepen one's autonomy. But because this integrating of dependence and autonomy is not easily achieved, there is bound to be struggle within any adult relationship. This is no cause for lament, however, for struggle is an essential ingredient of human life and human love.

To be sure, the analogy between a loving adult-adult relationship and that between human being and God is only an analogy. Humanity's dependence on God is of a different order than that within any purely human relationship. The creature cannot draw even one breath without its Creator's sustaining power. Nevertheless this does not negate the important positive aspects of the analogy that are lost in the child-parent model. The human person has much autonomy in this life, including whether to say yes or no to God's gift of love. Thus it is crucial that human beings not only recognize their autonomy, but learn to use it wisely, keeping it in tension with their dependence on God. In the process, struggle will inevitably erupt in this relationship as well. Far from being irreligious, such struggle is exemplified many times within the Hebrew Bible, paradigmatically in the story of Jacob wrestling with God (Gen. 32).

Just as Jacob received a wound along with God's blessing, so also did Adam and Eve attain autonomy at a price. For them, these losses and gains occurred both in the natural realm and in the moral order. Thus, the second tension in the story also points to the *inherent moral ambiguity of human life.* Visions of noble savages notwithstanding, from the first capable moment of life, human feelings, thoughts, and actions contain elements of both good and evil. Humanity begins and ends its existence *in medias res* — in the middle of the struggle between good and evil — where there is room for much that is better and much that is worse, but no room for achieved perfection. Humanity can never expect to have "clean hands" in this messy life; anyone who is self-righteous reveals only that she or he has not yet begun to understand or to help assuage the misery of the human condition. But if one does seek the good, even when it involves an implicated evil, one will discover that God's presence, grace, and forgiveness are found in the most unsavory circumstances.[24]

This situation is not the result of some particular fault committed at a specific time in human history; it is simply the way humans are created. This assertion evokes, of course, a controversial theological issue. Since Augustine, the moral ambiguity of the human race has been consistently affirmed, but solely as a result of the fall, not of creation.[25] Discussing the multiple issues raised by this idea requires that one address the third tension present in Genesis 2–3, that within God in relation to humanity.

One must remember that just as a difference exists between what can be said about God in narrative and in constructive theology, so also a difference exists between theological statements about God, and the Divine Mystery itself. In light of these differences I now will explore some theological implications of the portrayal of God-as-character in Genesis 2–3. The notion of *divine ambiguity* that the third tension produces is not totally alien to Christian doctrine. Traditional theology has typically expressed it through the symbol of the "wrath" of God, which is directed specifically against human sin and is ultimately justified by humanity's decisive rejection of God through Adam's and Eve's disobedience. On the view proposed here, however, the divine ambiguity simply *is*. It exists within God; it is not a reaction against a prior human action. This raises the theodicy problem.

When approached as a strictly rational matter, the problem of theodicy may be unsolvable.[26] This judgment holds even for the traditional position that lays the responsibility for all moral evil (and occasionally all natural evil) at the feet of humanity. The traditional position must confront the problem of how all humans "participated" in the sin of the first couple, and so how God can "justly" impose the consequences of their sin on the rest of the race. Further, as long as one claims that God is omnipotent as well as all-good, appeals to free will, aesthetic completion, pedagogical value, and retribution ring exceedingly hollow in the face of unthinkable catastrophes and intense personal suffering. Although numerous theodicies (some within the traditional framework, others revisionist) have recently been proposed, none of them has proved completely successful either in the scholarly community or in the hearts of suffering Christians. So, consequently, the way still appears to be open for one more approach to the issue.

My proposal is not, strictly speaking, a theodicy at all, for it does not attempt to absolve God of the responsibility for evil in the world. Instead, it seeks to encourage one to affirm the goodness of God in spite of the burden of evil, just as the Genesis 2–3 narrative encourages the reader to affirm that God-as-character is primarily Caring Creator despite the elements of the Evil Designer in the story's portrayal.

At the reflective level, then, this constructive proposal might be expressed in the following terms: God is the source of everything that is created. Since evil exists in God's creation, God shares in it. Evil is not solely God's "fault," nor is it solely the responsibility of any part of the created order. Rather, the entire created order participates with God in the production of evil during the course of creation. Since this production is a process, narrative — which uniquely links action and response — is the most adequate linguistic form for its expression. Genesis 2–3 carefully orchestrates the eruption of evil though the cooperation of all four realms represented in the story: the tree that "gave" its fruit; the serpent who tempted the couple; the humans who ate; and God-as-character who created the tree and the serpent, and issued the prohibition to the humans. Constructive theology, however, cannot simply paraphrase these narrative interconnections. It must find its own way of expressing this universal participation, but, in so doing, it must be attentive to the narrative quality of the source upon which it reflects.

We cannot know why evil is so pervasive in God's creation; we can only know that it is. We should not offer any explanations, for they will inevitably prove unworthy of God or of ourselves. We cannot of course claim that God is evil, for that is blasphemy. We must affirm God's goodness as preceding and encompassing (and, it is hoped, overcoming) evil in the world. At times this affirmation of God's goodness will be expressed in terms of its opposite, by our protest against God's participation in the evil that afflicts us. At times this affirmation will be expressed by our participation in action to overcome the evil that afflicts us or our sisters and brothers. At times the affirmation will be expressed by our renunciation (which no one else can make for or foist upon us) "of any and all complaint about evil."[27]

At no time, however, can we make this affirmation of God's goodness without the realization that God suffers with us.[28] This last and most crucial point goes beyond theological reflection on Genesis 2–3. Its root in Christianity is, of course, the cross, although the Hebrew Bible has its own sources as well.[29] The realization that God suffers evil with us is ultimately what allows us to live with the tension of God's ambiguity, even while we believe that God is good. Perhaps this is as close as a Christian can, or should wish to, come to a theodicy.

Each of the four constructive implications of the proposed interpretation of Genesis 2–3 and its world represents a significant departure from the traditional doctrine of creation. The goodness of creation is reinterpreted to mean that, from the very beginning of creation, goodness precedes (in priority though not in time) and encompasses the evil that also exists. The relationship between creature and Creator is no longer viewed as that between child and parent but rather as between adult and adult, allowing for the expression of human autonomy (as well as dependence) and for the inevitable struggle that occurs in the process of balancing both aspects. Humanity's moral situation is considered one of inherent ambiguity, stemming from creation itself; in this situation one's moral responsibility is to promote the good even at the price of involvement in evil. And, finally, God's connection to the evil in creation is addressed in the notion of the divine ambiguity, which admits the Creator's participation in the process, but still allows the affirmation of God's goodness.

Thoroughly grounding all these claims in careful theological argument would require investigating many other theological sources, such as other biblical and theological texts, modern experience, the secular disciplines. Much remains to be done with the four points suggested by the proposed reading of Genesis 2–3. But whatever the eventual evaluation of these specific suggestions, it is crucial that theological reflection begin to take more seriously the narrative form of Genesis 2–3. The story existed long before the doctrine and will outlast even the most profound systematic restatements. It thus deserves our concentrated theological attention. Even if a narrative approach does not convince God to love doctrine, we can hope that it will be sufficient.

NOTES

1. Elie Wiesel, *Gates of the Forest* (New York: Holt, Rinehart and Winston, 1966), pp. viii–xii.

2. See, for example Thomas Aquinas, *Summa Theologiae,* Ia, Q. 65, A. 2.

3. For a discussion of the rise of narrative theology, see Terence W. Tilley, *Story Theology* (Wilmington: Michael Glazier, 1985), chapter 2, and George W. Stroup, *The Promise of Narrative Theology: Recovering the Gospel in the Church* (Atlanta: John Knox Press, 1981), chapter 3.

4. Gilkey's two major works on creation are *Maker of Heaven and Earth: The Christian Doctrine of Creation in the Light of Modern Knowledge* (Garden City, N.Y.: Doubleday, 1959), and *Creationism on Trial: Evolution and God at Little Rock* (Minneapolis: Winston, 1985).

5. *Shantung Compound: The Story of Men and Women under Pressure* (New York: Harper & Row, 1966).

6. For a more detailed discussion of this interpretation, see my unpublished dissertation, "The Myth of Original Sin: A Hermeneutic Theology Based on Genesis 2–3," University of Chicago, 1983. ‡

7. Robert Scholes and Robert Kellogg, *The Nature of Narrative* (London: Oxford University Press, 1966), p. 4.

8. Robert Alter, *The Art of Biblical Narrative* (New York: Basic Books, 1981), pp. 157–158.

9. Aristotle, *Poetics,* 6. 1450a. 39–40.

10. Paul Ricoeur, *Time and Narrative,* vol. 1, trans. Kathleen McLaughlin and David Pellauer (Chicago: University of Chicago Press, 1984), pp. 66–67.

11. Ibid., pp. 42–45, 66–67.

12. Ibid., pp. 66–67.

13. Langdon Gilkey, *Naming the Whirlwind: The Renewal of God-Language* (Indianapolis: Bobbs-Merrill, 1970), pp. 57–61; 255–259.

14. The allusion to Tillich's "aroused freedom" is intentional. See *Systematic Theology,* 3 vols. (Chicago: University of Chicago Press, 1951, 1957, 1963), 2:35–36.

15. W. B. Gallie, *Philosophy and the Historical Understanding,* 2nd ed. (New York: Schocken Books, 1968). p. 48.

16. Ibid., pp. 46–47.

17. Although this is opposed to the traditional understanding of the text, it has been suggested in several recent psychological and biblical/theological studies. See, for example, Rollo May, *Man's Search for Himself* (New York: Norton, 1953), pp. 180–194; Richard Hanson, *The Serpent Was Wiser: A New Look at Genesis 1–11* (Minneapolis: Augsburg Publishing House, 1972), chapter 2; Dorothee Soelle, with Shirley A. Cloyes, *To Work and to Love: A Theology of Creation* (Philadelphia: Fortress Press, 1984), pp. 74–77.

18. Stephen Crites, "Angels We have Heard," in *Religion as Story,* ed. James B. Wiggins (New York: Harper & Row, 1975), pp. 25–27.

19. For a fuller discussion of these four "names" of God in the story, see Wismer, "The Myth of Original Sin," chapter 4.

20. Alter, *Art of Biblical Narrative,* pp. 116–117.

21. See Ricoeur, *Time and Narrative,* pp. 77–82.

22. The term is Gallie's. See *Philosophy and Historical Understanding,* p. 31.

23. See, for example, Sallie McFague, *Metaphorical Theology: Models of God in Religious Language* (Philadelphia: Fortress Press, 1982), chapter 5; and Rosemary Ruether, *Sexism and God-Talk: Toward a Feminist Theology* (Boston: Beacon Press, 1983), chapter 2.

24. Dietrich Bonhoeffer's experience in the assassination plot against Hitler is a good example of this. See his reflections in *Ethics,* ed. Eberhard Bethge (New York: Macmillan, 1955), and *Letters and Papers from Prison,* enlarged ed., ed. Eberhard Bethge (New York: Macmillan, 1971). See also Leonardo Boff's discussion of two situations in Brazil in *Liberating Grace* (Maryknoll, N.Y.: Orbis Books, 1979), pp. 103–105.

25. Irenaeus and Schleiermacher, however, present a minority position which see ambiguity as a result of creation itself. See John Hick's discussion in *Evil and the God of Love,* rev. ed. (San Francisco: Harper & Row, 1978), chapters 9–10. It should also be noted that the position argued here does not exclude original sin. Original sin adds to the ambiguity present in creation a positive (i.e., active) tendency to sin.

26. See Paul Ricoeur, "Evil, A Challenge to Philosophy and Theology," *Journal of the American Academy of Religion* 53 (December 1985): 644. His proposed response which combines thinking, acting and feeling was influential for my approach (see pp. 644–648).

27. Ibid., p. 647.

28. This notion of the "suffering God" is becoming prominent in many branches of Christian theology, including process, political, and various forms of liberation theology. See, for example, David Ray Griffin, *God, Power, and Evil: A Process Theodicy* (Philadelphia: Westminster, 1976); Jürgen Moltmann, *The Crucified God: The Cross of Christ as the Foundation and Criticism of a Christian Theology,* trans. R. A. Wilson and John Bowden (New York: Harper & Row, 1974); Jon Sobrino, *Christology at the Crossroads: A Latin American Approach,* trans. John Drury (Maryknoll, N.Y.: Orbis Books, 1978); Kazoh Kitamori, *Theology of the Pain of God* (Richmond, Va.: John Knox Press, 1965); Dorothee Soelle, *Suffering,* trans. Everett R. Kalin (Philadelphia: Fortress, 1975); James H. Cone, *God of the Oppressed* (New York: Seabury, 1975).

29. See, for example, Abraham Joshua Heschel, *The Prophets,* 2 vols. (New York: Harper & Row, 1962).

Chapter 10

"For Freedom Christ Has Set Us Free": The Christian Understanding of Ultimate Transformation

SCHUBERT M. OGDEN

I

THIS ESSAY ORIGINATED as a contribution to an ongoing dialogue between Buddhists and Christians in which Langdon Gilkey and I have recently had the privilege of participating. Even so, it speaks out of the much larger dialogue increasingly going on between Buddhists and Christians generally, and it takes the members of this much larger community as the primary audience to which its claims are addressed.

The general topic of the essay is "transformation," which I have taken the liberty of formulating still more precisely as "ultimate transformation." This I have done both because our Buddhist-Christian dialogue typically focuses on transformation in a quite precise sense and because of the precedent established by the well-known working definition according to which "religion is a means to ultimate transformation."[1] Pending such clarification as can come only as my argument develops, suffice it to say here that my principal assumption in so formulating our topic is that ultimate transformation is precisely what we as Buddhists and Christians are alike interested in discussing just because at the center of our respective self-understandings is that unique change in human life that may be formally characterized as the transition from inauthentic to authentic existence.

200

Given this assumption, my task is to state summarily the Christian understanding of this transition. Of course, the only way that I or anyone else can do this is to offer someone's understanding of this Christian understanding — in this case, my own. And recognizing this, you may have wondered why I have committed myself to state *the,* instead of, simply, *a* Christian understanding of ultimate transformation. There are, in fact, two reasons. In the first place, to claim to offer even *a* Christian understanding is either to beg the question of whether it really is a *Christian* understanding after all or else to assume the identical burden that must be borne by anyone who would offer *the* Christian understanding. In the second place, I can only suppose that what brings us together as Buddhists and Christians in inter-religious dialogue is not simply that we are all human beings who must somehow ask and answer the question about the meaning of ultimate reality but also that we are each a Buddhist or a Christian who as such bears responsibility for a certain answer to this question that is not only or primarily our own but also and primarily that of the religious community of which we are a part. For both reasons, then, it seems necessary to me to state, not what I understand by ultimate transformation, but what I understand to be the understanding of it that is normative for the Christian community.

On the other hand, I do not take mine to be the merely historical task of describing how Christians have in fact understood the transition from inauthentic to authentic existence. As much as I agree that what is normative for the Christian community is indeed given historically — namely, in the witness of the apostles by which the community as such was first constituted — I nevertheless insist on the difference between interpreting historically what Christians have said and meant in actually bearing their witness and stating systematically what they ought to say and mean if they are really to bear it. Because I take just such a statement to be called for here, I can only suppose that, if mine is a properly theological task at all, it is a systematic rather than a historical theological task.

In taking it to be properly theological, however, I understand it to be significantly different from preaching or teaching or any other form of Christian witness simply as such. Whereas all forms of Christian witness address others so as to summon them directly or indirectly to a Christian self-understanding, the proper task of theology is so to reflect on the claims to validity that are expressed or implied by such witness as to validate (or invalidate) these claims. More specifically, the proper task of systematic theology is to validate the claim of any instance of

Christian witness to be adequate to its content, in the twofold sense of being both appropriate to normative witness and credible to human existence. Thus, insofar as it is constructive, systematic theology consists in a formulation of the Christian witness that answers to the reflective questions about the appropriateness and credibility of this witness and not only to the existential question about the meaning of ultimate reality to which the witness itself is an answer. The same must be true, then, of the statement called for in this essay if it is to be the properly systematic theological statement that I take it to be.

This implies, of course, that the questions that are proper to criticizing the adequacy of my statement are essentially two: (1) Is its formulation in fact appropriate to the understanding of ultimate transformation expressed or implied by normative Christian witness? (2) Is its formulation really credible to human existence as such, in terms simply of our common human experience and reflection? Obviously, Buddhists have particular reason to ask the second question even as Christians will particularly want to press the first. But only a little reflection makes clear that we each have a stake in seriously asking both questions, lest we fail really to understand ourselves and our partners in dialogue or allow ourselves to believe what is not really worthy of our belief. This is not to say, however, that I shall offer the kind of evidence and reasoning for my claims that would be necessary to validate their appropriateness and credibility. On the contrary, one of the limitations of a summary statement is that it can do little more than clarify the claims that only a more developed statement can validate.

II

Having now defined the particular task of the essay, I want to return to what was said in provisionally clarifying its general topic. My assumption in formulating this topic as "ultimate transformation," I allowed, is that the transformation of common interest to us as Buddhists and Christians may be characterized formally as the transition from inauthentic to authentic existence. But a statement such as this cannot advance our discussion very far until its operative terms are themselves clarified or defined. The next step, then, is to explain what is meant formally by "the transition from inauthentic to authentic existence"; and this will require, in turn, at least some explanation of the whole terminology of which this term is a part and in which I, for one, find it helpful to think about our topic.

I would emphasize that this step, or one very much like it, seems necessary in making any contribution to our discussion. If we are to think and speak about one and the same general topic, we must concern ourselves with providing the formal terms in which this alone can be done.

I begin with the term "ultimate reality." According to the useful definition of William James, reality in general is "what we in some way find ourselves obliged to take account of."[2] Assuming this definition, I should say that "ultimate reality" refers to everything that we are all finally obliged to consider insofar as we exist humanly at all, whatever other things we may or may not have to take account of in each leading our own individual life. Thus ultimate reality includes everything necessary in our self-understanding, as distinct from all the other things that we understand that are merely contingent relative to our own existence simply as such. Whatever else it includes, then, ultimate reality includes our own existence as selves, together with everything that is in any way a necessary condition of the possibility of our existence, whether other human selves or a still larger world of subhuman or superhuman beings. Among the conditions that are thus necessary, obviously, is any reality that can be said to be "strictly ultimate" because it is a necessary condition of the possibility not only of human existence but of any existence whatever. Thus strictly ultimate reality is what not only we but any being that is so much as possible is obliged to take account of, if only in the completely general sense of being really, internally related to it and therefore dependent on it.

Of course, it is in a much more specific sense than this that we as human beings are obliged to take account of ultimate reality, including whatever is strictly ultimate. Recognizing this, philosophers have clarified an emphatic sense of the term "existence" in which it refers not merely to the actualization of essence generally but to the specifically human essence that can be actualized only by self-understanding. In this emphatic sense, then, if we exist at all, we exist understandingly, and so we are obliged to take account of our own existence as well as that of anything else ultimately real, not only by our being related to it and dependent on it but also by our somehow understanding it. Lest this claim be misunderstood, however, we should note that the understanding of existence and of whatever else is ultimate that is of the very essence of our humanity may or may not be fully explicated and so may remain only a more or less implicit understanding.

But now the capacity and the necessity somehow to understand ourselves and anything else ultimately real allow for yet another and more momentous contingency. It is also always possible that we may misunderstand them, both our own existence and everything else that is ultimate, including that which is strictly so. For this reason, to exist humanly at all is to be faced with the existential question about the meaning of ultimate reality, although, once again, we should note that one may very well ask and answer this question implicitly more than explicitly. In any event, the question about the meaning of ultimate reality simultaneously asks about both ultimate reality and ourselves. Thus it has two essential aspects, metaphysical and moral, in which it is distinctively different from, even while being closely related to, both properly metaphysical and properly moral types of questions.

The existential question about the meaning of ultimate reality is different from properly metaphysical questions because, while it indeed asks about ultimate reality, it asks about the meaning of ultimate reality for us, not about the structure of ultimate reality in itself. Even so, it is also related to metaphysical questions insofar as any answer to it necessarily implies some answer to them, the meaning of ultimate reality for us being correlated with the structure of ultimate reality in itself. On the other hand, it is different from properly moral questions because, while it indeed asks about ourselves, it asks about our self-understanding, not about our action. Still, it is also related to moral questions, insofar as any answer to it necessarily implies some answer to them, our self-understanding being correlated with how we are to act and what we are to do.

Notwithstanding its two essential aspects, the existential question is a single question. In asking it, we do not ask two different questions about ultimate reality and about our self-understanding; rather, we ask one and the same question about both — on the basic supposition that some understanding of ourselves is appropriate to ultimate reality in its structure in itself and, in this sense, is authorized by it. Thus, while we do indeed suppose that ultimate reality is prior to our understanding, we ask about ultimate reality only insofar as it authorizes our self-understanding, even as we ask about our self-understanding only insofar as it is authorized by ultimate reality.

To speak in this sense of an "authorized" self-understanding, however, is precisely what I mean by an "authentic" self-understanding; and seeing that we cannot exist humanly at all except by somehow understanding ourselves, I use the term "authentic existence" to distinguish that mode of being human actualized by an authentic self-understanding. Correspondingly, I hold that any self-understanding that is really a misunderstanding, because it is not appropriate to ultimate reality and in this sense is unauthorized, is properly called an "inauthentic self-understanding," and the mode of existence it actualizes, "inauthentic existence."

By "the transition from inauthentic to authentic existence," then, I mean either the process or an instance of change from an inauthentic to an authentic understanding of ourselves. Thus the import of my original assumption is that the ultimate transformation that we as Buddhists and Christians both claim to understand in our respectively different ways may be thought and spoken about formally as just such a change in self-understanding. Of course, any self-understanding is closely related both to certain metaphysical beliefs and to certain moral actions. Therefore, it is at least possible that the change from an inauthentic to an authentic self-understanding may involve still further changes in what we believe as well as in how we act and what we do. But even if we fully allow for this possibility, the implication of my assumption is clear: relative to this ultimate transformation in self-understanding, all other changes are at most penultimate transformations.

III

The question now is as to the material understanding of ultimate transformation that is expressed or implied by normative Christian witness. It will be clear from my title that I shall be guided in answering this question by the theology, or, more exactly, christology, of freedom classically formulated by Paul. But if accepting Paul's guidance is only to be expected of someone who stands in my theological tradition, it in no way settles the issue of the appropriateness of my answer. On the contrary, even Paul's theology is in principle exactly like my own in being the formulation for a particular situation of the witness of the apostles that is the sole primary norm of witness and theology alike. Thus the question remains whether, or to what extent, his theology itself is appropriate to this norm as well as credible in terms of his situation. In any event, what is called for here is not an exegesis of Paul but a systematic theological statement for our situation today; and this I intend to provide even if it is in the tradition constituted by Paul's theological reflections that I shall follow in doing so.

The proper starting point for such a statement is the constitutive claim of the Christian witness that Jesus is the Christ, in the sense that through Jesus the meaning of ultimate reality for us is decisively re-presented. I say "*re*-presented" here in order to bring out that, given what "ultimate reality" has been explained to mean, any meaning of ultimate reality that could be explicitly represented through Jesus must have always already been implicitly presented in our self-understanding simply as human beings. Nevertheless, because our self-understanding can be fully ours only insofar as it becomes explicit and because it can always be really a misunderstanding, there are good reasons why what is first presented in our existence itself should also be presented again, and so *re*-presented, through particular historical events. Moreover, given the plurality of such re-presentations as have emerged in the course of history, there is equally good reason why there should be some decisive re-presentation whereby one can responsibly decide between their con-flicting claims. In any case, the claim constituting the Christian witness is that the event of Jesus is just such a decisive re-presentation — hence its qualification of this event by christological titles like "Christ" — and that, therefore, the meaning of ultimate reality that we always already understand, if only implicitly or by misunderstanding it, is none other than that which this event makes fully explicit.

In this sense, the Christian witness is and must be "christocentric." But there is a difference between thus claiming that the only meaning of ultimate reality for us is that which is decisively re-presented through Jesus and claiming that only in Jesus is the meaning of ultimate reality for us constituted. In my view, the kind of christocentrism that makes or implies this second claim is profoundly incompatible with the Christian understanding of human existence. Jesus is rightly said to be the Christ because he *de*-fines the ultimate reality he re-presents, not because he *con*-fines it, just as, by analogy, certain elements, once consecrated, are rightly said to be a sacrament because they *de*-fine the grace they signify, not because they *con*fine it. On the other hand, I take it to be also incom-patible with a Christian self-understanding to allow any event other than Jesus to be the decisive re-presentation of the meaning of ultimate real-ity for us. Although a Christian, in my view, can and must allow that the same meaning may indeed be re-presented through other events, which for non-Christians may well be its decisive re-presentations, the chris-tocentrism proper to the Christian witness must take Jesus alone to be thus decisive, just as, by analogy, a Christian may very well allow that even the most ordinary meal may be a real means of grace for certain persons, and yet insist that only the Lord's Supper rightly administered is a proper Christian sacrament.

But if we start with the christological claim thus understood, we proceed by asking about the answer to the existential question that is decisively re-presented through Jesus. What does this answer assert about the meaning of ultimate reality for us and, therefore, about our own self-understanding?

Its assertion about the meaning of ultimate reality for us is determined by the claim that the only strictly ultimate reality, which not only we but anything that is so much as possible is somehow obliged to take account of, is the reality of God, which itself is understood to be the utterly boundless love both of itself and of everything else. Thus, according to this answer, the sole primal source both of ourselves and of any even merely possible world of other persons or things is the same unbounded love that is also the sole final end of all things. This means that our self-understanding can be authentic only insofar as it is appropriate to this love, and so authorized by it, whence the assertion that we are to understand ourselves through faith in God's love.

By "faith" here is meant, in the first place, the relatively passive moment in our self-understanding that consists in trust — trust in the love of God alone as the primal source and the final end of our own lives as well as of everything else. I speak of such trust as "relatively passive," because, while it is indeed a moment in our own self-understanding, it is that moment in which we accept the always already prior reality of God's love for us and all other things as the only strictly ultimate reality. In other words, the trust that is the relatively passive moment in our faith corresponds to the aspect of God's love in which it is relatively active, and unsurpassably so, because it does all that any love could conceivably do for all others as well as itself. We can and should trust in God's love without reservation because it unceasingly acts not only to create a world in which we and all other creatures can exist and act in turn, but also to redeem this world by embracing each and every creature in God's own unending life. But "faith" also means, in the second place, the other relatively active moment in our self-understanding that consists in loyalty — loyalty to God's love as the integral cause that all existence and action are to serve, our own as well as all others'. This moment of faith is "relatively active," because, even though it, too, presupposes the prevenient action of God's love as the only strictly ultimate reality and is possible at all only where there is a prior trust in this love, it is that moment in our faith that is the proximate ground of our own returning action. As such, loyalty corresponds to the aspect of God's love which is relatively passive, albeit unsurpassably so, because it accepts all that

could be conceivably done or suffered by anyone, whether itself or any
other. We can and should be loyal to God's love without qualification
because it unfailingly suffers all that we or anything else could possibly
do or suffer as something that is also done to God.

Faith in God's love in this twofold sense of unreserved trust and unqualified loyalty is decisively re-presented through Jesus as our authentic
self-understanding. But this means that any other self-understanding in
which something besides God's love alone is the object of our trust and
loyalty and, therefore, is also taken to be strictly ultimate is an inauthentic understanding of our existence. The term for such an understanding
in traditional Christian witness and theology is "sin," whose meaning
is seriously misunderstood when, as commonly happens, it is used only
in the plural to refer to moral transgressions. As true as it is that moral
transgressions are the inevitable consequence of sin, sin as such and
properly so-called is not a matter of action, of how we act or what we
do, but a mode of existence — namely, that mode in which we do not
accept but rather reject the always already prior reality of God's love
for us and for all as the only strictly ultimate reality. Of course, being strictly ultimate, God's love is such that not only we but anything
whatever is obliged somehow to take account of it; and for this reason
neither we nor anything else could ever simply reject it. But so to understand ourselves as to direct our trust and loyalty to anything alongside
of God's love is precisely to reject it as the only strictly ultimate reality.
In this sense, sin is indeed the rejection of God's love, which may be
described either negatively as "unfaith," with its two moments of distrust in God's love and disloyalty to it, or else positively as "idolatry,"
with its two moments of trusting in and being loyal to something besides
God's love as the only reality that is strictly ultimate.

In the Christian understanding, then, ultimate transformation as either the process or an instance of change from an inauthentic to an
authentic self-understanding is the change from sin to faith, from unfaith and idolatry to trust in God's love and loyalty to it alone as strictly
ultimate. The name generally given to this change in the Christian tradition is "salvation," although other terms are sometimes also used to
describe it, such as "redemption" and "regeneration." The Protestant
tradition has also commonly spoken of it in terms of "justification" and
"sanctification." Insofar as these terms are not simply other metaphors
for thinking and speaking about one and the same change — as they
often are in Luther's usage, for example — they usually refer to two different aspects of the one transformation effected by God's love insofar

as it is accepted in faith. In the case of "justification," the reference is primarily retrospective in that it has to do with overcoming the guilt of sin from the past, while in the case of "sanctification," the primary reference is prospective because it has to do with overcoming the power of sin over the future.[3]

But however one describes it, the possibility of such change is constituted solely by God's prevenient love, which, being boundless, embraces each and every human existence, even though it has previously rejected God's love through the distrust and disloyalty of idolatrously trusting and serving other gods. To be sure, the decisive re-presentation of this possibility is through Jesus, who is said to be the Christ just because he is the love of God itself made fully explicit. But as we have seen, it is one thing thus to re-present our authentic possibility, something else again to constitute it; and as surely as the right kind of christocentrism demands that the first be attributed to Jesus, it just as surely demands that the second be attributed to Christ, by which I mean the prevenient love of God which Jesus decisively re-presents and for which "Christ," like all other christological titles, is a more or less adequate expression. Properly speaking, we must say that the only agent of ultimate transformation from sin to faith is Christ, in the sense of God's own prevenient love, which can be decisively re-presented through Jesus only because it is implicitly presented in human existence as such.

But now it is just this understanding of ultimate transformation that Paul formulates when he says, "For freedom Christ has set us free" (Gal. 5:1). In the nature of the case, the mode of existence actualized by the self-understanding of sin is an existence in bondage — namely, to all of the things that we take to be strictly ultimate by making them the objects of the trust and loyalty that rightly belong solely to God's love. By trusting and serving our various idols, we deliver ourselves into dependence on them and, to this extent, are not free but bound in our relations both to them and to everything else. On the other hand, the mode of existence actualized by the self-understanding of faith is just as naturally an existence in freedom — namely, both from and for everything other than God's love, in which alone we place our trust and to which alone we seek to be loyal. By trusting and serving nothing besides God's love, we are delivered from dependence on all other things and, to this extent, are not bound but free in our relations both to ourselves and to everything else. This means that, in making possible the change from a self-understanding of sin to the self-understanding of faith, God's love frees us from existence in bondage to existence in freedom. And it is this that Paul has in mind when he tells us that it is for freedom that Christ has set us free.

Not the least merit of his formulation, however, is to bring out that the existence *in* freedom that is actualized by faith is, as he says, also existence *for* freedom. In fact, Christ sets us free from existence in sin for existence in faith only insofar as we exist and act for the freedom of others. This is the clear implication of my earlier statement that faith in God's love consists not only in trusting in it without reservation but also in being loyal to it without qualification. For, clearly, to be loyal to God's love is also to be loyal to all to whom it is loyal, and this, naturally, is everyone. Moreover, as certain as it is that there cannot be any such loyalty unless there is first an unreserved trust in God's love, it is equally certain that such prior trust can be really present only where there is also this unqualified loyalty to all whom God loves. Paul himself makes this point in the immediate context of formulating his christology of freedom by speaking of the faith for which Christ sets us free as "faith working through love" (Gal. 5:6). The very nature of such faith, he attests, is that it can be passive to God's love for us only by being active in our own love for others.

However formulated, the point is that we cannot ourselves be freed from the bondage of sin for the freedom of faith except by participating actively as well as passively in God's liberating love. So the gift and demand of our own ultimate transformation involve us in the ultimate transformation of all other human beings who can be in any way affected by our action as well as in such penultimate transformations as are thereby also given and demanded by God's love.

IV

The last step in the argument is to clarify in principle exactly what penultimate transformations are involved in ultimate transformation. This we may do by recalling, first of all, something on which we have touched more than once in the preceding discussion — namely, that any self-understanding, being at least implicitly an answer to the existential question about the meaning of ultimate reality, is closely related both to metaphysical belief and to moral action. Thus understanding oneself in a certain way always involves one's believing certain beliefs and performing certain actions. But if this can be said formally of any self-understanding, it might well appear that among the other changes involved in one's ultimate transformation from sin to faith is a change both in one's beliefs about ultimate reality and in one's actions toward others.

The difficulty in drawing this inference, however, is that one's self-understanding is not only closely related to one's beliefs and actions, but, as was also pointed out above, distinctively different from them. Because of this difference one can believe what faith believes and can act as faith acts even without having undergone the transition from sin to faith. Recognizing this, we must always allow that undergoing this transition may not involve any change in what one believes or in what one does but only in how one understands one's existence in believing and acting alike.

Nevertheless, self-understanding necessarily involves both believing and acting; and in most instances, certainly, ultimate transformation involves penultimate transformations in beliefs as well as in actions, including the actions whereby we bear explicit witness to our beliefs. This explains why, in the language of the tradition, one rightly says that faith must always find expression in good works — works of piety as well as works of mercy — even as sin inevitably expresses itself in sins — sins of impiety and irreligion as well as sins of moral transgression. Good works in this sense are always necessary because we can *exist* for the freedom of faith only insofar as we *act* for it — namely, by bearing witness to others in all that we say and do that it is for just such freedom that they, too, have been set free.

The question that arises in our situation today — and to which we now need to give special attention — is whether such penultimate transformations in individual beliefs and actions exhaust the changes that ultimate transformation involves. In a recent book that effectively argues for a negative answer to this question, Nicholas Wolterstorff employs a typology of religions in which he distinguishes "salvation religions" generally into the two main types of "avertive" and "formative" religions. Although religions of both types "look forward to salvation from what is defective in our present mode of existence," avertive religions typically acquiesce in what is defective and then turn away from it to unite with a higher reality, while formative religions typically seek to reform what is defective in obedience to a higher will.[4] But even among religions that are dominantly formative rather than avertive, there can be important differences. Thus Wolterstorff argues that, even though Lutheranism was sufficiently different from the more avertive religion of medieval Christianity to be classified as formative, "the focus of its formative efforts was mainly on ecclesiastical structures and on individual 'inwardness.' "[5] On the other hand, "the emergence of early Calvinism represented a fundamental alteration in Christian sensibility, from the vision and practice of turning away from the social world in order to seek closer union with God to the vision and practice of working to reform the social world in obedience to God."[6]

I have two reasons for directing attention to Wolterstorff's argument. First of all, it makes clear that the "world-formative Christianity" that he traces to early Calvinism and that he himself wishes to advocate as appropriate today is certainly not the only understanding of ultimate transformation by which Christians have been guided. Even if one would want to qualify his characterizations of the different types of Christian religion, one could not seriously question that there have been such types and that the differences between them have indeed had to do with whether, or to what extent, ultimate transformation has been understood to involve penultimate transformation of the social world. My second reason for considering Wolterstorff's argument is that even his account of the relatively late emergence of world-formative Christianity in early Calvinism is not completely free of anachronism. Anyone acquainted with the contemporary movements in Christian theology called "political theology" and "theology of liberation" will be familiar with an apologetic that seeks to show that already in the New Testament, because in the witness of Jesus himself, there is an understanding of ultimate transformation as involving more than a change of individuals, indeed, as more or less explicitly political. On the other hand, exegetes and historians of early Christianity continue to give compelling reasons for dismissing such an apologetic as anachronistic. The fact is that the understanding of the scope of human power and responsibility that underlies our contemporary concern with politics can be read out of the New Testament only by first being read into it. Something like the same reasoning, I believe, can be urged against Wolterstorff's apologetic for early Calvinism. Even if he is surely right in insisting that this type of Christianity stressed the active as well as the passive moment in faith and the need for faith always to find expression not only in religion but in all the rest of human life, one may nevertheless question whether its understanding of the scope of human power and responsibility was not still subject to constraints that are even more obviously present in earlier types of Christianity.

My point, in short, is that an understanding of ultimate transformation as also involving penultimate transformation of social and cultural structures depends not only on normative Christian witness but also on a distinctively modern historical consciousness. Wolterstorff himself recognizes this insofar as he reckons among the factors that account for the emergence of early Calvinism "the drastic alteration in social relations taking place in Western Europe in the sixteenth century." "In this situation," he allows, "it was only natural that people would begin to reflect on alternative social structures and that the idea of social structure as part of the givenness of their surroundings would begin to seem entirely implausible."[7] But how much more is this true after the bourgeois revolutions of the eighteenth century and the proletarian revolutions of our own. What makes a world-formative Christianity indeed appropriate to our situation today is the historical consciousness that is ours as contemporary men and women. We are aware as earlier generations were not that even the most basic structures of social and cultural order are neither divinely ordained nor naturally given but humanly created — by historical beings like ourselves who have the power and the responsibility to change them, given the moral demand implied by faith. Because this demand governs the whole of our action, we can understand ourselves as Christians and as the historical beings we know ourselves to be only by acknowledging our specifically political responsibility for social and cultural change.

So in the Christian understanding for which I have argued, the existence for freedom for which we are freed by God's love involves our action not only for the freedom of faith of all our fellow human beings but also for their freedom from unjust social and cultural structures that oppress them and keep them in bondage. In this way, our ultimate transformation involves penultimate transformations in the social and cultural orders for which we are responsible as well as in our individual beliefs and actions. Even so, having also argued that our ultimate transformation is one thing, all other changes, something else, I must insist on this final point: as surely as ultimate transformation may indeed involve radical social and cultural change, even the most radical such change can never be more than penultimate in relation to the freedom of faith for which Christ has set us free.

NOTES

1. Frederick J. Streng, *Understanding Religious Life,* 3rd ed. (Belmont, Calif.: Wadsworth Publishing Co., 1985), p. 2.

2. William James, *Some Problems of Philosophy: A Beginning of an Introduction to Philosophy* (New York: Longmans, Green and Co., 1911), p. 101.

3. Philip S. Watson, "Luther and Sanctification," *Concordia Theological Monthly* 30 (1959): 243–259.

4. Nicholas Wolterstorff, *Until Justice and Peace Embrace* (Grand Rapids: Eerdmans, 1983), p. 5.

5. Ibid., p. 10.

6. Ibid., p. 11.

7. Ibid.

PART III

THEOLOGY INTERSECTS
RELIGIOUS PLURALISM

Chapter 11

The "Last Enchantments": Religion, Nature, Home

RAY L. HART

T HE RANGE OF LANGDON GILKEY'S THEOLOGICAL PURVIEW, like that of his mentors Reinhold Niebuhr and Paul Tillich, has been extensive. That range has included nothing less than the sea changes visited upon humankind by Western modernity. Few theologians of his generation have insisted as resolutely as Gilkey that we cannot genuinely behold without being beheld by what we behold. (Says Gaston Bachelard, the exotic historian of science: anything we really look at, looks back.) A fundamental theological mistake reduced Western modernity to a deposit of secular questions with which unreconstructed theological questions are to be paired up. No, it is not and cannot be a matter of secular "them" and theological "us," for the theological *persona* has been as corroded by the acids of modernity as has any other. To have kept this fact in the forefront of theological consciousness, without becoming paralyzed by it, is one of Langdon Gilkey's signal achievements.

And another is that he has not retreated in vague references to the "modern" or "secular" mind, but rather has worked tirelessly to identify the parameters by which theology has been, or must be, most severely qualified and expanded. While no single essay could recapitulate his life-work, I believe these parameters are that the effects of Western modernity are most clearly visible in (1) the pure and empirical sciences and their methods, (2) the rise and aggrandizement of historical consciousness, and (3) the loss or failure of metaphysical nerve.

217

I honor Langdon Gilkey here not by protracting his analysis of modernity or by assessing his theological response to that analysis. He and every other thinker of like distinguished attainment is most appropriately honored in the effort to extend his project.

It is an astonishing fact in the history of consciousness that things can be as clear at the beginning of an epoch as at its end. No one subsequently, not even a William Blake or a Friedrich Nietzsche, saw more perspicuously the shape of modernity than John Donne at its dawn. Just a year after Galileo announced his shift of the cosmic center, not only from the earth but from humankind as well, to the sun, John Donne was expressing his horror in "An Anatomie of the World":

> 'Tis all peeces, all cohaerance gone
> All just supply, and all Relation...

The "cohaerance gone" was the sense of natural status and natural relatedness. Now come the haunting words:

> Every man alone thinkes he hath got
> To be a Phoenix, and that then can bee
> None of that kinde, of which he is, but hee.

Man alone, away from home, a grounded bird, aspiring to be a phoenix, homesick for the cosmic nest. Others would compound elegiac poignancy, but is there a great distance from Donne to Matthew Arnold at the end of modernity and the latter's lament at humankind's being deprived of "the last enchantments"?[1]

I wish in what follows to ponder the multiply locative bird that the modern person is, and I shall do so by meditating on three enchantments, three rudimentary nouns in our language and the verbs cradled in them: religion, nature, home. I seek to stimulate (even if I cannot instantiate) the imagination of the verbality of the noun, the imagination of religion, of nature, of home.

Religion

The English noun "religion" has two verbal roots with a common stem. Classical Roman thinkers derived *religio* from *religere;* the Christian Fathers derived it from *religare*. In both cases the central stem is *lig-* (*ligere, ligare*), which suggests "binding."[2] This sense survives in such

English nouns as ob*lig*ation, *lig*ament, *lig*ature. It was a sense still evident for Gladstone in the third quarter of the nineteenth century when he condemned "religion . . . with a debased worship appended to it . . . but no *religating*, no binding power." If one takes this classical sense of Roman civil religion, religion means scrupulous attention to what claims and binds, to what holds us together (personally and socially) and obliges us to the source or sources of ultimate sponsorship in the world.

If one adds to the classical Roman the special sense of the Christian Fathers, above all that of Augustine, one calls attention to the *repetitive* and *changing* character of ligation as the essence of religion. It is not binding alone or simply, but loosening from former bonds and rebinding, *re*-ligare, that is at the heart of religion. Religion that does not stop religating involves a combination of binding and freeing, of the fixed and the variable, of the same and the different, of the one and the many. To the classical sense of binding is added, in all three of the surviving western religions (Judaism, Christianity, Islam), the religative significance of *time* and *memory*. Since selfhood is given in concert with time and memory, with space and place, we can say, in a reversal of the French adage, that the more things are the same, the more they are different.

In his *Confessions*, the first rudimentary autobiography and document of self-consciousness — in the modern sense — in the Western world, Augustine lays out the "binds" in which he has found himself. The mere knowledge of these "binds" — with the Manichees, his mistress, his bastard son, Adeodatus, his pious mother, Monica, the stealing of pears as a youth — was not religious. Not one's knowledge but what one *ack*nowledges (confesses: *confiteor*) is the stuff of *re*-ligation, of one's religious story. Long before Max Scheler, Augustine recognized that there is no possibility of forgiveness or salvation if the past is fixed. For Augustine the past is not bound but is subject to re-binding as one's story unfolds, folds out, and folds up in the coincidence of past, present, future. What seemed binding in the past proves for Augustine in the course of mnemonic probing not to have been so, while many trivial events in the past show themselves, in concert with an accumulating selfhood over time, to be provident. What one was *negligent* of shows itself as *religent*, as affording religation. In his and in every human memory, Augustine saw occasions neglected for their providential power. These occasions provided (providence) obliging surmises or evocations that now, through re-ligation, become invocations. Thus in a religated life, the repressed never loses its pertinence to what may be obliged, and that which is obliged is not to be formulated apart from what has happened — and continues to happen in the ligaments of story.

Religion, religating, so understood makes for an intense interior dialogue, a coincidence of opposites, a relentless tension between the elements of historically placed selfhood. Augustine conducted such a tensioned dialogue in the presence of One who is absent to our surest speech and audiently present to our negligence. Religation, our tensioned acknowledgements, is an unending effort to know even as we are known by One who will not let us rest in the binds of fate. The temptation of the human heart is to rest in its own identities and identifications. Because religion *ligates,* it makes for duty, the fixed, the conservative; because it *re*-ligates, it makes for release, change, radicality. The temptation of religion in the West, often historically realized, is to split the tension between these tendencies, becoming either radically conservative and thus the ideology of a *status quo* or a *status quo ante* (as in today's American "Moral Majority"), or radically anarchic and thus the ideology of an *avant garde* (as in various forms of mysticism in the West, and in modern "liberalisms"). Religion with real religating power is shot through with dialectic: it is at rest and restless, at home and homeless, bound and free. Insofar as "religion" becomes a hardened, non-dialectical ligation, and the scholarly study of religion is directed only to the substantialization of such ligations, I believe our departments of religious studies in the university or college might more honestly be called: The Department of *Negligious* Studies!

Home

When one uses the word "home" one gives to it a valorization almost as unique as one's own body odor. We cannot pause over "home" without an agitated reflexiveness for it is accompanied in speech by a private onrush/ uprush of *images,* what Bachelard called "sudden saliences on the surface of the psyche." Few words so steadily reflect their reflexivity, so immediately betray their imaginal peripheries, so directly embody the wistful or the alienated. In its unstudied utterance there is an idiosyncratic variation in which the cradle of the body rocks all sound. The catch in the throat, the sigh that carves the breath, give to "home" its tonality, its sonority. It is one of the few words left in our language in which the memory and the imagination of the body interdict all calculation. We can perhaps see why by looking to the primal verbal activities that the noun comprises.

The English word "home" is of Teutonic origin, and back of that there are probably Indo-European (*Em* or *M:* connoting "mine") and Sanskrit (the mantric *Om* or *Aum*) roots. And as a noun "home" is a compact of the re-verberations of several Germanic and old English verbs. There is the sense of Old Prussian *keimen:* to germinate; split the seed; be separated from the universal stock in one's own place, soil, and blood; thus to arise, start, begin in one's radical individuality. That sense pervades the German noun *Heimat:* the place of nativity, where things began, and where one fundamentally is *settled,* where one dwells, the *geography* of one's founding imagination. To settle, however, does not mean merely to dwell in, merely to inhabit. The Middle English verb *dwellen* (like Old High German *twellen*) adds another nuance: to intercept, to hold up, to stay, to tarry; so home is not only a place one dwells in, but also a place of dwelling on. That dwelling in and dwelling on is further amplified and racinated in the Old English verb *abidan,* which means both to go on being and to await, to "bide the time" expectantly, and so pertains to an abode one can or cannot abide. Finally, the Latin *residere,* to reside, suggests not only to settle or sink, but to be inherent in, to vest, to belong. To reside is not alone to domicile, but to settle down to what rises up as an initiating, originating, intrinsic claim or bond, a cumulative and aggrandizing *residuum.*

Certain reverberations in the word "home" chime with those in "religion"; and one may call attention to them even in advance of bringing the word "nature" into listening range.

We have seen that religion comprises a sense of ligation or binding, and have found a like sense in home as the place in which we inhere, in which we are vested, that which claims us. We have further heard that religion comprises the sense of *re*-ligation, the loosening of bonds that cannot accommodate rebinding, as we have heard in "home" a starting that continues, a dwelling that dwells on, a founding imagination that accommodates an expanding residuum. To get a tap root down, and thus a plant, the seed must split (in something like the current vernacular sense: when we get away from here, we "split"). Man or woman is not a plant, however. The original place, however formative, cannot accommodate the perduring human home. Because ligation, to remain binding, to make present what is obliged, requires an unending re-ligation, one is driven from home into uncharted homelessness, from the domestic into the wild. A person, as H. Richard Niebuhr once observed, is like a migratory bird: one cannot be all that one is in one climate, one place. There is a doubleness, a multiplicity in one's locative ground.

Not by accident, then, the "religious" in the world's religions — peripatetics, wanderers, wayfarers, vagrants, mendicants, saunterers — have been at home in homelessness, have made home and homelessness coincide. All holy walking, said Thoreau, is sauntering.[3] The saunterer, he said, is the *Sainte-Terrer,* the one on the way to the Holy Land. Thoreau himself was such a one; his errand into the wilderness was to find a home for his homelessness. He believed that "in Wildness is the preservation of the world." We should remember that before our *American* foreparents were settlers they were Pilgrims. The dialectic of home and homelessness in American Christianity has been thematic from the beginning: the dialectic of the uprooted and the rerooted, the uprouted and rerouted, the unligated and the religated. And not only from American beginnings. The anonymous author of the Letter to Diognetus in the second century enjoined the Christian to make of every foreign land a homeland, and of every homeland a foreign land.

Parenthetically, one may refer to *the* great philosopher of home in the twentieth century, Martin Heidegger. For him the estranged, alienated, vagrant person quests for home as *dwelling.* For the American, however, and I believe this owes in some large measure to his or her experience of nature, home must embrace the dialectic of home *and* homelessness, the canny and the uncanny, the domestic and the wild. If Thoreau counseled settling down through the alluvion that extends from Paris to Concord, below freshet and frost, to rocks in place, where one might set one's Realometer, he suggested that one not merely dwell or abide there, but have as well a place where one could get the hell away from and awake in different climes. Only with such a place and only by leaving it, only by being simultaneously at home and homeless, can one dwell *on* the abiding abidingly.

The reader will have noticed that I have not developed the dialectic between home and homelessness in one of the classical Western theological ways, by resort to this-worldly and other-worldly categories. The hegemony of time and history as the framework of religious consciousness has pressed Western theology into the use of those categories. It is otherwise with religions (including Christianity) that have not lost their ligations and religations with nature. Religions that are staked in nature — as Heidegger says: that preserve the earth, receive the sky, await the divinities, and escort the mortals — have no need for a bifurcation of worlds to account for an inner-world reality. For *other* American foreparents (and mine), the American Indians, the house is the home of homelessness: the lodgepole or the smokehole opens the way for movement between planes, for the ascent and descent of the migratory, multiply located bird that we are.

Nature

In these last comments we have begun to trench our third noun, nature, and we may now bring its verbal resonance into range. Etymologically, nature derives from *natus,* past participle of *nascor,* to be born, to be begotten. Nature then is the whence of things aborning, of things coming to be — and, by extension, of things decaying and passing away. Nature, then, is *genesis.*

Regrettably, little account has been taken of the history that prevails over our hearing of the three nouns: religion, home, nature. That lack cannot be rectified in a few sentences; but I risk a few observations on the history of "nature."

Before the rise of modern mechanics in physics and Enlightenment deism in philosophy, nature was understood on an organic model, as a living organism. Nature was the *creative* effect of intelligent soul, whether in mythological expansion that intelligence was understood, as in Christianity, to transcend the cosmic body, or to be embodied demiurgically *in* the cosmic animal, as in Greek natural philosophy. In both cases nature was not a *self-conscious* creativity because, as Plotinus said, nature lacks imagination: it cannot transcend its own becoming. The creative and creating effect of intelligence, nature cannot *be* intelligent. An intelligent, self-conscious rendering of nature's creativity is precisely the charge of human culture. Only a human culture unreligated to a nature so understood could forget a maxim that was unquestioned over two millennia of glorious cultural achievement: "Art imitates nature."

In early modernity, in a sea change of paradigms both for science and cosmology, nature is seen as the *created* (not creative) effect of an Intelligence that is not only remote but retired. "Creativity" becomes a buzzword in the language in respect of humankind. As the cosmos becomes centered on the sun, creativity becomes centered in the human being (who is at best an imitator of superannuated Deity). Creativity is delivered into human hegemony and is exercised upon nature as its all-encompassing stuff. With the presence of the stuff of regularity and the concomitant absence of the Regulator, everyone is usufructory creator. Omitting many important steps, we can see the philosophical apogee of this view in Fichte. For him, nature is the realm of the Not-I and exists as the counter against which the reality of self-consciousness of the I is shaped. In the very ecstasy of the differentiated ego, Fichte exclaimed: "I do not exist for Nature, but Nature exists for me."[4]

I shall bring these brief historical observations to a head with some comments about a genius of the first rank who negotiated the paradigm changes between the Enlightenment and the nineteenth century, and who anticipated their issue in the twentieth. Goethe was perhaps the last towering figure in Western culture to make signal contributions both to letters and to the sciences. He identified and deplored the split between spirit and nature that emerged in the nineteenth century and the consequent dichotomy between the "two cultures" following on the assignment of spirit to the humanities (*Geisteswissenchaften*) and nature to the sciences (*Naturwissenschaften*). Attracted as they are to mathematics as their fundamental language, the sciences would lead to a quantification of all qualities and thus to an alienation of humankind from nature as concrete process. As for the Romantic humanities, their energies would be siphoned off to feed "the hot paroxysms" (Erich Heller) of the human heart, unnourished by the amplitude of a nature rich in self-diffusion.[5]

While *Faust* stewed on the back burner of his mind for sixty years, Goethe entered the scientific lists and did experimental work in botany, anatomy, biology, and the optics and physiology of color. In something like the classical Greek sense, he set out to "save the phenomena" of nature. What would become of humankind alienated from the concrete experience of nature, estranged from the very geneses that nourish human life? The fundamental phenomenon, the *Urphänomenon,* was metamorphosis (a word Goethe introduced into the language), that morphogenesis by which "nature is constantly creating new forms. What now exists, never was before; what was, will never come again. All is new, and yet always the same."[6] Explaining unity within nature's variety and change within its continuity, Goethe anticipated evolution nearly eighty years before the appearance of Darwin's *Origin of Species.*

The phenomena of genesis everywhere exhibit two irreducible principles for Goethe. The first of these is polarity (*Polarität*). Every concrete phenomenon in nature is an interplay of tensions, a coincidence of opposites, a fusion of centrifugal and centripetal tendencies. The same polarity works in the arts and all affairs of the human heart. In his poetry and drama and novels Goethe ceaselessly alternates between the images of *Wanderer* and *Hütte,* one who roams and philanders, one who longs for home and family: at home and homeless, bound and free.

The second principle of nature's geneses is *Steigerung,* an all but untranslatable term. However much "polarity" accounts for unity within change, the one and the many, the same and the different, it cannot account or be responsible for the creation of new genetic forms in which there are *changes of quality. Steigerung* is that "intensified heightening" that gives rise to a new term, and thus to a new round of polar relationships. The same principle is at work in the arts. The justification for a work of art is that it establishes the human spirit at a new level of quality: nature and culture remain in tandem only as the *geneses* of nature chime with the *poieses* of spirit. And Goethe contended against the Romantics generally and Schiller particularly that such a *Steigerung* is not a matter of "idea." Because heightening in nature is a matter of concrete fact, science is inescapably experimental and empirical. Because heightening in the human spirit is a function of individual stories, Goethe tells of roaming and homing in connection with the *realia* of Wilhelm Meister's life; and he tells of Faust and his dog. The tendency to become specific (*Spezifikationstrieb*), which is the tendency of all becoming (genesis) in both nature and spirit, and which shows itself when nature and spirit are ligated and religated, is protection against the unhappy consciousness of the bad infinite, to use Hegelian language. (And if *Polarität* and *Steigerung* sound like Hegel's *Dialektik* and *Aufhebung,* that is because he got them from Goethe.) As Goethe suggested in *Wilhelm Meister Lehrjahre,* "If we can believe it possible that the creator of the world took upon Himself the form of what He made, and for a time lived with men on earth as *they* live ...," we can only revere the specific in both nature and man.

How Shall We Dispose Ourselves to Nature Religatively?

Earlier I called attention to reverberations in the words "religion" and "home" that chime with each other. From what has been adduced from "nature," it will be clear that that word emits echoes that join the chorus of like resonances: to homing and roaming, to ligating and re-ligating, to heightening and aborning. To be held in the embrace of nature, as we just now noted from Goethe, is to be joined to the specific (that is, to what is manifest, what is phenomenal, what shows itself, or appears). And so I come to a thesis, that a fresh settling in the specificity of nature (scarcely the same thing as "a natural setting") may afford a human home for human homelessness and thus a religation of the multiple locatives of religious sensibility. This thesis arouses two questions to be taken up in conclusion. *How* shall we dispose ourselves to nature religatively? And if we do, *what* are some of the re-ligations that might ensue?

First then, how shall we dispose ourselves to nature in its religating potentialities? Not, as Goethe warned against the Romantics, in hankering for the primitive, as though we had or could shed our civilized hides. There is an irony in Thoreau's admonition to get our feet out of the cultural alluvion of Paris and Harvard College, while he sits on his pumpkin at Walden reading books in Greek and Latin! If we are lucky enough to meet the raw, it will be from the standpoint of the cooked. An original innocence is closed for us; we are at best suppliants of a second innocence, in Paul Ricoeur's phrase, suppliants of a "post-critical naiveté." That means we cannot ignore *that* and *what* we know, and so we cannot follow Goethe in excoriating the sciences of the day (unless, like him, we do them better). But we can aspire not to ignore that and what we do *not* know, knowingly. When humanists knew what they were about, they trafficked in learned ignorance (Nicholas of Cusa's *docta ignorantia*).

Let us revive an old idea: The religative potency of nature awaits our being disposed to it as to a *text*. A text that invites our audience again and again is one that expands our learned ignorance. In developing the venerable notion of disposing ourselves religatively to nature as text, I am conscious of drawing explicitly upon Goethe and Thoreau. (To their horror, one could add Calvin, though I do not.)

Said Goethe: "To be enjoyed, to be turned to account, Nature herself must be present to the reader, either really, or by the help of a lively imagination." The phenomena of nature reveal and conceal themselves "...as a text, in the first instance, — partly as they appear unsought, partly as they may be presented by contrivance..." — that is, by human culture.[7] In a paraphrase of Italo Calvino's paraphrase of Descartes, we may say that nature expresses itself as long as someone can say "I read, therefore it writes."

Thoreau went into the woods to transact some private business in nature's public. He traveled light, with only a few classical texts at hand. But his attentiveness discovered him in a vast circulating library where sentences were written in bark, where "much is published, little written," the source of sentences "merely copied from time to time on to linen paper." (Nature's motto: publish or perish!) In such a circulating library, words might indeed be "nailed to their primitive senses" and the *poieses* of human culture be replenished with the *geneses* of nature. So Thoreau:

> A town is saved, not more by the righteous men in it than by the woods and swamps that surround it. A township where one primitive forest waves above while another primitive forest rots below — such a town is fitted to raise not only corn and potatoes, but poets and philosophers for the coming ages. In such a soil grew Homer and Confucius and the rest, and out of such a wilderness comes the Reformer eating locusts and wild honey.... Alas for human culture! Little is to be expected of a nation, when the vegetable mould is exhausted, and it is compelled to make manure of the bones of its fathers. There the poet sustains himself merely by his own superfluous fat, and the philosopher comes down on his marrow bones.[8]

Without nature's *genesis* human *poiesis* is bereft of religative nurture.

Well then, if we are to be nurtured in the *re*-ligative potencies of nature, we are to be disposed to nature not only as text but as a text of a certain kind. We are, as post-critical persons, to be disposed to nature as to the text of poetry. Not as sheer genesis, the matrix of becoming and passing away, does nature present itself as a text fraught with religative potentiality. (Without *poiesis,* nature is in bondage to a saturated discourse.) Only when *genesis* is met by a commensurate *poiesis* does such a text emerge. Only then does space afford an alveolic place that can rebind us, one in which we are obliged to settle, dwell in and dwell on. In such a meeting of *genesis* and *poiesis* the tropes of nature arouse our latent capacity for parable, and the migratory bird in us finds its nest.[9]

We should of course remind ourselves of the restraints of a hermeneutic of texts. I have not said that nature *is* poetry, not even (as perhaps in Schelling) that nature is *unconscious* poetry. The tropes of genesis that nature polarizes and heightens are those in which we are not complicit; at least, we are not more complicit in them than is any other natural force. If nature did not retain the lead in this respect, if it did not steal initiative in the text that emerges at the junction between its genesis and our poiesis, we would have nothing to expect from that text but our own projections. (We would have, as in Romanticism, the psychoanalysis of nature.) When a text is honored as text, it sets a limit to velleity and arouses the imagination: as Bachelard says, we aspire to repeat its cre-

ativity and continue its exaggeration. What religative poetry does with
nature is what poetry does with everything it holds in view. To follow
Bachelard once more, "poetry puts language in a state of emergence, in
which life become manifest through its vivacity."[10]

What Are the Religative Potentialities
of a Fresh Reading of Nature?

Our final question is: *What* re-ligations might we expect from such a
reading of nature?

(1) We might expect to be re-bound to *variation:* we might expect the
potency for variation that lies at the heart of natural process to involve
us in ceaseless rebinding. Nature like religion has its ligations — its
continuities, regularities, patterns. Scientists as much as theologians
(and for the same reason) have a conservative streak; they attend to
these regularities as affording an enduring human home.

But the essence of modern science, for which "evolution" is only
the code word, is that nature has packed its trunks with potentialities
for variation. Being the matrix of genesis, nature embodies both the
fundaments of creativity, the need to limit and the need to keep options open. A human culture that attended to the religations of nature itself would be one in which culture's classical practitioners and
guardians, the humanists, would pack the attics and basements of the
university with potentialities for human variation. In such a university students might wander into the attics and basements and, as the
young will, try on the clothes. Many a new life might be found in such
play.

(2) Ligated to nature's religations, we would no longer be able to
avoid *one* potentiality for variation, and that is the possibility, some
would say the accelerating likelihood, of *nature without humankind.*

One of the most fascinating and still unfinished chapters in the history of modern science is the resistance to an evolutionary theory of
nature's religations. I refer not to the understandable resistance of
some "fundamentalistic" theologians, trapped in old ligations, but to
the resistance of some scientists, repressing the same or similar ligations. Human terror lies at the base of this resistance. If species
come and go, there is no reason to suppose that *homo sapiens* may
not be among them. Nature got along for millions of years without humankind; and we must assume it could do so again. This recognition
and its repression (as Loren Eisely and others have claimed) account

for the delay of the explicit formulation of the theory of the origin of species, a theory known to have hovered in the consciousness of scientists long before Darwin. And is it not the case that, having finally acknowledged an evolutionary account, scientists look to the stages of evolution in order to see how nature was teaching itself to make *homo sapiens,* thereby giving scientific vindication of the myth of Narcissus?

In 1937 Eric Gutkind, a sadly neglected Jewish theologian and philosopher, questioned "whether man is, perhaps, a kind of blind alley of nature, into which the cosmos has run. Is man, perhaps, a kind of natural monster, destined to die out?"[11]

Have we begun to meditate the religations coincident with this potentiality, what some call this prospect? One who has, E. M. Cioran, opines in *The Fall Into Time* that "one is never so much man as when one regrets being so." The Western person is incorrigibly an accomplice of time and is afflicted with the awareness of it; thus we are tempted to exist in the Fichtean sense, so that all existence, even that of nature is centered on our own. Yet the surprise of being in contiguity with nature is that

> ...the surprise of being precedes the surprise of being human...; it is less natural to be man than simply to be. We feel this instinctively: it is the source of our delight each time we manage to sidestep ourselves and participate in the blissful sleep of objects.... He who has never envied the vegetable has missed the human drama.[12]

In nature, if I may paraphrase Bachelard, something is always praying to be born. Were we attentive to nature, we might overhear what is praying to be born *after* humankind. What can stop the stopping of humankind that humankind's stopping of nature (*per impossibile*) entails? I repeat: have we the surmises out of which we could rebound and be re-bound to such a variation, to humankind as marginal to the cosmos?

(3) A fresh disposition to nature would involve us in a religation of self-identity and self-diffusion.

Tillich and others have often said that human beings cannot evade the ultimate since that is the person's root concern. But neither can the person endure the ultimate very long at a stretch, especially if "the ultimate" does not include one as one has come to perceive oneself. If the Malthusian prospect is in large measure the result of human competition for an ever more individuated ego consciousness, we should be surprised only if the ego did *not* suppress and repress such a prospect and every other counter-variation.

There can be little doubt that, in the West, time and history have afforded the medium of differentiation and individuation for everyone. Western culture, with rare exceptions, is the story of an accelerating repudiation of human anonymity, is the work of authors more than that of authorization, is a crescendo of rage for the signature of the unique. The passion for clarity and certainty that arose with modernity and that has persisted throughout its day was itself in the service of certifying the *ego* and its *sum:* clarity and certainty came to be the sum of its *sum.* Moreover, our very sociality came to be the founded in the shared complications of individual ego — hence the hegemony of Freud and Marx over contemporary social theory.

In a reversal of Eric Gutkind, we may say that as the "I" (or the Ego) was the aim of history and its latter-day Western civilization, so the "I am not" as a distinctively human potentiality lies in the lees of nature. However specific the religations of nature may be and are, with respect to individuality it is red in tooth and claw.

In calling for a religation between self-identity and self-diffusion as a distinctive *human* potentiality, we must emphasize that this is a *re*ligative potentiality. It is not that old ligation, that first solitude in mere animality from which we decline (and for which Romantics pine). It conduces rather to a second and last solitude to which we may aspire and accede, one that carries the accumulations of the course through history. Practicing ourselves in diffusion, we may be located in that last anonymity in which, through religations we cannot now foresee, we might find our signature.

(4) Juxtaposition with nature would involve us in a religation of proper selfhood and property.

The connection between "proper" (*propre:* one's particular ownmostness) and "property" is intimate. The ego and its competition for uniqueness is at the root of possession and property; property conduces to propriety. Nature too is miserly, discarding nothing that ever worked, but never to the end of individual aggrandizement. At the same time it is profligate in waste, in service of the total fund of variation.

What religations of religions themselves will be necessary if we are to enter nature and if nature is to enter us with potentiating force? As the patrons of individuality, have not Christianity and Judaism, of course against their intention and will, made us frenetics of possession, fueling civilization with infinite desire, want, and need? Surely one of the doors natures opens to us is an apprenticeship in dispossession.

I am well aware how incompletely developed these potentialities for religation are as cited. And I may be told that it is a little precious to garner them by recourse to nature when one could get them directly by booking Pan Am to Benares or Kyoto. While it may be true that these potentialities have something in common with religions that hold a different view of selfhood and sustain a different relation to nature than those in the West, I believe there are crucial hermeneutical reasons why Americans cannot detour their own history in gaining access to them. In some deeply residual sense we are still what the Puritan Fathers and the Republican Founders called (in different senses) Nature's Nation, readers of the Book of Nature.

On this note we may turn once more, and concludingly, to Thoreau. He thought the passage over the Atlantic occasioned potentiality for the new American to wake in a New Creation, where one might "travel a great deal in Concord," climb the Mt. Katadins of the inward morning, and grow beans for the tropes they arouse in the parable-maker. His inner compass pointed always west, his central metaphor for the home of homelessness and in which he saw the preservation of spirit and nature sourcing and sponsoring each other. Among his spare rations for the journey into wilderness were (in addition to the Western classics) the Vedic scriptures; he knew that if you go far enough west it becomes east. Should the noble American experiment fail, there is one more ocean to cross. *That* eventuality he viewed with mixed and troubled emotions:

The Atlantic is a Lethean stream, in our passage over which we have had an opportunity to forget the Old World and its institutions. If we do not succeed this time, there is perhaps one more chance for the race left before it arrives on the banks of the Styx; and that is the Lethe of the Pacific, which is three times as wide.[13]

NOTES

1. For the relation of early modern poetry to early modern science, see Stephen Toulmin, *The Return to Cosmology* (Berkeley: University of California Press, 1982). He treats of Donne on pp. 217–236.

2. These are, of course, matters of continuing scholarly debate. The common stem aside, Marie-Louis von Franz has recently has recently pointed out that *ligare* and *ligere* have distinguishable and perhaps distinct meanings. She points out that in common parlance *ligere* meant "to pick up" or "to collect," as in picking up or collecting wood, or "to read," as in gathering up or putting together individual letters (Marie-Louis von Franz, *Alchemy: An Introduction to the Symbolism and the Psychology* [Toronto: Inner City Books, 1980], pp. 97f. I am grateful to Professor David Miller for calling this discussion to my attention.) Yet I do not see that very much rides on this distinction, nor is much gained or lost by insisting upon it. All grant that *ligare* carries the nuance of binding, tying, gathering together, connecting; and the nuances are close to those of *ligere*.

3. Henry David Thoreau, "Walking," in *Walden and Other Writings,* ed. Brooks Atkinson (New York: Modern Library, 1950), p. 597.

4. Johann Gottlieb Ficthe, *The Vocation of Man* (*Die Bestimmung des Menschen*) (New York: Liberal Arts Press, 1956), p. 153.

5. Erich Heller, *The Disinherited Mind* (New York: Meridian Books, 1969), p. 32.

6. Johann Wolfgang von Goethe, "Die Natur" (Fragment), in *Goethe Werke*, Bd. XIII, *Naturwissenschaftliche Schriften* (Hamburg: Christian Wegner Verlag, 1971), pp. 45–47.

7. Johann Wolfgang von Goethe, *Theory of Colors* (*Die Farbenlehre*), trans. by Charles Locke Eastlake (Cambridge: MIT Press, 1976). Preface to first edition, p. xlviii.

8. Thoreau, "Walking," p. 617. These lines from Thoreau remind me of others from William Butler Yeats: "God guard me from those thoughts men think/ In the mind alone,/ He that sings a lasting song/ Thinks in a marrow bone."

9. I have developed these cryptic suggestions more thoroughly in "The Poiesis of Place," *Journal of Religion* 53 (January 1973), pp. 36–47.

10. Gaston Bachelard, *The Poetics of Space,* trans. Maria Jolas (Boston: Beacon Press, 1969), p. xiii.

11. Eric Gutkind, *The Body of God: First Steps toward an Anti-Theology* (New York: Horizon Press, 1969), p. 136.

12. E. M. Cioran, *The Fall into Time,* trans by Richard Howard (Chicago: Quadrangle Books, 1970), pp. 34–35, 52, 178.

13. Thoreau, "Walking," p. 608.

Chapter 12

Fides Quaerens Intellectum as Basis of Pluralistic Method

ROBERT P. SCHARLEMANN

THE THEME TO BE EXPLICATED IN THIS ESSAY is the following: When the formula "faith seeking understanding" is understood as the statement of a hermeneutical method, and not as the foundation of a metaphysical theology, it is a formulation of the pluralistic structure of thinking.

Prior to Friedrich Schleiermacher, the hermeneutical aspect of theological methods was not so obvious as it has become since then, even if it has always been implicit in the notion of *fides quaerens intellectum.* In the medieval as well as the early Protestant conceptions of theology, the question of method was treated in terms of the Platonic-Aristotelian notion of *methodos,* with its double movement of analysis and synthesis, though with refinements and elaborations. Today, however, the question of theological method almost always includes a consideration of how theological language is to be interpreted. This may be more true of descriptions of method that one finds in, say, Paul Tillich and Langdon Gilkey than in Karl Barth; but scarcely anyone can avoid the matter of how that "strange" language of theology is to be understood. That is one of the ways in which theology today is still in the heritage of the Kantian and post-Kantian critiques of the meaning of religion and theology.

Method as such does not imply anything hermeneutical. It means only a path that the mind can retrace in order to arrive at a goal. In this sense, a reflection on the divine names constitutes a method; for, at least since the time of Pseudo-Dionysius's *De divinis nominibus,* the purpose of reflecting on the meaning of divine names was to arrive at

233

the knowledge of the one meant by those names. To search for the right name of God is in effect to search for the best path to a knowledge of God. So, for example, Nicholas of Cusa proposed the formulation "not other" (*non aliud*) as the name most adequate to lead the mind to a knowledge of God as a map leads a traveler to a city. Anselm's formulation of the name of God as "that than which a greater cannot be thought" is an earlier example of the same intention.

In his *Church Dogmatics,* Karl Barth criticized the way in which the conception of theology as a practical science came to prevail in Protestant thought and to lead to an anthropologizing of theology.[1] The chief debate about method in early Protestantism — it is to Protestant scholasticism in the seventeenth century that we owe the term "methodology" — did not involve a question of interpretation but a question of the nature of theological science; it centered on whether theology was a theoretical or a practical science, and the terms of the discussion were those already found, if not in Aristotle and Plato, then at least in the *Dialectica* of John of Damascus. If theology was considered to be a practical science — the science of diagnosing and healing the soul, as medicine was the science of healing the body — then it followed the method of practical sciences. This method required identifying the goal (health of soul), the subject (the human sinner), and the means through which health could be brought to the sinful soul. Typical is Johann Friedrich König, who claims: "The method of treating theology, since this is among the practical habits, is analytical, proceeding from a cognition of end and subject to principles from which and means through which the end is introduced [into the subject]."[2] If, on the other hand, theology was treated as a theoretical science, its method was to proceed from principles to consequences. Initially, among the Protestants, the Lutherans adopted the practical conception, despite Melanchthon's opposite position, and the Calvinists adopted the other; but the practical conception gradually gained dominance all around, and with Schleiermacher's *Christian Faith* it took a decided hermeneutical turn.

Yet there is a hermeneutical component even in the discussion before Kant and Schleiermacher to the extent that the way in which one thought of theology involved an understanding of what theological statements were to mean. At least to that degree, theological thinking seems always to have involved a hermeneutical procedure rather than a strict method, that is, a definable procedure to arrive at certain goals by employing certain means or, more specifically, the rules and criteria according to which one arrives at scientific knowledge and which knowledge must satisfy in order to be regarded as scientific. I mean "science" here as secured knowledge in the broadest sense, and not only as referring to the natural sciences. Thus, the dialectical method, which, after a period when method was taken rather loosely to mean a quick path into a subject matter (and was equivalent to "summa," "discipline," "art," and the like), was incorporated into theological science in the Middle Ages, constituted only part of the theological procedure. It is self-consciously the way in which Thomas Aquinas, for example, explicates the questions and answers in his *Summa theologiae.* A question is posed, the apparent answer and the contrary positions are stated, the answer is reached by making the distinctions through which the opposing sides of the answer can be seen to be true, and the discussion concludes with replies to specific objections. *Veritas in distinctionibus* — truth is in the distinctions. All of this is dialectical method. But, fundamentally, the theological method as such was more; it included the hermeneutical procedure of interpreting propositions about God by reference to propositions about being at the same time that it gave to dialectical method a certain adjudicating role. This is the procedure made legitimate in principle by the notion that faith seeks understanding.

Much has been made of this conception in twentieth-century theology, not least of all because of the major role it played in the thought of Karl Barth but also because of Heidegger's critique of ontotheology. In the present essay, my purpose is to show how a certain kind of pluralism is contained in this principle if it is understood as the formulation of a hermeneutical method, based upon an irreducible duality that belongs to thinking as such, and not as a principle of metaphysics. When it is so understood, it does not fall victim to a Heideggerian critique of the "onto-theo-logical constitution of metaphysics."

What "Faith Seeking Understanding" Means

The scope of the conception of faith as seeking understanding becomes apparent only when it is spelled out as the identity in difference between *understanding being* and *believing in (or trusting) God.* To see the hermeneutical import of the formulation, one must say more than that faith seeks understanding; one must also call attention to the difference in the activities and the intentions that are meant by the words *faith* and *understanding.* Understanding always means understanding being; and faith always means trusting God. Hence, "faith seeking understanding" is a matter of the way in which a believing in God "seeks" an understanding of being. What is understood is fundamentally always namable as "being," and what is trusted is always in the end "God." The acts are different and the intentions are different; yet there is an identity in this difference that makes it possible for the one to "seek," or be open to, the other. (The converse formulation, which was used after Anselm as a description of speculative philosophy, is "understanding seeking faith" — *intellectus quaerens fidem*.)

Moreover, from a post-Kantian point of view, one must also say what "understanding" and "trusting" mean in relation to the other aspects of epistemological theory. If the act of knowing consists of putting together perception and thought (so that, for example, when we say that something is a dog we are putting together the concrete sensations that we have of the object with the abstract notion of the same thing),[3] then what understanding is, in contrast both to perception and to conception, is the uniting of the two by reference to a form of the word *being*. This is to say that understanding is distinct from both perceiving and conceiving, although it is related to both of them and accompanies them — there is no understanding apart from percepts and concepts. It is also to say that its proper "object" is not the thing as concretely perceived nor the thing as abstractly thought but precisely the being that unites the two. The being of the dog that we see and know is not, then, a reference to how we perceive it or class it; it refers, rather, to the factor that makes it possible for us to unite our particular perception and our general thought of the thing. Much confusion about the meaning of the correspondence theory of truth can be avoided if one bears this in mind. When it is said that truth consists of the agreement between understanding and reality, this does not mean the agreement between the mental concept of a thing and the physical appearance of the thing — it is not, in other words, the agreement between an idea and a thing. Rather, it is, more exactly, the agreement or correspondence between the understanding and the reality, that is, between the copula through which the mind grasps the unity of the object ("understanding," or *intellectus*) and the be-ing through which the object is what it is on its own ("reality," or *res*). More simply, it is the correspondence between the "is" ("was," "are," "were," "will be") of the judgment and the "is" of the thing. In that way it can also be said to lie in the distinctions. To understand is, in any case, always to understand being — the being of the thing that is the definite object of perceiving and knowing; and what is meant by the "being" of a thing is different from the thing as such. This is not to say that we always need to attend to the difference. In everyday circumstances, nothing of importance hangs on whether we are concerned with the being of a thing or with the thing — in a bakery, one does not have to distinguish between the bread, and the being of the bread, that one buys.

If understanding involves a uniting of singular percepts and universal concepts in the way just described, the principle that faith seeks understanding suggests that believing in God "seeks" to understand being. It suggests, in other words, that the understanding of being is also an interpretation of the trust in God. My suggestion here is that to "seek" means to "look for an interpretation." One language seeks another language to provide an interpretation of its own meaning; one act looks toward another act for its own completion. The language of faith can be transposed into the language of understanding in the sense that what we understand when we understand anything is an interpretation of the one we trust when we trust anyone. But this would seem to imply that trusting is, like understanding, an act of thinking in which two different aspects are synthesized. So we must ask: If understanding brings together percepts and concepts, what is brought together in *fides?* If the "being" of a thing means the unity of its singular and universal aspects, what unity is implied in the name *God?*

A guideline for seeing the sameness in the difference between the two is offered by the fact that our understanding of being always accompanies our perception and conception; our understanding is one of the three moments included in our thinking anything at all. The same can be applied to the act of trusting God. For just as being is not some invisible, other "thing" besides the things that we normally perceive or know, but is, instead, the be-ing of those very things, so God is not some other invisible object of trust besides the persons (or things) that we otherwise trust, but is, rather, the one that we are trusting when we trust anyone or anything at all. Being is not a Kantian noumenon or thing in itself, and God is not an invisible person.

A more difficult question concerns the other parallel between being, as what we understand, and God, as whom we trust. Being unites a singular and a universal. Everything that is anything at all is a singular ("this") and a universal ("kind of thing") in one. Hence, to understand being is to think of this thing *as* the kind of thing *it* is. If faith can seek understanding because faith and understanding are the same in the different, then the God who is the object of trust must, like being, bring together two different moments in the act of trust. The two moments brought together in understanding are those of perceiving (the singular) and conceiving (the universal). What are the two moments brought together in *fides?*

To answer this question, there is available, so far as I know, no critique of faith comparable to the critique of knowledge that Kant provided; and Kant's own placement of faith depends on his viewing faith as something between opining and knowing. Opinion, in Kant's description, is subjectively and objectively uncertain; knowledge is subjectively and objectively certain; and faith is subjectively certain but objectively uncertain. In faith one can be as certain of what one believes as one can be certain that one is moral. This is another conception of faith, however, than the *fides* that seeks understanding. Using this other conception of faith, we cannot see how faith and understanding are the same in the different as two modes of an original thinking. For such *fides* is not defined by comparison with opining and knowing but by its relation to understanding; God who is the object of its intention is the same as being which is the object of the intention of understanding. In that sense, *Deus est esse.* Schleiermacher's analysis will not do either; for if faith is prereflective feeling, then reflection can interpret expressions of faith, but expressions of faith do not interpret reflection. Wilhelm Herrmann's analysis of the role played by trust in the formation of moral being may offer a better guide than Kant's alignment of faith between opinion and knowledge or Schleiermacher's identification of it with immediate feeling. But even Herrmann did not provide the kind of critique of the act of trust that could supplement Kant's critique of knowledge or provide a basis for seeing faith and understanding as the difference of an identity. The work I have in mind is his *Ethik,* in which Herrmann explains the emergence of spiritual life out of natural life by reference to trust.[4] Ethos, or *Sittlichkeit,* is, he says, a behavior "in which human life is to transcend the species (*Art*) given by nature and to gain a new species of life through its own activity."[5] In that sense, ethos and its vitality are supra-natural. Such a life is first made possible in us, Herrmann goes on to say, by someone who elicits trust from us. One could even say, without violating Herrmann's argument, that it is the trustworthiness of another, when we become aware of it, that implants in us this new species of life. What is set forth in the present essay is only the preliminary sketch of a different conception.

The question is, then, whether we can see three moments in the act of trust that are analogous to the three moments in the act of understanding. Does the constellation of *notitia, assensus,* and *fiducia* in the traditional definition of faith provide help? I propose the thesis that trusting always unites a particular self (the self that "I" am) with the universality of selfhood at all, so that the act of believing is always one in which the human and divine are united (just as the act of understanding unites percept and concept). To put it differently: what occurs when we find it possible to trust anyone or anything at all is that we as isolated individuals are enabled to identify ourselves with a selfhood that is universal. This uniting of singular and universal is different from that of perception and conception but has the same structure, the structure of an act of *thinking*. To be able to trust or to believe means to be able to identify ourselves with a self that is "larger" than our own self. Radical trust is the identity of the I (the human) and the not-I (the divine). (It is possible that further distinctions need to be made between the community of an individual with universal selfhood and the community of the human and divine. But they do not seem to be necessary for the main point being made here.) The *notitia* is a "notice" of the other, "assent" is a sense of community with the other, and *fiducia* is the unity of the notice and assent. (I do not wish to suggest that this is how theologians who used those terms in the past to define elements of faith understood them, since they clearly did not so understand them.) That by reference to which the identifying is done is "God" (in the same way that "being" is that by reference to which the unity of singular percept and universal concept is achieved). Hence, to trust at all is to trust God, just as to understand at all is to understand being. Understanding being is the possibility of bringing together perception and conception, and trusting God is the possibility of bringing together the individuality of our self-awareness and the universality of selfhood as such, or the human and the divine. *Fiducia* is to notice and assent as understanding is to perception and conception. Mistrust is, similarly, the failure to unite, or the wrong uniting of, the human and the divine, just as misunderstanding is the failure to unite, or the wrong uniting of, percept and concept.

If the principle that faith seeks understanding is the principle of hermeneutical method in theology, it states the possibility of using the understanding of being as a way of interpreting the trusting in God. The language in which the understanding of being is expressed can thus be interpreted by the language in which the believing in God is expressed. What we are doing when we trust God is interpreted by what we are doing when we understand being; for to understand being is a different mode of trusting God. This is a different reading of the relation between God and being from the one that treats "God" and "being" as two names for the same metaphysical object. It is a reading that accentuates the hermeneutical aspect of the method implied in the fact that there are two basic modes of *thinking*—that of *fides* and that of *intellectus*—and that thinking as such is enacted only in one or both of these modes. If there is an identity between the believing in God (in the sense of trusting God) and the understanding of being, then the propositions in which faith is formulated can be translated into propositions in which understanding is formulated, and conversely; and they can interpret and test each other even though they cannot replace each other.

The basis for that reciprocity is that they are both modes of *thinking*. In one sense, understanding is the opposite of trusting, for to trust seems to mean a kind of not-understanding—I trust that things will come out all right but I do not understand how they can do so. Despite that apparent difference, the principle that faith seeks understanding, as a hermeneutical principle, means that the opposition between the two does not exclude their identity. The act of understanding being is not the act of trusting God; that is true. Yet, because they are both modes of thinking, there is an identity between them so that they not only "seek" each other but "find" each other when the one interprets the other. Each completes the other. *How* the completion takes places can be explained in various ways. Tillich's version of it, which is characteristic of Gilkey too, appeals to the correlation of questions and answers. Understanding being eventuates in a question to which trusting God provides an answer—or, in Tillich's terms, a question of being to which the symbol of God is the answer. Put in its most basic theoretical formulation, the correlation means that we can grasp everything by reference to being (in the unity of its singular and universal moments), but we cannot grasp being as such; hence, being ends as a question, to which an answer has to be provided by something other than what we can grasp.

Other versions of the method do not appeal to the structure of question and answer. Aquinas had recourse instead to a name that is intermediate between being as such and God, such as the names "prime mover," "first cause," and the like. As Thomas put it, everyone understands or calls the one the other—God the prime mover and the prime mover God. This is to say that in our understanding of things we reach a point at which understanding being coincides with trusting God and, conversely, trusting God coincides with understanding being. It is not entirely clear how that connection is made in Thomas. Gerhard Ebeling, for example, explains it as a linguistic phenomenon: A connection is made in language between the name of God and the name of the first cause.[6] But that must imply that something in the meaning of "God" is the same as something in the meaning of "the prime mover." What is that something? Very probably it has to do with the fact that we can at least understand that nothing in the world is a prime mover. To be the first cause or prime mover, and the like, is in any case to be *not* this or that or any other thing that is part of our experience of the world. But this is what we understand "God" to mean as well. Whoever or whatever God is, we understand the name to mean that God is *not* the world or anything in it and not I either. Thus, to the extent that we understand the prime mover to be nothing in the world or the world itself we can make a connection between the meaning in that idea and the meaning in the name of God. "Everyone" would call the prime mover (first cause, and the like) "God" to the extent that both God and such a mover are understood to be *not* this or that or any other definable thing.

Is the Unity of Faith and Understanding an Understanding?

The question that arises when one speaks in this way of *fides* and *intellectus* as two basic modes of thinking, irreducible to each other but interpretable by each other, is whether the thought that makes that connection is itself an exercise of faith or of understanding or of both. If believing in God and understanding being are said to *be* two modes of thinking, the very language we use to describe the relation between them suggests that it is understanding, rather than believing, that provides the connection between the two. This is, of course, understanding of a second degree — not an understanding of the being of things but an understanding of what thinking is. But understanding, even when thus potentiated, or raised to the second degree, is still understanding, so that the point of view from which we regard believing and understanding is that of understanding. We "understand" that our understanding and our believing are two modes of thinking; we "understand" the "being" of thinking.

Accordingly, although the very way in which we describe the matter does suggest that the difference that exists between believing in God and thinking of being at the first level does not apply at the second level, we should exercise further scrutiny before accepting this suggestion. True, when we say what faith and understanding are, we give expression to an understanding of their being; and, in the nature of the case, hermeneutical reflection will constitute an exercise of understanding. But it is also possible that the difference between understanding and believing is also effective for second-order understanding. If it is effective there, then our understanding of what understanding and believing are is but one side of our thinking of them; the other side is an activity that has the nature of *believing* our believing and understanding. Believing in believing may initially suggest the kind of empty action that critics of "faith in faith" rightly contemn: the view that it is important to believe that believing is important but not so important to have this rather than that content of believing. But that is not what is at issue here. Rather, the present concern focuses on the question of whether believing in God (what we are doing when we believe in, or trust, anything) can be raised to the second degree as can the understanding of being. The suggestion being made here is that believing in God can be so raised and that, therefore, the hermeneutical reflection, through which we understand the identity and difference in understanding being and trusting God, is itself not only an understanding of being (the being in our thinking) but also a trusting of God (the God in our trusting).

This is a subtle but important point. For it affects the question of whether our second-order thinking (in which we think about our think-ing) is enclosed in itself. If it is enclosed in itself, then the being of our thinking—the being of what we are doing—is likewise enclosed in itself, different from and unconnected with the being of the things that are other than our thinking. But our thinking process "is" something; it is a process among other processes, and, though it may require an agent, it does not require any particular person as an agent. The activ-ity in which I engage when I think is the same as the activity in which another person engages when he or she thinks. For that reason, even second-order thought—the understanding of our understanding as be-ing something—is directed toward the being that is other than thinking (even when it is the being of thinking). The meaning of the term *being* is different from the meaning of the term *thinking* even when we are speaking of the being of thinking. If that were not so, we could not tell the difference between the sense of the phrase "the being of thinking" and the sense of the phrase "the thinking of being."

The same considerations can be applied to the question of whether we both understand and believe the unity of believing and understand-ing. If it is true that the understanding of understanding is still directed toward being (even though it is the being of understanding rather than the being of things understood), it is also true that believing in believing is still directed toward God (though it is the God of believing rather than the God of things or persons believed). At the primary level we understand being by understanding things as being what they are (this as a tree, that as a rose, another thing as a dog, and so on); at the secondary level, we understand being by understanding our understanding as being what it is. Similarly, we trust God, in the primary sense, by trusting the community in things or persons (alien egos as expressions of selfhood); at the second level, we trust God by trusting our trusting as an expression of the community of self. And just as it is "being" that remains the object of understanding at both levels, so it is "God" who remains the object of trust at both levels.

In that sense the unity of faith and understanding is itself both faith and understanding.

Is This Onto-Theo-Logical Metaphysics?

By explicating the hermeneutical dimension of the notion that faith seeks understanding, or that believing in God is to be interpreted by understanding being, we determine that the "God" who is "being-itself" in this scheme is not the "God" about which Heidegger raised questions in his essay "The Onto-Theo-Logical Constitution of Metaphysics."[7] In that essay, Heidegger criticized the identification of God with being and suggested that the atheistic philosophy of the present century might be closer to the true God than is theistic metaphysics. He asked how it was that God even got into philosophy at all, and he answered the question by reference to the unthought difference between being and entities as well as between being in general and supreme being. God could get into metaphysics because Western metaphysics, thanks to the *Austrag,* or arrangement, by which it was carried out at all, did not think the thought that being as being is not the same as the supreme being nor did it think the thought that being-itself (*esse; das Sein*) is not the same as a supreme being or the supreme being (*ens supremum; das Seiende*). One might even read Aquinas's five ways as a confirmation of Heidegger's point despite their inclusion of a certain kind of difference. For Aquinas identifies God with being-itself and simultaneously with the first mover, prime cause, and the like; and he can do so at least by reference to our understanding that God and the prime mover are both *not* the world or ourselves. That *not* does introduce a difference between being and beings. But Thomas does not consider the difference in the ways that the two are "not" the world. That difference he leaves unthought.

Heidegger was not the first to enunciate this theme, though his was a distinctive variation on it. In the 1920s the dialectical theologians had raised similar questions about the identification of God and being, and there is an even older tradition of placing God beyond being and non-being altogether. But Heidegger has received recent attention through the work of the deconstructionists, and his questioning most directly challenges the identity of God and being on a philosophical, not only a theological, basis. It does so partly by severing the connection between God and being and partly by substituting ontological reflection on poetic words for the self-reflection of faith. What I have tried to show is that the challenge that is thus directed to a theistic, metaphysical God does not affect the hermeneutical conception of faith as seeking understanding. Instead, this identity in difference is the basis of a certain pluralism to the extent that it means we cannot say what God is, only what being is, and we cannot trust being, only God; but both our understanding of being and believing in God are modes of thinking. Far from being the basis of an ontotheological metaphysics, the principle holds God and being apart. If it joins them, it is not by means of the proposition "God is being" but by means of the proposition "God is God as (what is) not God." It is through such a being-as-not that a connection is made between God and entities and, from there, of God with being. If God and being are not identifiable except by reference to the difference between understanding and believing, then the notion of faith as seeking understanding, or conversely, is the basis of recognizing the pluralist constitution of human thinking and human being at all.

To say that human thinking is pluralistic is to say more than that each of us is a different perspectival point for the way we think of the world. That we are such perspectival points is no doubt true. Every act of thinking is an act emerging from a point, an agent, that has perspectival uniqueness. But the pluralism of thinking, strictly taken, means more than that; it means that thinking as such is expressed in at least two fundamental modes that can never be reduced to each other. Thinking as thinking appears only in the form of understanding being and of believing God. The two acts are different from each other; their intentions (being; God) are different from each other; the difference between them cannot be collapsed or absorbed into a higher mode of thinking. In all that, they are irreducibly two. To put the matter differently, ontology and theology are equally original and irreducible. Yet the two "seek" each other because the one provides an interpretation of the other. What it means to understand being is made clear by trusting God, and what it means to trust God is made clear by understanding being. What connects the two is not some third mode but the metaphorical power of moving between them. That this metaphorical power has some connection with the negative, or with difference as difference, is indicated by the way in which God's not being the world or anything in it and being's not being a being of any kind provide the path, in the world or among entities, for moving between them. That we can recognize the one we trust ("God") and the one we understand ("being") to be other than the world or anything in it, other than an entity, is the path, the *hodos* of the *methodos,* along which we move from the one to the other.

"Faith seeking understanding" would not be the principle of pluralism if it meant that the object of believing can be made an object of understanding or if meant that there were a mode of thinking in which the difference between faith (in God) and understanding (of being) were not longer present. It would not be a principle of pluralism, in other words, if it meant that "God" can be identified with "being." It is a principle of pluralism, however, if it is the formulation of a hermeneutical method that reflects the metaphorical nature of thinking itself which arises out of the "not," or difference as difference.

NOTES

1. *Kirchliche Dogmatik* I/1: 199f.
2. Johann Friedrich König, *Theologia positiva acroamatica* (1664), §55.
3. This does not necessarily imply that the act of putting the two together is one of "subsuming" a particular under a universal. It means only that, however one further explains the synthesizing, what is involved is that we put together concrete perceptions with abstract conceptions in order to form the whole judgment. The term *subsumption* does, however, point to the connection with understanding (like the term *substance,* which, literally, means under-standing).
4. Wilhelm Herrmann, *Ethik* (Tübingen: J.C.B. Mohr/Paul Siebeck, 1901, 1913).
5. Ibid., p. 12.
6. "Existenz zwischen Gott und Gott," *Zeitschrift für Theologie und Kirche* 62, 1:100.
7. English and German text published in *Identity and Difference,* trans. Joan Stambaugh (New York: Harper & Row, 1969),

Chapter 13

The Question of Criteria for Inter-Religious Dialogue: A Tribute to Langdon Gilkey

DAVID TRACY

IT IS DIFFICULT TO THINK OF A MAJOR THEOLOGICAL OR CULTURAL IS-
SUE not addressed in the theology of Langdon Gilkey. In his extraordinary theological career he has consistently spotted, formulated, and addressed the questions demanding Christian theological attention in our
ever-changing cultural and historical situation. With the exception of
Paul Tillich, it is difficult to name another twentieth-century theologian
who so straightforwardly addresses the major issues that the incredible history of our century forces upon our attention. Grounded in his
first love, historical theology, Gilkey (like his two great mentors Reinhold Niebuhr and Tillich himself) has fashioned a theological method
or correlation of "message" and "existence" that has been addressed
to all the major "situational" issues (process, science, history, politics,
the "death of God" movement, secularity, reason, culture, symbol, and
most recently, the world religions) in direct relationship to all the major
Christian symbols.[1]

In rereading Gilkey's major works for this article I became increasingly aware how much I (and a great number of others) have learned
from, even often been shaped by, his unfailing ability to raise the next
major situational issue in direct relationship to an exceptional grasp of
the entire history of Christian theological reflection. Who but Gilkey
would have spotted so clearly and so early the difficulties of the "God

who acts" biblical theology? The "mythical" dimension of science? The importance of the "death of God" movement for all theology? The need to retrieve the doctrine of providence in the heyday of eschatology? The crisis of Western culture become the crisis of Western notions of rationality? The challenge of religious pluralism to all Christian theological symbols, not only the doctrine of Christ?

The list could easily be expanded but these examples may suffice to warrant my contention: No theologian of our time has been clearer or more daring in acknowledging the ever new questions that must be asked nor more persuasive in responding to those questions theologically. In this essay I have adopted a somewhat peculiar strategy: rather than analyzing Gilkey's own analysis of the question of religious pluralism, I have chosen to pay tribute to his influence by writing my own present response to the question of religious pluralism. The fact is that Langdon Gilkey first persuaded me to address this question in our joint courses on the subject for the last three years. His brilliant proposals — on "rough parity," "relative absolutes," and the category of the "intolerable" — have clearly influenced my own present formulations. Our differences lie mostly in his typical recourse to dialectics and dialectical categories, like those cited above, in contrast to my own typical recourse to analogy and analogical-pluralistic categories, like those developed below. These different strategies represent two distinct but related strategies (perhaps classically Protestant and classically Catholic) in the Christian theological tradition.[2] But however serious these differences in response may, in the long run, prove to be, the similarity is what most strikes me now. I find no better way to indicate the profound influence of my friend, colleague, and mentor, Langdon Gilkey, than to provide an example of the kind of response that his questions and his responses have provoked in my own theology. Whether he fully approves of that influence, I do not know. But the existence of his influence may serve to suggest this text of an alternative but related response to the latest question he has formulated for us all — the question of religious pluralism and its import for Christian theology.

As any theologian involved in serious inter-religious dialogue soon learns, her or his earlier theological thoughts on the "other religions" soon become spent. There is no more difficult or more pressing question on the present theological horizon than that of inter-religious dialogue. Part of that question must be the question of possible criteria for the dialogue itself. Such criteria, if available, must not claim to replace the dialogue but, at best, heuristically to inform it.

My own risk in this essay is to attempt to formulate some general criteria. I am painfully aware of their inadequacy but just as painfully aware of the need to attempt them. That awareness, in my case, arises from four sources: first, the development of modern Western hermeneutics modelled on dialogue and conversation and the pressing question of its applicability or non-applicability to the questions of cross-cultural dialogue and, even more difficult, inter-religious dialogue;[3] second, my own involvement for some years in Jewish-Christian dialogues and Buddhist-Christian dialogues as well as in ancient Greek religion; third, the impact for me of the work of Mircea Eliade and the challenge of his great retrieval of the archaic religions for all theological thought; and fourth, as noted above, the impact of the daring and groundbreaking work of my colleague, Langdon Gilkey, with his categories of "parity," "relative absolutes," and the "intolerable."[4]

My strategy — a groping one, I admit — is as follows: to return to a thinker who tried honestly to face this question in early modernity, William James, in order to see what revisions may be needed in the general criteria he once advanced. Accordingly, the present essay has two parts: first, an interpretation of James's own position and then a reformulation of his criteria for contemporary discussions. If these criteria fail, that too can be a gain: to learn one road not to travel can sometimes be as fruitful as learning the right one. But that, of course, only the conversation itself can tell.

William James on Describing and Evaluating Religion

The most notable fact about William James on religion remains the multiplicity of his responses and interests — indeed to the point where the notion "fact" dissolves as clearly as the "substantial self" dissolves into multiplicity in *The Principles of Psychology*. There is no one Jamesian view on either describing or assessing "religion." There is no single and recognizably Jamesian argument on religion with which, as with, say, Kant, one can argue. James's position is less like an argument and more like a rather diverse and sometimes rambling conversation. It is a conversation filled with valuable and sometimes extraordinary insights on how to describe religion in all its variety and how to assess it in all its complexity.

In the *Varieties of Religious Experience* James named his own final position on religion "piecemeal" supernaturalism. My own interpretation of his position(s) here might be named a "piecemeal" interpretation largely for the same reasons that he resisted a "wholesale" supernaturalism. The latter seems improbable. The former seems both possible and promising. I shall, therefore, in these brief reflections signal a few typically Jamesian moves on religion, at least those that seem most characteristically James and most worth discussing. These two criteria for reflection usually go together but not always: for example, James's actual description and defense of "pragmatism" (as distinct from that of Peirce) is, however, central to James's overall position, less insightful, and surely less persuasive, than he thought.

One factor above all strikes one about James on religion that distinguishes him from most Western philosophers of religion: his insistence on variety. To read *The Varieties* is to be exposed to a remarkable range of religious options: from classics like Wesley and Teresa of Avila or Luther and Al-Ghazzali to a whole range of then contemporary memoirs collected by Starbruck and others. The insistence on the variety of religion to the point that it may be difficult even to use the word "religion" has now become something of a commonplace among several scholars in contemporary religious studies (e.g., W. C. Smith and John Cobb). James felt at home with the word "religion," even defining its common characteristics, although in three quite different ways, in *The Varieties* alone. He did believe that in all that difference there was enough commonality to allow us to speak coherently of "religion" as "the feelings, acts, and experiences of individual men in their solitude, so far as they apprehend themselves to stand in relation to whatever they may consider the divine."[5]

But granted that the commonalities delineated by James now have been controverted, it is clear that the sheer variety — the "republican feast" side — of religion attracted James most. And his same insistence on variety attracts most of his later readers. There is truth to the various charges that James's own "variety" was highly limited. In one sense, his choices, however various, were very late Victorian: many selections from Christianity, some from Judaism and Islam, some comments on the other "high" religions (Buddhism, Hinduism) with most other religions thrown together as "pagan" (the Greek and Roman religions) or "savage" (the primal or archaic religions). At the same time one must note James's clear interest in and commitment to the then nascent "science of religions" as the discipline (far more than theology or philosophy) on which James pinned his hopes both for describing religions *and* for eventually assessing them.

What consistently interested James in the religions was religious ex-

perience, especially the "feeling" element. What interested him was
what he named a "full fact": "a conscious field *plus* its object as felt or
thought of *plus* an attitude towards the object plus the sense of a self to
whom the attitude belongs."[6] The best of James's thought on religion,
I believe, is found in his insistence on personal experience as *the* locus
for religion and as that which needs both describing and assessing. It
is true, of course, that such an insistence exacts a price — namely, a
failure to account for other crucial aspects of the religious phenomenon,
such as the institutional, or even social (recall von Hügel or Royce or
Troeltsch among James's own contemporaries) or the more strictly intellectual expressions in philosophies and theologies (recall the Hegelians
and neo-Kantians among James's contemporaries). It is odd, I admit,
that the great proponent of the variety of religious experiences neglected
such crucial aspects of religion as the institutional and the intellectual.

Odd, but not fatal: for James clearly knew that here he was par-
tial, but for a reason. The reason remains worth dwelling upon: Many
philosophers and theologians seem finally not very interested in what
religious persons may experience (or think they experience). Rather
they are interested only in whatever cognitive claims religious experience might entail. Somewhat like the theologians of the Roman Curia,
most philosophers seem interested *only* in the cognitive *beliefs* implied
or entailed by religious *faith* rather than trying to describe and assess
the experience which that faith as a fundamental orientation involves.
It is not that James was not interested in the assessment of cognitive
claims; as we shall see below, he was very interested and, I think, very
interesting. It is, rather, that he believed that most philosophical and
theological attempts at assessing religion analyze only the side of religious experience identified as "cognitive claim" (or "belief") and fail to
recognize that this is exactly what they are doing. The "religion," as
analyzed by many philosophers and theologians, often becomes a phenomenon that involves some rather strange, not to say odd or bizarre,
"beliefs" that demand assessment. At its clearest, this becomes a "religion is really x" position. Recall Santayana, for whom "religion is poetry
which intervenes in life; poetry is religion which supervenes upon life."
Recall Braithwaite, for whom religion is really morality with some stories added to help one internalize the morality. Recall W. C. Clifford
(James's adversary in *The Will to Believe*) for whom religion seems to
be an immoral credulity in odd and unpersuasive cognitive claims or
beliefs.

Above all William James conceived religion as some kind of personal experience: at its best, a "full fact" experience. Because religion as experience is what must first be described before being assessed, we need to try to describe those classic documents that describe religious experience. Because religious experience needs to be described in its distinctive characteristics *as* religious (rather than by means of those characteristics it shares with morality, art, metaphysics, etc.), James appealed to the "extreme cases" (e.g., the "saints" and the "mystics"). But James was not interested only in the "extreme cases" because of their extremity. Indeed, if that were so, why would he have provided so generous an account of the "healthy-minded?" Why not only the "extreme cases" of the "healthy-minded" (like Walt Whitman or Emerson) rather than such less extreme versions as the "mind-cure" movements or "liberal Christianity"? Those interested in extreme cases, after all, are usually interested principally if not exclusively in James's "sick-soul" types. They are tempted to think of the "healthy-minded" examples of the "moral" rather than the "religious."

Any analyst of religious experience should, I believe, at some point follow James's advice and study *first* (not *only*) the "extreme cases" in all their variety — from "sick-soul" to "healthy-minded," from James's mystic and saint to Eliade's shaman and guru to Buber's prophet. In one sense, James's strategy follows a suggestion often voiced: "I may not be able to define religion but I know it when I see it." Whatever *else* Wesley or Luther or Teresa of Avila or John of the Cross are, they are recognizably religious. If we can, in some descriptive manner, analyze their experience by interpreting their texts, we have good candidates for characteristics that may prove recognizably religious.

The logic of James's move from analyzing "personal experience" by interpreting "extreme case" documents purporting to describe that experience remains, I think, a plausible strategy for anyone wishing to describe one crucial aspect of religion: viz., the individual's experience of religion insofar as others can understand that experience by interpreting the documents (e.g., of "conversion" — one of James's favorite topics) that claim to describe it. Such descriptions, if successful, would admittedly not cover the institutional and the strictly intellectual aspects of religion. Nevertheless, such descriptions would cover, for James, the heart of the matter: those experiences which are distinctively religious. Most of the *Varieties* is concerned with description of those experiences — the latter, to repeat, is interpreted through various documents. The *Varieties* (as well as James's other works) also includes assessments of this religious experience worth noting.

James's enterprise of assessing or evaluating religious experience was as various as were his descriptions of religious experience itself. I make no claim to interpret exhaustively all his many strategies of assessment; and they were many: from the *Principles of Psychology* through the *Pragmatism* essays to *A Pluralistic Universe* to the final (or was it?) position of *Essays in Radical Empiricism.* My own belief is that to render James's position of assessing or evaluating any phenomenon, especially religion, strictly coherent would not do justice to the "buzzing, blooming confusion" of the experience that William James was intent on communicating with all his rhetorical skill.[7]

Nevertheless there are still some moves for evaluation that are characteristically Jamesian, both early and later. The first set of typical moves may be found in what might be named James's essays on assessing religious belief for oneself, in what might be called psychological and sometimes philosophical reasons for religious belief. The most famous of such criteria are, to be sure, those in the *Essays in Morality and Religion,* especially the famous "Will to Believe" essay.[8] As James later recognized, this essay (and the larger project in the other related essays) should have been named "The Right to Believe." By his haste (and perhaps his wish to provoke) James handed his critics an easy charge: that he was defending sheer "fideism" with his "will to believe." Indeed, the furor over the "will to believe" phrase was analogous to the clamor over this equally unfortunate phrase, the "cash-value" of an idea.

What James really attempted to defend about "religious belief," however, was the "right to believe." In general, for James we have such a right whenever the beliefs in question are "live," "forced," and "momentous." By a "live" hypothesis James meant a real possibility that could guide one's conduct. If a belief could not guide a person's conduct, then a decision for or against that belief is no decision at all: It is dead.

Decisions are "forced" only if they are live as well as possessing the characteristic that it is impossible not to choose one of two logically distinct options presented. Such "live and forced" options present the imperative: "Either accept this truth or go without it."

"Momentous" decisions, as distinct from trivial ones, are characterized by their ability to show a difference that the person can experience. For James, true decisions on all beliefs, including religious beliefs, should be live, forced, and momentous.

I have recalled this familiar Jamesian position in the larger argument of "Will to Believe" in order to indicate the kinds of moves James was wont to make: not, for example, how for him "live" options tended towards criteria of conduct, "forced" options to criteria of logical coherence, and "momentous" options to criteria of personal experience. What interests me here is that, on this reading at least, there can be a "rough coherence" between James's basic position on evaluating religious belief "from within" in "Will to Believe" and his assessment of religious experience from "outside" in his similar criteria in the sometimes disparate comments on criteria of assessment in the *Varieties* itself. Indeed, I believe that such a rough coherence was present in James all along or, as he liked to say, "on the whole." On the whole, I read James (who once quipped that his position should be named "on the wholeism") as holding to the same *kind* of criteria whether judging nonreligious phenomena (as the *Principles* or in the *Pragmatism* essays) or religious phenomena (either from "within" as in "Will to Believe," or from "outside" as in the *Varieties*).

These general criteria are delineated in psychological and philosophical terms. In psychological terms, best expressed in *The Principles of Psychology*, one can find an adequate psychological description of a given reality only when one can account for (1) perceptions (including experience in the broad sense — i.e., feelings, moods, attitudes, and not only "sense-experience" as in classical empiricism), (2) conceptions, and (3) volitions. And in philosophical terms, which are, for James, largely terms of assessment just as psychological terms are largely terms of description, one needs (1) criteria of a full empiricism — indeed, finally, a radical empiricism where his notion of experience is given full sway; (2) criteria of logical coherence — James's weakest link as critics from Royce to Russell and even frustrated allies like Peirce insisted, and as James himself conceded; and (3) criteria of pragmatism — in the sense of the consequences for action of all ideas.

My claim is that psychologically and philosophically these roughly coherent criteria for both description and evaluation of any phenomenon are also the criteria present in James's actual descriptions and evaluations of religious experience in the *Varieties*. In brief, note the rough coherence of the psychological and philosophical criteria cited above with James's insistence in the *Varieties* [9] that "on the whole" the criteria for assessment of religious experience remain: (1) "immediate luminousness" (i.e., perception and personal experience in the broad, even radical sense); (2) coherence with what we otherwise know or believe to be the case (as in the description of live, forced, momentous options); and (3) individual and social practical consequences.

If my reading is correct here, then it may also partly illumine three remaining puzzles in James. First, his concern with mysticism is a concern, above all, to try to describe and assess any claims to "immediate luminousness" for mystics and for others observing mystics. Second, the concern with "saintliness" is principally a concern with consequences and (interestingly enough, for so famous an individualist) principally for the *social* consequences of the "saint." Third, the whole of the assessment of religion in the *Varieties* must cohere with what one otherwise knows and believes (e.g., in psychology and philosophy). This is why, I think, James believed that mystics would find their experience irrefutable but the rest of us could not accord it that status. But we could affirm that mystics' accounts of their experience do allow us to affirm our belief (which coheres with but is clearly not identical with theirs) in the reality of "something more."

In sum, James remains intriguing because he seems so basically fair to the variety of religious experiences he describes and so multiple, subtle, and coherent in his tentative assessments of these experiences. On the whole, I think that James not only seems fair, but fundamentally he succeeds: he *is* a good interpreter and assessor of the variety of religious experiences, for William James is often immediately luminous in what he says, he is roughly coherent in the ways suggested above, and he does provide good practical consequences — like allowing the plurality of religious experiences to yield to a genuinely pluralistic attitude to religion like his own. He remains the classic early modern student of religious pluralism.

A Rethinking of Jamesian Criteria

However suggestive James's classic study of the variety of religious experiences may be, it is equally important to emphasize its severe limitations. Much has happened since his study — in philosophy, in theology, in history of religions, and, above all, in history itself. His candidates for religious pluralism, however generous for the early twentieth century, seem now clearly limited — Western, and even parochial. It is not merely the relative lack of attention he accords the great traditions of Asia, especially Buddhism in all its plurality and Hinduism with its traditions of pluralism; it is the fact that these great traditions have now also become genuine "live" options for Westerners. Western Buddhists, especially those in the United States, have changed traditional Asian forms of Buddhism in notable ways. Recall Jeffrey Hopkins, Robert

Thurman, and the thinkers at the Naropa Institute in Tibetan Buddhism, or Francis Cook and others in Zen Buddhism. Recall as well the fruitfulness of the many Buddhist-Christian dialogues (including the one organized by Maseo Abe and John Cobb, which I have been honored to participate in with Langdon Gilkey.[10] The Western Buddhists have not merely rendered Buddhism a live option for many Westerners but have subtly changed Buddhism itself as radically as the earlier classic shifts from India to Thailand, Tibet, China, and Japan once did. The power and attractiveness of many gurus and Hindu philosophical thinkers among Westerners has also yielded yet new Western forms of both Hinduism and Sikhism.

Moreover, the magisterial work of Mircea Eliade on the great archaic and primal traditions and their challenge of an archaic ontology as well as the explosion of work by historians of religions and anthropologists on many religious locative traditions in Oceania, Africa, and the Americas has exponentially increased the radical variety of religion beyond James's imagination. In Christian theology alone, the number of theologians who now acknowledge that Christian self-understanding can no longer treat the question of religious pluralism in either tradition exclusivist or, often, even inclusivist categories has increased greatly: from the pioneering work and often conflicting proposals of Raimundo Panikkar, W. C. Smith, John Hick, and John Cobb to the recent work of Julia Ching, Langdon Gilkey, Paul Knitter, Gordon Kaufman, Leonard Swidler, Rosemary Radford Ruether, Will Oxtoby, Schubert Ogden, Hans Küng, Wolfhart Pannenberg, and many others. The list of strictly theological proposals for serious inter-religious dialogue is now at the point where it is difficult to understand how any serious theologian in any tradition cannot accord the issue of religious pluralism a central role in her or his thinking. The expanding list of "live options" and conflicting proposals either for dialogue or resulting from dialogue make contemporary theology more and more genuinely pluralistic amid a conflict of interpretations.

On the philosophical side, moreover, James's relatively sanguine contentment with the categories "experience" and "religious experience" has now been properly (and, I have argued elsewhere, correctly) challenged by the linguistic turn in all its permutations and conflicts. Those conflicts include the recent centrality given to radical plurality in post-structuralist thought (centered around the category *difference*) and the increasing sense of the ambiguity of all traditions exposed by history itself and by the many new forms of ideology-critique and dialectical thought (centered around the category "the other"). Even the category "religion," as is well known, has come under increasing suspicion for its Western (more exactly Romano-Christian) overtones.

In such an intellectually parlous situation, it may seem an odd choice to return to one of the earliest modern attempts to deal intellectually with religious pluralism, William James. My apologia for my choice must be a brief one: James's *Varieties of Religious Experience* is, I continue to believe, a classic. Like all classics, it combines a curious datedness with an excess and permanence of meaning that yield fruitful reflection for later interpreters. Such, at least, is my belief on classics in general and on the *Varieties* in particular. I will now risk that belief by trying to show how James's very general, flexible, and fruitful criteria might be reformulated for our present concern for some criteria for serious inter-religious dialogue.

First of all, James's category of "immediate luminousness" can be usefully shifted to the wider hermeneutical category of "possibility." Insofar as hermeneutics since Gadamer is itself grounded in the category of conversation and dialogue, and insofar as hermeneutics is fashioned to relate experience directly to language, hermeneutics proves a fruitful philosophical tradition for all concerned with the meaning and import of all serious dialogue and the indirect (i.e., through language) character of all the "experiences" available for interpretation. (Even James, after all, had to rely on texts to interpret the "religious experiences" he believed he was interpreting).

Moreover, as post-Gadamerian hermeneutics has yielded its own history-of-effects, there is now available, *pace* Gadamer, a greater role both for explanatory methods (Ricoeur), ideology-critique (Habermas), and plurality than an earlier hermeneutics envisaged.[11] A notion of "dialogue" that has no place for these central intellectual, moral, and even religious demands tempts one, alas, by too easy notions of "similarity" or even "sameness," and too sanguine a notion of the complementarity of all the religions.

Granted these important caveats, hermeneutics shows how dialogue remains the central hope for recognizing the "possibilities" (and, therefore, the live options) that any serious conversation with the "other" and the "different" can yield. It matters relatively little whether the dialogue is through person-to-person dialogue or through that peculiar form of dialogue we call serious reading of texts, rituals, or events. To recognize the other *as* other, the different *as* different is also to acknowledge that another world of meaning has, in some manner, a possible option for myself. The traditional language of analogy may still prove that, in admittedly a new form, one way to formulate how, after any genuine dialogue, what once seemed merely other now seems a real possibility and thereby, in some manner, now seems similar to what I have already experienced (including religiously). I acknowledge that I and others who are trying to formulate "an analogical imagination" as one strategy for envisioning religious pluralism must be not only wary but downright suspicious of how easily claims to "analogy" or "similarity" can become subtle evasions of the other and the different. Similarity cannot be a cover-word for the rule of the same.[12] Hence we still need to remind ourselves linguistically of this great danger by speaking not of "analogies" as "similarities" (*simpliciter*) but of analogies as always already similarities-in-difference.

But whatever the fate of the strategy of "an analogical imagination" for rendering the possibilities discovered through dialogue into similarities-in-difference, the larger issue is elsewhere: viz., in the category of "possibility" itself. My earlier shift from James's category of "immediate luminousness" to the category of "suggestive possibility" suggests that the adjective "suggestive" is meant to serve as a reminder that "possibility" need not be a "live, momentous, and forced" option for the interpreter in order to prove a genuine possibility. As reception-theory (Jauss) in hermeneutics reminds us, a whole spectrum of responses to any classic is available. That spectrum can range all the way from a shock of recognition (in aesthetic terms) or "faith" or "enlightenment" (in religious terms) to a sense of tentative response to a genuine, i.e., live, but not forced or momentous option, on the other end of the spectrum. The spectrum remains a real spectrum (and not a mere *congeries* of responses) insofar as any genuine *possibility* evoked by the conversation itself is produced. What little I understand of Buddhist "compassion" I do not understand on inner-Buddhist grounds of enlightenment. Yet I can respond and have responded to that classic notion with a resonance to the challenge it poses to my own Christian notions of love.

A further advantage of the hermeneutical category of suggestive possibility produced by serious inter-religious dialogue is the fundamentally aesthetic rather than ethical character of the category "possibility." The hermeneutical tradition from Heidegger through Gadamer and Ricoeur has defended the primordial notion of truth-as-manifestation (not correspondence, strict coherence, or empirical verification or falsification). This notion of truth as manifestation (more exactly, with Heidegger, as disclosure-concealment)[13] has two singular advantages for this first general set of criteria for inter-religious dialogue. The first advantage is that the notion of truth-as-manifestation more closely fits both notions of "revelation" or its analogues in many religions and notions of "enlightenment" in other religions or ways. The same notion of religious manifestation, like the experience of truth in works of art, also frees this first set of criteria to have a more aesthetic rather than either ethical or "scientific" cast. The advantage here (as James with his category of "immediate luminousness" and his focus on the "mystics" for "cognitive" issues also implicitly recognized) is that the question of criteria for truth in religious dialogue will not only be ethical-pragmatic or scientific-metaphysical. Although the later criteria remain relevant, as we shall see below, the imposition (especially by Western partners to the inter-religious dialogue) of solely ethical (e.g., justice or social-political liberation) or solely verificationist or Western metaphysical notions would be challenged.

The truth of religion is, like the truth of its nearest cousin, art, primordially the truth of manifestation. Hermeneutical thought, with its defense of this notion, is, I believe, well-suited to defending anew this primal insight of both art and religion. In that sense, such thought (with its attendant criteria) is useful for reopening the highly complex questions of mysticism, of revelation, of enlightenment. Such thought may also reopen the question of why so many Buddhist thinkers (especially Zen) refuse too sharp a distinction between the aesthetic and the religious.

As further developments within recent Western hermeneutics indicate, however, one need not and should not stop in the dialogue with the first set of criteria any more than James stopped with "immediate luminousness." But one should dwell there long enough to allow the truth of the other to become, somewhere along the spectrum, a genuine possibility for oneself, in however transformed a form. "To understand at all is to understand differently." To understand at all is to understand from and within genuine dialogue allowing real manifestations of the other's truth and thereby mutual transformation. The kind of further questions appropriate for the dialogue and, thereby, the kind of further general criteria available can now be clarified by a return to and reformulation of James's other two sets of criteria.

Let us name the second set of criteria a rough coherence with what we otherwise know or more likely believe to be the case. The danger here is that, especially for Western conversation-partners, this set of cognitive criteria (under rubrics, for example, like strict verification and strict falsification) will so quickly take over the conversation that notions of truth in art and religion as manifestatory will become distant memories.

But here, surely, several recent Western philosophical discussions of reason itself are enormously helpful for fighting that scientistic (not scientific) temptation. In an intellectual situation where even philosophers of natural science (e.g., Kuhn and Toulmin) have challenged earlier reigning paradigms of scientism and "rationality," many (but, to be sure, not all) in the philosophical community have far more flexible notions of "truth" and "reason" than was once the case in the heyday of positivism.[14] Science itself is now acknowledged as also a hermeneutic enterprise. What one now finds is a historically and hermeneutically informed philosophy of science (Toulmin) as well as philosophically informed history of science. It is not merely the case, as Hegel insisted, that the fact that reason has a history is a problem for reason. It is also the case that the history of reason includes the history of relatively adequate (e.g., Aristotle) and inadequate (e.g., positivism) accounts of reason. Hence the emergence of historically informed "consensus" theories of rationality (Apel, Habermas, Bernstein). I do not pretend by these brief references to imply that the problem of an adequate notion of reason is readily available. Of course, there is no *de facto* consensus among contemporary philosophers on what rational consensus in principle is. But this, for the purposes of the inter-religious dialogue, is not necessarily unfortunate. If, in fact, philosophers like Bernstein show a genuinely rational way to recover the classical resources of reason (e.g., Aristotelian *phronesis* and Peirce's "community of inquiry") then, minimally, the discussion of "reason and religion" should be freed from what Bernstein nicely labels both "objectivism" and "relativism." Those two options, which are so familiar in the recent past and so fatal for serious dialogue of any sort, are spent. Rather we are left with more flexible but no less rational criteria for the rough coherence of what truth-as-manifestations we may glean from art and religion with what we otherwise know reasonably from science or, more likely, believe in accordance with the present consensus of rational inquirers.

The situation for inter-religious dialogue (as for comparative studies in history of religions) has become, in sum, far more flexible. Many of us believe that the best step forward (in keeping with Aristotelian *phronesis*) is to find concrete examples for dialogue on comparison (e.g., Christian love and Buddhist compassion). We should dialogue on such concrete issues in order to see, by fidelity to the logic of the questioning set loose by the subject-matter, what ensues. This strategy, which has proved so fruitful in contemporary philosophy of science, is surely a more promising step forward than one more round of bringing all religious claims to truth once more before the "bar of rationality." If the demands of reason in concrete cases are observed, if a rough coherence between the truths of religion and art and the truths of science and philosophy does obtain in the dialogue, that can, for the moment, suffice. This *"solvitur ambulando"* strategy, so congenial to James, can provide a proper strategy forward for the contemporary inter-religious dialogue with the crucial proviso that the demands of reason, however chastened from earlier positivist notions of rationality, must be allowed full sway in every conversation worthy of the name.

As any participant in serious inter-religious dialogue soon discovers, moreover, a further set of criteria will and should emerge — generically ethical-political criteria.[15] These criteria, so familiar to the prophetic trajectories of the religions, enter the conversation by two routes. First, the religions themselves, especially but not solely in their prophetic strands, demand them. Secondly, our very nature as human beings demands ethical assessment. For example, it is noteworthy how frequently Jewish, Christian, and Islamic conversation partners, in fidelity to both their prophetic heritages and to their contemporary ethical-political concerns, raise these issues in inter-religious dialogues: Recall John Hick's recent work, or Hans Küng's criteria of the *humanum,* or Emil Fackenheim's Jewish post-Holocaust "return to history," or Fazlur Rahman's revisionary Islamic theology, or Rosemary Radford Ruether's Christian feminist concerns, or Rita Gross's Buddhist feminist concerns, or Paul Knitter's liberationist emphasis.

The "pragmatic" turn of hermeneutics itself, as indeed of much contemporary philosophical discourse, fully shares in this insistence on the need for ethical-political criteria. In that sense, we are all the heirs of James's insistence on the criteria of "ethical, humane" fruits, or consequences for action — both individually and societally. Even here, however, our situation is more difficult and more parlous than the one James envisaged. On the "individual" side, the rampant problems of individualism (Bellah *et al.*) have become a major ethical dilemma for modern Western societies. More difficult still, the very notion of the "self," so cherished in almost all Western philosophies and theologies (even those, like process thought, that are highly critical of earlier "substantialist" notions of the self), has become a central problem in inter-religious dialogue where several highly sophisticated Buddhist and Hindu notions of "no-self" enter to radicalize all more familiar Western (e.g., James or even Lacan) revisionary notions of "self."

The ethical-social-political criteria meet similar challenges: above all, from the philosophical discovery of the inevitability of socio-political realities embedded in all discourse and the Jewish-Christian-and-Islamic reformulation of the prophetic strands of these traditions into several distinct and often competing liberationist theologies. Here too, only a *"solvitur ambulando"* approach grounded in dialogue and faithful to the demands of the dialogue itself can hope to yield much fruit. In the meantime, James's pragmatic criteria of ethical (and, by implication, social and political) consequences for action (recall his analysis of "saints") remains a necessary set of general and flexible criteria for serious inter-religious dialogue.

That these criteria themselves need further reflection and refinement beyond the brief analysis given above (or beyond even my more extended reflections on them elsewhere) is obvious. Even if these criteria are, on the whole, sound, they still cannot replace the actual inter-religious dialogue but only inform it with the kind of questions and some general heuristic criteria for those questions. Moreover, the criteria illuminate but, on their own, do not resolve the inner-theological issue of the nature of Ultimate Reality: one or plural, God or Emptiness, Atman or the One?

However, such criteria may still aid us all as we struggle on the *terra incognita* of our present acknowledgment of religious pluralism as a question for all religious thinkers in all traditions. Prior to serious inter-religious dialogue, we cannot in principle rule out "inclusivism" or even "exclusivism." But, for many of us, as the dialogues become more serious and more a part of our everyday way of thinking religiously and theologically, some envisionment of radical religious pluralism becomes a live option.[16] Only the further conversations can show the way forward for any of us — on the whole.

NOTES

1. For an example of Gilkey's own method of correlation, see his *Message and Existence: An Introduction to Christian Theology* (New York: Seabury, 1980). For one example of his recent work on inter-religious dialogue, see the essays in *Society and the Sacred* (New York: Crossroad, 1981), pp. 121–170.

2. Is it entirely accidental, I wonder, that modern secular French thinkers choose the category "difference" and modern secular German thinkers choose the dialectical category "the other." For examples, see Gilles Deleuze, *Difference et repetition* (Paris: Presses Universitaires de France, 1968), and Michel Theunissen, *The Other: Studies in the Ontology of Husserl, Heidegger, Sartre and Buber* (Cambridge: MIT Press, 1984).

3. For my own development of these categories see *Plurality and Ambiguity: Hermeneutics, Religion, Hope* (San Francisco: Harper & Row, 1987).

4. See Gilkey's recent, forthcoming essays on these categories — essays that I have been privileged to hear in our joint classes on religious pluralism.

5. William James, *The Varieties of Religious Experience* (Cambridge: Harvard University Press, 1985), p. 34.

6. Ibid., p. 393. The best study of James's notion of a "full fact" remains John Wild, *The Radical Empiricism of William James* (Garden City, N.Y.: Doubleday, 1969).

7. For a good study see Henry Samuel Levinson, *The Religious Investigations of William James* (Chapel Hill: University of North Carolina Press, 1981). There remains a need for a full study of James as a rhetorical thinker.

8. William James, *The Will to Believe and Other Essays* (Cambridge: Harvard University Press, 1982).

9. *The Varieties of Religious Experience*, p. 23.

10. The papers for these conferences are being published in the journal *Buddhist-Christian Studies*. See also John B. Cobb, Jr., *Beyond Dialogue: Toward a Mutual Transformation of Christianity and Buddhism* (Philadelphia: Fortress, 1982), and Langdon Gilkey, "The Mystery of Being and Nonbeing," in *Society and the Sacred*, pp. 123–139.

11. For two good, recent studies of the developments in this tradition, see Robert Hollinger, ed. *Hermeneutics and Praxis* (Notre Dame: University of Notre Dame Press, 1985), and Price R. Wachterhauser, ed., *Hermeneutics and Modern Philosophy* (Albany: State University of New York Press, 1986).

12. For these categories, see David Tracy, *The Analogical Imagination: Christian Theology and the Culture of Pluralism* (New York: Crossroad, 1981), pp. 405–457.

13. I have tried to clarify my own interpretation of this important category in Heidegger in *Plurality and Ambiguity*, pp. 20–31.

14. The most comprehensive recent study here is Richard J. Bernstein, *Beyond Objectivism and Relativism: Science, Hermeneutics and Praxis* (Philadelphia: University of Pennsylvania Press, 1983).

15. I understand Langdon Gilkey's category of "the intolerable" to be this kind of ethical-political category, just as his category "relative absolutes" is analogous to the concerns of my first two sets of criteria.

16. Here Gilkey's category of "rough parity" is especially helpful.

Bibliography

PUBLICATIONS OF LANGDON GILKEY

Books

Maker of Heaven and Earth. New York: Doubleday and Company, 1959. 298 pp. Chapter 2 is reprinted in part in Ian Barbour's *Science and Religion,* New York: Harper Forum Books, Harper and Row, 1968, pp. 159–181. German edition: *Der Himmel und Erde gemacht hat,* Munich: Claudius Verlag, 1971. 304 pp.

How the Church Can Minister to the World Without Losing Itself. New York: Harper and Row, 1964. 151 pp.

Shantung Compound. New York: Harper and Row, 1966; London: Anthony Blond, 1968. 242 pp.

Naming the Whirlwind: The Renewal of God-Language. Indianapolis: Bobbs-Merrill, 1969. 451 pp.

Religion and the Scientific Future. New York: Harper and Row, 1970; London: SCM Press, 1970. 193 pp. Also published in Reprint ed., Macon, Ga.: Mercer University Press. Italian translation: *Il destino della religione nell'era technologica,* trans. P. Prini. Rome: Armando Armando Editore, 1972. 223 pp.

Catholicism Confronts Modernity. New York: Seabury Press, 1975. 211 pp.

Reaping the Whirlwind: A Christian Interpretation of History. New York: Seabury Press, 1976. 446 pp.

Message and Existence: An Introduction to Christian Theology. New York: Seabury Press, 1979. 257 pp.

Society and the Sacred: Towards a Theology of Culture in Decline. New York: Crossroad, 1981. 170 pp.

Creationism on Trial: Evolution and God at Little Rock. Minneapolis: Winston Press, 1985. 301 pp.

263

Contributions to Books

"Neo-Orthodoxy," *A Handbook of Christian Theology,* ed. Marvin Halverson and Arthur Cohen. New York: Meridian Books, World Publishing Co., 1958, pp. 256–261.

"The Imperative for Unity — A Re-Statement," *Issues in Unity.* Indianapolis: Council on Christian Unity, 1958, pp. 11–32.

"Theology," *The Great Ideas Today,* 1967. Chicago: Encyclopedia Britannica, Inc., 1967, pp. 239–270.

"Modern Myth-Making and the Possibilities of Twentieth-Century Theology," in *Theology of Renewal,* vol. 1, ed. L. K. Shook. Montreal: Palm Publishers, 1968, chap. 14, pp. 238–312.

"The Contribution of Culture to the Reign of God," in *The Future as the Presence of Shared Hope,* ed. Maryellen Muckenhirn. New York: Sheed and Ward, 1968, pp. 34–58.

"Evolutionary Science and the Dilemma of Freedom and Determinism," in *Changing Man: The Threat and the Promise,* ed. K. Haselden and P. Hefner. Garden City, N.Y.: Doubleday and Co., 1968, pp. 63–76. Also published in *The Christian Century,* 84 (March 15, 1967): 339–343.

"Unbelief and the Secular Spirit," in *The Presence and Absence of God,* ed. C. F. Mooney. New York: Fordham University Press, 1969, chap. 4, pp. 50–68.

"New Modes of Empirical Theology," in *The Future of Empirical Theology,* ed. Bernard E. Meland, vol. 7 of *Essays in Divinity,* gen. ed., Jerald C. Brauer. Chicago: University of Chicago Press, 1969, pp. 345–370.

"The Universal and Immediate Presence of God," in *The Future of Hope,* ed. Frederick Herzog. New York: Herder and Herder, 1970, pp. 81–109.

"Empirical Science and Theological Knowing," in *Foundations of Theology: Papers from the International Lonergan Conference,* ed. Philip McShane. Dublin: Gill & Macmillan, 1971, pp. 76–101.

"Biblical Symbols in a Scientific Culture," in *Science and Human Values in the 21st Century,* ed. Ralph W. Burhoe. Philadelphia: Westminster, 1971, pp. 72–98.

"The Problem of God: A Programmatic Essay," in *Traces of God in a Secular Culture,* ed. G. E. McClean, O.M.I. Staten Island, N.Y.: Alba House, 1973, pp. 3–23.

"Addressing God in Faith," in *Liturgical Experience of Faith,* ed. Herman Schmidt and David Power. New York: Herder & Herder, 1973, pp. 62–76.

"The Spirit and the Discovery of Truth through Dialogue," ed. Paul Brand, *Festschrift for Edward Schillebeeckx: Leven uit de Geest.* Hilversum, Holland: Gooi en Sticht, 1974. Also published in French as "L'Esprit et la decouverte de la verité dans le dialogue," in *L'experience de l'Esprit: Melanges E. Schillebeeckx.* Paris: Beauchesne, 1976, pp. 225–240. Also in *Experience of the Sacred,* ed. P. Huizing and W. Bassett. New York: Seabury, 1974, pp. 58–68.

"Reinhold Niebuhr's Theology of History," *Journal of Religion* 54 (October 1974): 360-86, and in *The Legacy of Reinhold Niebuhr,* ed. Nathan A. Scott, Jr. Chicago: University of Chicago Press, 1975, pp. 36–62.

"The Structure of Academic Revolutions," in *The Nature of Scientific Discovery,* ed. Owen Gingerich. Washington, D. C.: Smithsonian Institution Press, 1975, pp. 538–546.

"The Crisis of the Word 'God,' " in The *Contemporary Explosion of Theology: Ecumenical Studies in Theology,* ed. and introduced by Michael D. Ryan. Metuchen, N.J.: Scarecrow Press, 1975, pp. 20–26.

"The Crisis of 'God' Language," in *The Contemporary Explosion of Theology: Ecumenical Studies in Theology,* ed. and introduced by Michael D. Ryan. Metuchen, N.J.: Scarecrow Press, 1975, pp. 27–33.

"God: Eternal Source of Newness," in *Living with Change, Experience, Faith,* ed., F. A. Eigo, O.S.A. Villanova: Villanova University Press, 1976, pp. 154–166.

"The Future of Science," address given to Nobel Laureates at St. Olaf College, October 1975, published as *The Future of Science: 1975 Nobel Conference,* ed. T. C. L. Robinson. New York: John Wiley and Sons, 1977. Also published as "The Creativity and Ambiguity of Science," in *Society and the Sacred,* chap. 6, pp. 75–89.

"The Covenant with the Chinese," in *China and Christianity: Historical and Future Encounter,* ed. J. D. Whitehead. Notre Dame: Center for Pastoral and Social Ministry, 1977, pp. 118–132. Appears in *Society and the Sacred,* chap. 10, pp. 139–156.

"Toward a Religious Criterion of Religions," in *Understanding the New Religions,* ed. Jacob Needleman and George Baker. New York: Seabury, 1978, pp. 131–137.

"The Dialectic of Christian Belief: Rational, Incredible and Credible," in *Rationality and Christian Belief,* ed. C. F. Delaney. Notre Dame: Notre Dame University Press, 1979, pp. 65–83. Also in *Society and the Sacred,* ch. 3, pp. 26–41.

"Idea of God Since 1800," in *Dictionary of the History of Ideas,* ed. Philip P. Wiener. New York: Charles Scribner's Sons, 1973, vol. 2, pp. 351–366.

"The Religious Dilemmas of a Scientific Culture: The Interface of Science, Technology, and Religion," in *Being Human in a Technological Age,* ed. Donald M. Borchert and David Stewart. Athens, Ohio: Ohio University Press, 1979. Appears in *Society and the Sacred,* chap. 7, pp. 90–103.

"The Political Dimensions of Theology," in *The Challenge of Liberation Theology: A First World Response,* ed. Brian Mahan and L. Dale Richesen. Maryknoll, N.Y.: Orbis, 1981, pp. 113–126. Reprinted with slight editing from *Journal of Religion* 59 (April 1979): 154–168. Appears in *Society and the Sacred,* chap. 4, pp. 42–56.

"Is Religious Faith Possible in an Age of Science?" in *Unfinished . . . Essays in Honor of Ray L. Hart,* ed. Mark C. Taylor. A thematic series of the *Journal of the American Academy of Religion* 48 (1981): 31–44.

"Tillich: The Master of Mediation," in *The Theology of Paul Tillich*, 2nd ed., ed. Charles W. Kegley. New York: Pilgrim, 1982, pp. 26–59.

"The Creationist Issue: A Theologian's View," in *Cosmology and Theology*, ed. David Tracy and Nicholas Lash. New York: Seabury, 1983, pp. 55–69.

"Creationism: The Roots of the Conflict," in *Is God a Creationist? The Religious Case Against Creation-Science*, ed. Ronald M. Frye. New York: Scribners, 1983, pp. 56–57. Adapted from an article that appeared in *Science, Technology, and Human Values* 7 (Summer 1982). A version also appears in *Christianity and Crisis* 42 (April 26, 1982): 108–115 and *Creationism, Science and the Law*, ed. M. La Follette. Cambridge: MIT Press, 1983, pp. 129–137.

"Can Art Fill the Vacuum?" in *Art, Creativity, and the Sacred: An Anthology in Religion and Art*, ed. Diane Apostolos-Cappadona. New York: Crossroad, 1984, pp. 87–92. Also in *Criterion* 20 (Autumn 1981): 7–9.

"Scripture, History, and the Quest for Meaning," in *History and Historical Understanding*, ed. C. T. McIntyre and Ronald A. Wells. Grand Rapids: Eerdmans, 1984, pp. 3–16. Also in *Humanizing America's Iconic Book*, ed. Gene M. Tucker and Douglas A. Knight. Chico, Calif.: Scholars, 1982, pp. 25–38 and *Society and the Sacred*, chap. 5, pp. 57–72.

"Theology of Culture and Christian Ethics," in *The Annual of the Society of Christian Ethics*, ed. Larry L. Rasmussen. Vancouver: Society of Christian Ethics, 1984, pp. 341–364.

"God," in *Christian Theology: An Introduction to Its Traditions and Tasks*, revised and enlarged ed., ed. Peter C. Hodgson and Robert H. King. Philadelphia: Fortress, 1985, pp. 88–113.

"Theology as the Interpretation of Faith for Church and World," in *The Vocation of the Theologian*, ed. Theodore W. Jennings. Philadelphia: Fortress, 1985, pp. 87–103.

"The New Being and Christology," in *The Thought of Paul Tillich*, ed. James Luther Adams, Wilhelm Pauck, and Roger Shinn. New York: Harper and Row, 1985, pp. 307–329.

"Theological Frontiers: Implications for Bioethics," in *Theology and Bioethics*, ed. E. E. Shelp. Dordrecht: Reidel Publishing, 1985, pp. 115–133.

"The Role of the Theologian in Contemporary Society," in *The Thought of Paul Tillich*, ed. James Luther Adams, Wilhelm Pauck, and Roger Shinn. New York: Harper and Row, 1985, pp. 330–350.

"Religion and Science in an Advanced Scientific Culture," in *Knowing Religiously*, ed. Leroy S. Rouner. Notre Dame: University of Notre Dame Press, 1985, pp. 166–176.

"An Appreciation of Karl Barth," in *How Karl Barth Changed My Mind*, ed. Donald K. McKim. Grand Rapids: Eerdmans, 1986, pp. 150–155.

"Reinhold Niebuhr as Political Theologian," in *Reinhold Niebuhr and the Issues of Our Time*, ed. Richard Harries. Grand Rapids: Eerdmans, 1986, pp. 157–182.

Journal Articles

"Academic Freedom and the Christian Faith," *Christianity and Crisis* 12 (December 22, 1952): 171–173.

"Morality and the Cross," *Christianity and Crisis* 14 (April 5, 1954): 35–38.

"The Christian Response to the World Crisis," *Christianity and Crisis* 15 (August 8, 1955): 107–111.

"In Faith... Praise, Thanksgiving and Joy," *Christianity and Crisis* 16 (December 10, 1956): 168–169.

"Christ and the City," *Motive* 17 (April 1957): 2, 3, 29.

"Darwin and Christian Thought," *The Christian Century* 77 (January 6, 1960): 7–11. Reprinted in Ian Barbour's *Science and Religion* (New York: Harper Forum Books, Harper and Row, 1968), pp. 159–181.

"Calvin's Religious Thought," *Motive* 20 (February 1960): 5–6.

"Cosmology, Ontology, and the Travail of Biblical Language," *The Journal of Religion* 41 (July 1961): 194–205. Reprinted in *Concordia Theological Monthly* 33 (March 1962): 143–154.

"The Concept of Providence in Contemporary Theology," *The Journal of Religion* 43 (July 1963): 171–192.

"Stewards of the Mysteries of God," *Criterion* 3 (Winter 1964): 29–31.

"Is God Dead?" and "God is Not Dead," *The Voice* (Bulletin of Crozier Theological Seminary) 57 (January 1965): 4–11.

"Dissolution and Reconstruction in Theology," *The Christian Century* 82 (February 3, 1965): 135–139. Reprinted in *Frontline Theology,* ed. Dean Peerman (Richmond: John Knox Press, 1966), pp. 29–38. Also translated and reprinted as "Abbau and Wiederaufbau in der Theologie," in *Theologie im Umbruch* (Munich: Chr. Kaiser Verlag, 1968), pp. 32–41.

"Holy, Holy, Holy," *The Baptist Student* 44 (January 1965): 24–27.

"Secularism's Impact on Contemporary Theology," *Christianity and Crisis* 25 (April 1965): 64–67. Reprinted in *Witness to a Generation,* ed. Wayne Cowan (Indianapolis: Bobbs-Merrill, 1966), pp. 127–132. Reprinted also in *The Theologian at Work,* ed. A. Roy Eckardt (New York: Harper and Row, 1968), pp. 192–197. Reprinted again in *Radical Theology: Phase Two,* ed. C. W. Christian and Glen R. Wittig (Philadelphia and New York: J. B. Lippincott Co., 1967), pp. 17–23.

"The Authority of the Bible: The Relation of the Bible to the Church," *Encounter* 27 (Spring 1966): 112–123.

"Evolutionary Science and the Dilemma of Freedom and Determinism," *The Christian Century* 84 (March 15, 1967): 339–343. Reprinted in *Changing Man: The Threat and the Promise,* ed. K. Haselden and P. Hefner (Garden City, N.Y.: Doubleday and Co., 1968), pp. 63–76.

"If There Is No God...," *Criterion* 6 (Spring 1967): 5–7.

"Social and Intellectual Sources of Contemporary Protestant Theology in America," *Daedalus* 96 (Winter 1967): 69–98. Reprinted in *Religion in America,* ed. William McLaughlin and Robert Bellah (Boston: Beacon Press, 1968), pp. 137–166.

"American Policy and the Just War," *Criterion* 7 (Winter 1968): 9–16.

"Religious Dimensions of the Secular," excerpts from a lecture delivered at Barat College, March 7, 1968. Published in *The Barat Review* 3 (June/September 1968): 106–109.

"Religion and the Secular University," *Dialog* 8 (Spring 1969): 108–116. Reprinted in *Religious Education* 64 (November–December 1969): 458–466.

"Trends in Protestant Apologetics," *Concilium* 6 (June 1969): 59–72. Also published in *The Development of Fundamental Theology,* ed. J. B. Metz (New York: Paulist Press, 1969), pp. 127–157.

"Religious Dimensions of Scientific Inquiry," *Journal of Religion* 50 (July 1970): 245-67. Reprint of Chapter 2 of *Religion and the Scientific Future,* pp. 35–64.

"Theology in the Seventies," *Theology Today* 27 (October 1970): 292–301.

"Comments on Emmanuel Levinas' *Totalité et Infini,*" in *Algemeen Nederlands Tijdschrift voor Wijsbegeerte,* 64e (Amsterdam, 1971).

"Ervaring en Interpretatie van de Religieuze Dimensie een Reaktie," *Tijdschrift voor Theologie* 11 (July/August/September 1971): 292–302.

"Process Theology," *Vox Theologica* (Gronigen, The Netherlands) 34 (January 1973).

"Robert Heilbroner's Morality Play," *Worldview* 17 (August 1974): 51–55.

"Christian Theology" (the study of, at the University of Chicago Divinity School), *Criterion* 13 (Winter 1974): 10–13.

"Religion and the Technological Future," *Criterion* 13 (Spring 1974): 9–14.

"Symbols, Meaning, and the Divine Presence," *Theological Studies* 35 (June 1974): 249–267.

"Robert S. Heilbroner's Vision of History," *Zygon* 10 (September 1975): 215–233.

"On Going to War Over Oil," *The Christian Century* 92 (March 12, 1975): 259–260.

"Theology and the Future," *Andover Newton Quarterly* 17 (March 1977): 250–257.

"Anathemas and Orthodoxy: A Reply to Avery Dulles," *The Christian Century* 94 (November 9, 1977): 1026–1029.

"A Covenant With the Chinese," *Dialog* 17 (1978): 181–187.

"Responses to Berger," *Theological Studies* 39 (September 1978): 486–507.

"The Political Dimensions of Theology," *The Journal of Religion* 59 (April 1979): 154–168.

"The AAR and the Anxiety of Non-Being," *Journal of the American Academy of Religion* 48 (March 1980): 5–18.

"The Roles of the 'Descriptive' or 'Historical' and the 'Normative' in our Work," *Criterion* 20 (Winter 1981): 10–17.

"Theology for a Time of Troubles: How My Mind Has Changed," *The Christian Century* 98 (April 29, 1981): 474–480.

"A New Watershed in Theology," *Soundings* 64 (Summer 1981): 118–131. A revised version appears in *Society and the Sacred,* chap. 1, pp. 3–14.

"Some Words from the Faculty" (on ministry studies at the University of Chicago Divinity School), *Criterion* 21 (Autumn 1982): 21–22.

"Response to Ross Reat's Article, 'Insiders and Outsiders in the Study of Religion,'" *Journal of the American Academy of Religion* 51 (1983): 484–488.

"The Political Meaning of Silence," *Philosophy Today* 27 (Summer 1983): 128–132.

"Events, Meanings and the Current Tasks of Theology," *Journal of the American Academy of Religion* 53 (1985): 717–734.

Book Reviews

"Great Good Sense," review of Nathaniel Micklem's *Ultimate Questions,* in *The Christian Century* 72 (August 3, 1955): 896.

"Biblical Theology and Historical Reality," review of John Knox's *The Death of Christ* and Richard R. Niebuhr's *Resurrection and Historical Reason,* in *Encounter* 19 (Spring 1958): 214–218.

Review of George H. Tavard's *Paul Tillich and the Christian Message,* in *Union Seminary Quarterly Review* 18 (March 1963): 283–284.

Review of Paul M. Van Buren's *The Secular Meaning of the Gospel,* in *The Journal of Religion* 44 (July 1964): 238–243. Reprinted in *New Theology,* no. 2, ed. Martin Marty and Dean Peerman (New York: Macmillan Co. 1965), as "A New Linguistic Madness," pp. 39–49.

"Is God Dead?", review of Daniel Jenkins's *The Christian Belief of God,* in *The Christian Century* 82 (January 6, 1965): 18–19.

Review of Alexander J. McKelway's *The Systematic Theology of Paul Tillich,* in *Foundations* 8 (July 1965): 18–19.

Review of John Cobb's *A Christian Natural Theology,* in *Theology Today* 22 (January 1966): 530–545.

"Seeds of Malaise," review of Karl Lowith's *Nature, History and Existentialism,* in *The Christian Century* 83 (November 2, 1966): 1341–1342.

Review of James Luther Adams's *Paul Tillich's Philosophy of Culture, Science and Religion,* in *Theology Today* 23 (January 1967): 565–569.

"The Integrity of History," review of Philip Hefner's *Faith and the Vitalities of History,* in *Una Sancta,* 24 (Pentecost 1967): 67–71.

"A Paganized Judaism," review of Richard Rubenstein's *After Auschwitz,* in *The Christian Century* 84 (May 10, 1967): 627–628.

"A Theology in Process: Schubert Ogden's Developing Theology," *Interpretation* 21 (October 1967): 447–459. This is an extended review of Ogden's *The Reality of God and Other Essays.*

"Standing on the Promises," review of Jürgen Moltmann's *The Theology of Hope,* in *The Christian Century* 84 (December 20, 1967): 1630–1632.

"Anatomy of Reconciliation," review of Emil L. Fackenheim's *The Religious Dimension in Hegel's Thought,* in *The Christian Century* 86 (January 8, 1969): 52–53.

Review of Karl Rahner's *Spirit in the World,* in *Journal of Ecumenical Studies* 7 (Winter 1970): 138–144.

"That Mysterious Sleeping Dragon," review of *Understanding Modern China,* ed. Joseph M. Kitagawa, in *The Christian Century* 87 (August 26, 1970): 1019–1020.

"Pannenberg's *Basic Questions in Theology,* vols. 1 and 2; A Review Article," in *Perspectives* (Pittsburgh, Pa.) 14 (Spring 1973): 34–55.

"A Theological Voyage with Wilfred Cantwell Smith," *Religious Studies Review* 7 (October 1981): 298–305.

Contributors

Thomas J.J. Altizer is Professor of English at the State University of New York at Stony Brook, where he also was the first chair of an interdisciplinary program in religious studies. His books include *Oriental Mysticism and Biblical Eschatalogy, The Gospel of Christian Atheism, The Descent into Hell, The Self-Embodiment of God,* and with Myers, Rashke, Scharlemann, Taylor, and Winquist, *Deconstruction and Theology.*

John B. Cobb, Jr. is Ingraham Memorial Professor of Theology at the School of Theology at Claremont and Avery Professor of Religion at the Claremont Graduate School. Director of the Center for Process Studies, he is author of, among other titles, *A Christian Natural Theology, Living Options in Protestant Theology: A Survey of Methods, Christ in a Pluralistic Age, Process Theology: An Introductory Exposition* (with David R. Griffin), and, with David Tracy, *Talking about God.*

Langdon Gilkey is Shailer Mathews Professor of Theology at the Divinity School of the University of Chicago. He is past president of the American Academy of Religion. A complete bibliography of his works appears as the Appendix in this volume.

Ray L. Hart is Professor of Religious Studies at the University of Montana. A former editor of the *Journal of the American Academy of Religion,* he is author of, among other works, *Unfinished Man and the Imagination: Toward an Ontology of a Rhetoric of Revelation.* A version of his essay also appeared in *The Critique of Modernity,* edited by Julian N. Hartt and published by the University Press of Virginia.)

Hans Küng is Professor of Theology at the Institute for Ecumenical Research in Tübingen, West Germany. His works include *On Being a Christian, Does God Exist?, Infallible?: An Inquiry, Freud and the Problem of*

271

God, and *Structures of the Church.* Another version of his essay is included in *Paradigm Change in Theology,* ed. Hans Küng and David Tracy (Edinburgh: T. & T. Clark, forthcoming); it is included here with permission of T. & T. Clark Ltd., Publishers.

Donald W. Musser is Associate Professor of Religion at Stetson University. His essays and reviews have appeared in *Zygon, Soundings, Journal of Religion, Christian Century,* and *International Journal for Philosophy of Religion.*

Schubert M. Ogden is University Professor of Theology and Director of the Graduate Program in Religious Studies at Southern Methodist University. Past president of the American Academy of Religion, he has also served as the Sarum Lecturer at Oxford University. His books include *On Theology, The Point of Christology, The Reality of God, Christ without Myth,* and *Faith and Freedom.*

Wolfhart Pannenberg is Professor of Systematic Theology at the University of Munich. His numerous books include *Anthropology in Theological Perspective, Theology and Philosophy of Science, Jesus–God and Man, The Idea of God and Human Freedom, Ethics, Basic Questions in Theology, I & II,* and *Theology and the Kingdom of God.*

Joseph L. Price is Associate Professor of Religion at Whittier College. His essays and reviews have appeared in *Soundings, Christian Century, Foundations, The Journal of Religion,* and *Religious Studies Review.*

Robert P. Scharlemann is Commonwealth Professor of Religious Studies at the University of Virginia. Past president of the North American Paul Tillich Society, he has served as the editor of the *Journal of the American Academy of Religion.* His books include *Thomas Aquinas and John Gerhard, Reflection and Doubt in the Thought of Paul Tillich, The Being of God: Theology and the Experience of Truth,* and with Thomas J. J. Altizer et al., *Deconstruction and Theology.*

Nathan A. Scott, Jr. is the William R. Kenan, Jr., Professor of Religious Studies and Professor of English at the University of Virginia. Past president of the American Academy of Religion, he is a Fellow of the American Academy of Arts and Sciences. His many books include *The Broken Center: Studies in the Theological Horizon of Modern Literature; Negative Capability; The Wild Prayer of Longing: Poetry and the Sacred; The Poetry of Civic Virtue: Eliot, Malraux, Auden;* and *The*

Poetics of Belief: Studies in Colerdige, Arnold, Pater, Santayana, Stevens, and Heidegger. His essay first appeared in the Spring 1987 issue of the *Journal of the American Academy of Religion.*

David Tracy is the Andrew Greeley Professor of Theology at the Divinity School of the University of Chicago. A co-editor of the *Journal of Religion,* he also serves on the editorial boards of *Religious Studies Review, Concilium,* and *Theology Today.* He is past president of the Catholic Theological Society of America. His books include *The Achievement of Bernard Lonergan, Blessed Rage for Order: The New Pluralism in Theology, The Analogical Imagination: Christian Theology and the Culture of Pluralism, Pluralism and Ambiguity,* and, with John Cobb, *Talking About God.*

Charles E. Winquist is Thomas J. Watson Professor of Religion at Syracuse University. Formerly the Executive Director of the American Academy of Religion, he is on the editorial board of the *Journal of the American Academy of Religion,* and he is the author of *The Transcendental Imagination: An Essay in Philosophical Theology, The Communion of Possibility, Homecoming: The Dynamics of Individuation, Practical Hermeneutics: A Revised Agenda for the Ministry,* and, with Thomas J. J. Altizer et al., *Deconstruction and Theology.*

Patricia L. Wismer is Assistant Professor of Theology and Religious Studies at Seattle University. She previously taught at the University of Notre Dame and the College of Wooster. Her recent work includes presentations at the College Theology Society of America and the American Academy of Religion.

Also from Meyer•Stone Books...

LIBERATION THEOLOGY
Essential Facts about the Revolutionary Religious
Movement in Latin America and Beyond

Phillip Berryman

"Phillip Berryman writes clearly and convincingly about what may turn
out to be the most important religious movement since the Protestant
Reformation. Persuasive and provocative, *Liberation Theology* should
be read by everyone who wants to understand the preferential option
for the poor and the spiritual revolutions going on in Latin America."
— Robert F. Drinan

"...just the book I've been searching for. As the basic text for my course
on liberation theology, it is everything I need: concise, well written,
balanced. It gives some real attention to the critics of liberation theology,
which any fair text must do." — Harvey Cox

Phillip Berryman is the author of *The Religious Roots of Rebellion* and
Inside Central America.

Theology 240 pp.

Paperback: ISBN 0-940989-03-4, $6.95

NAMING THE IDOLS
Biblical Alternatives for U.S. Foreign Policy

Richard Shaull

Foreword by Richard Falk

"I would rather entrust the foreign policy of this country to Richard Shaull than to our present State Department, no matter which party is in the White House and regardless of who is selected to serve as Secretary of State.... Shaull offers us much wisdom with great clarity... a valuable and exhilarating book."

> — Richard Falk, Center of International Studies,
> Woodrow Wilson School for Public and International Affairs,
> Princeton, New Jersey

"...a superb, even stunning job! Richard Shaull knows and understands the Bible, and brings it to bear with rare compassion and competence. I am a lifelong biblical scholar; but he leaves me in wonder at his gifts in opening my eyes to what I have failed to see, or failed to see clearly."

> — B. Davie Napier, Professor of Bible, Yale University, Emeritus

"Richard Shaull is ideally equipped to evaluate U.S. foreign policy in light of scriptural and especially prophetic teaching. He has worked for many years in Colombia, Brazil, and Central America. We have here the fire, the vision, and the wisdom of a true prophet."

> — Gary MacEoin, author of *Sanctuary: A Resource Guide*...

Richard Shaull is Henry Winter Luce Professor of Ecumenics, Emeritus, Princeton. For over forty-five years he has been involved in helping North Americans learn from and be changed by their encounter with Third World realities.

Social Concerns   160 pp.

Paperback: $9.95 (ISBN 0-940989-32-8)

MYSTERY WITHOUT MAGIC

Russell Pregeant

"If you have been looking for a sound introductory religious studies text for undergraduates, your search is ended. Pregeant's *Mystery Without Magic* is truly exceptional. He anticipates the questions and problems that students commonly raise and addresses them clearly, logically, and with good sense. I was certain this book would speak to my students, but I found that it began to speak to me as well. I wish I'd had Pregeant's book when I was beginning my study of religion."

— Suzanne C. Toton, Ed.D.,
Associate Professor of Religious Education and Christian Living,
Villanova University

"Rejecting the dualism at the heart of Western theology, Pregeant offers us a way of discovering meaning and direction by going deeper into our world rather than looking beyond to another. This is an important next step in the kind of theological reconstruction initiated by Paul Tillich."

— T. Richard Snyder, Professor of Theology and Ethics,
New York Theological Seminary

"Russell Pregeant has written a very strong, persuasive, and imaginative book."

— William A. Beardslee,
Professor of Religion, Emeritus, Emory University

Russell Pregeant is an ordained minister in the United Methodist Church. He is currently Chaplain and Professor of Religion and Philosophy at Curry College, Milton, Massachusetts, where, he says, he struggles to interest his students by gearing religion and philosophy to real-life questions.

Religious Studies/Spirituality   180 pp.

Paperback: $12.95 (ISBN 0-940989-19-0)

THE WAY OF THE BLACK MESSIAH
The Hermeneutical Challenge of Black Theology

Theo Witvliet

With a Foreword by Gayraud Wilmore

"Theo Witvliet is one of the most astute interpreters of black theology writing today. He has worked long and studied hard to understand black theology within the context of the black community and of the entire Third World. I highly recommend his perspective and deeply respect his critique. *The Way of the Black Messiah* is the most important critical assessment of black theology yet published. It is must reading for both black and white theologians."
— James H. Cone

"Theo Witvliet has not only taken pains to try to understand the theology that erupted from the dark underside of the English-speaking world, but is sensitive to its peculiar sins and considerable virtues as a theology of human liberation.... He has made a manifestly important contribution to the study of the black religious experience.... As a black historian-theologian what is my final word about this unusual *tour de force* by a Dutch journalist-theologian who has a nose for what we in the United States call 'religious news' and an ear for the black story as a pointer to the universal narrative of human liberation? My final word is that he belongs with us."

— Gayraud Wilmore, from the Foreword

Theo Witvliet is Lecturer in Ecumenism at Amsterdam University. He is the author of *A Place in the Sun: An Introduction to Liberation Theology in the Third World.*

Theology   352 pp.

Paperback: $19.95 (ISBN 0-940989-04-2)
Library Binding: $39.95 (ISBN 0-940989-09-3)

———————

Order from your bookstore
or from
Meyer • Stone Books
2014 South Yost Avenue,
Bloomington, IN 47403
Tel.: 812-333-0313